MY FATHER'S GUN

MY FATHER'S GUN

One Family, Three Badges,
One Hundred Years in the NYPD

Brian McDonald

A DUTTON BOOK

DUTTON
Published by the Penguin Group
Penguin Putnam Inc., 375 Hudson Street, New York, New York 10014, U.S.A.
Penguin Books Ltd, 27 Wrights Lane, London W8 5TZ, England
Penguin Books Australia Ltd, Ringwood, Victoria, Australia
Penguin Books Canada Ltd, 10 Alcorn Avenue, Toronto, Ontario, Canada M4V 3B2
Penguin Books (N.Z.) Ltd, 182–190 Wairau Road, Auckland 10, New Zealand

Penguin Books Ltd, Registered Offices:
Harmondsworth, Middlesex, England

First published by Dutton, a member of Penguin Putnam Inc.

First Printing, May, 1999
10 9 8 7 6 5 4 3 2 1

REGISTERED TRADEMARK — MARCA REGISTRADA

LIBRARY OF CONGRESS CATALOGING-IN-PUBLICATION DATA:
McDonald, Brian (Brian Vincent)
   My father's gun / Brian McDonald.
      p.   cm.
   ISBN 0-525-94396-X (alk. paper)
   1. Police—New York (State)—New York—Biography.   2. Irish Americans—New
York (State)—New York—Biography.   3. Irish American families—New York
(State)—New York.   4. Fathers and sons—New York (State)   I. Title.
   HV7911.A1M33   1999
   363.2'092—dc21
   [B]   98-51156
                                                                CIP

Printed in the United States of America
Set in Janson

This book is printed on acid-free paper. ∞

For Mom

I would like to express my gratitude to the many people whose guidance, knowledge, and candidness helped make this book possible. First, I'm indebted to the police officers who worked alongside the members of my family. In my mind, they are heroes all. I would also like to thank archivist Daphne Dennis, the Bronx Historical Society, Inspector Michael Collins, and authors Thomas Repetto, Robert Daly, Luc Sante, and Peter Maas whose research made my job infinitely easier. I was blessed with the extraordinary assistance of editor Rosemary Ahern, Jane Dystel (the Jerry McGuire of literary agents), Sam Freedman, and Miriam Goderich.

Most important, I would like to thank my family, especially my father and my brother Frankie. I love them. Warts and all.

CONTENTS

PROLOGUE

On the evening of January 18, 1987, my brother Frankie sat at a desk in the 48th Precinct house, the borough command center for the Bronx Task Force, and absently gazed out the window at the crawling traffic on the Cross-Bronx Expressway. The snow, which had begun falling lightly the day before, had taken on a steady slanting trajectory and the fat, swirling flakes clicked against the window. He thought of the young patrolman's body lying in the foyer of the building on Fordham Road. He thought of the surrounding neighborhood. He'd run past that building a thousand times as a kid. He played Johnny-ride-the-pony on those sidewalks every day. Yet this neighborhood no longer even remotely resembled the one that lived in his recollections.

My brother and his partner, Detective Edward Blake, had worked three solid days on the investigation into the murder of off-duty patrolman Michael Reidy. Both of them had been assigned to the Major Case Squad, a kind of detective all-star team. My brother was frequently picked for this elite squad, and routinely worked high-profile and high-priority cases. In November

1986, he, along with one hundred other detectives, was assigned to the case of Larry Davis, the drug dealer stickup artist who shot and seriously injured six cops and initiated the largest manhunt in the history of the NYPD. Now, it was a cop-killer the Major Case Squad was after.

At first, their information was thin. They knew Reidy, a rookie cop assigned to the 41st Precinct, had been shot and killed as he was robbed in the vestibule of his mother's building across from St. Nicholas of Tolentine Church. They knew that Reidy had cashed his paycheck at a check-cashing place on Fordham Road. They surmised that someone had followed him home. They knew, too, that there had been a struggle, and that Reidy had emptied his five-shot revolver. But, they had no witnesses, and three days into the investigation, very few leads.

Then a patrolman named Powers walked into the office with his girlfriend. He had asked to see the detectives assigned to the Reidy case. It seemed to my brother and Blake that Powers had an agenda, that the patrolman wanted to use his girlfriend's information as currency, to trade for a possible promotion into the detective division. In a way, you couldn't blame Powers. For patrolmen, opportunities like this one didn't happen often. It was a golden opportunity. After Powers made his opening play, he stood for a few moments in an uneasy silence. He was well aware that my brother and Blake were the ones who would let the appropriate bosses know how important his information was—if, in fact, it was important. But what the patrolman didn't know was that he couldn't have made a worse choice in picking a champion for his cause. My brother took on just about every case—especially the killing of a cop—on the deepest of personal levels. In his job, in his life, he always led with his heart, the way Muhammad Ali led with his left—a personality trait that made him a great cop, led to mistakes, and, ultimately set him up for disappointment after disappointment. The NYPD is the all-time heavyweight champion of disappointing people. My brother pushed the cold container of coffee across the desk and sat on the desk's corner and felt his stomach turn—from the bad coffee, Powers' blatant careerism, or both. I'll promise him anything, he thought, hear what the girl has to say, then forget him like yesterday's New York *Post*.

Initially, it seemed what the girlfriend had wasn't really much. She said that her brother overheard someone bragging about murdering a cop. Frankie and Blake were leery, but interested. As seasoned detectives, they knew many murders were solved on such seemingly vague information; criminals like to brag, their fatal flaw. Yet countless other investigations are steered down the wrong street when detectives take these kinds of tips too seriously. Still, after three days of absolute nothing, my brother and Blake were willing to grab on to even the most tenuous of threads. They pulled their coats from the backs of their chairs and headed to the address of the brother of Patrolman Powers' girlfriend.

The brother told the detectives that he knew the man who had bragged about killing a cop only by his street name, Ski. But, he said, he knew that Ski had a half-brother, with a different last name, who was in prison upstate.

By ten p.m. the detectives were back in the office, canvassing the upstate prison system by phone. In those days, before computer links, such work was arduous. They called dozens of prisons, without success. At this time of the night, most of the prisons' administrative offices were manned by skeleton crews. Some officials they reached that night didn't have access to files; others told the detectives to call back the next morning. My brother didn't have time to wait.

The break in the investigation came when a watch warden from an upstate prison, who'd promised to phone back after he looked through his files, did. It was six a.m. My brother well remembers the exact time. He had looked at his wristwatch often during those early morning hours because he had an eight a.m. appointment at One Police Plaza—the most important trip to headquarters in his police career. Now, with the fresh lead, he wondered if he'd make the appointment at all. He wondered, as he and Blake again grabbed their coats, if he really wanted to make it.

Under "Siblings" the prison files on the half-brother listed Ski's full name, Angel Maldonado. It also listed his last known address. The building superintendent answered the bell, dressed in raggy jeans and wearing an undershirt. He wiped sleep from his eyes as he looked at my brother's shield through the glass of the building's front door. Yes, the super said through the glass, he knew who Maldonado was; but no, he didn't live in the building anymore. The super turned and began to shuffle down the hall. My brother slammed his shield against the glass and screamed to the man in the undershirt to open the door.

"He moved out two weeks ago," the super said over his shoulder, unimpressed by my brother's credentials. In this neighborhood, in those years when crime was more regular than trash collection, a police badge, even a gold one, had about as much juice as an expired credit card.

From experience, having witnessed his anger, I can see, in my mind's eye, my brother's face, fiery red, like a full summer setting sun, the veins in his neck like cord, as he continued to slam the window with the gold shield, screaming at the super: "To where?"

For a moment the man hesitated in the hallway, his back to my brother. Finally, he turned and opened the door.

Back at the Command Office there was much activity. Quickly a stakeout was planned at the address the superintendent had grudgingly given, 190th Street and Morris Avenue. The captain of the Task Force, John Ridge, called my brother and Blake into his office to congratulate them. He told the two detectives that a press conference was planned for later that morning, as soon as they brought Maldonado in, and that he wanted them there. My brother looked at his watch; it was nine a.m. "I'm going to have to miss it," he told the captain. "I'm already an hour late for my appointment downtown."

As he drove his ten-year-old Nissan through the heavy snow down the East Side Drive, my brother thought back over the past twenty years of his life. The storm provided extraordinary solitude; the crunch of the snow underneath the tires, and the squeaking beat of the wipers, which fought in vain to keep up with the flakes smashing against the windshield, added a rhythm to his thoughts—memories, which came to him revised, edited like a eulogy. In them there was no frustration, no bureaucracy, no demotions or heart-wrenching unsolved cases; just the pure contentment he had always felt as a cop.

He had been to his share of cop retirement parties held in rooms above fake Irish bars. He had even made some of the farewell speeches himself: What a great guy, a terrific cop, and the rest of the happy horseshit that goes along with such oratory. He had chipped in many times for the cheap-gold shield ring, the parting gift, and had slapped the retiree on the back and promised to keep in touch, to meet regularly for a few beers. But after each of these parties, my brother knew that the relationship would just not be the same. He was about to leave a job that not only defined him as a man, but also delineated his world. Many years later, he told me that a cop was the only thing he'd wanted to be; in many ways—tradition, circumstance, environment—it was the only thing he could have been.

He turned off the Drive at the Houston Street exit, far north of the exit for One Police Plaza, and pulled the car over to a phone booth. Money had been the determining factor in his decision, and he hated that. I'll call them, he said to himself, just tell them I've changed my mind. But as he sat there in his Nissan, his thoughts went to his wife, Pam, and their two daughters. For so much of the past twenty years they had struggled together just to get by. The offer he had would mean the struggle would be over. He realized that he had no choice. He had to do it, for them. He tugged at the wheel of the Nissan and made a slow U-turn back onto the Drive.

Later that morning, about the time that Angel Maldonado was being arrested in the Bronx for the murder of Michael Reidy, my brother handed in his gold shield, Kevlar vest, and service revolver to the pension check at police headquarters and retired. And so ended nearly one hundred years of police service in my family.

I was not one of them, although I took the entrance exam to the New York City police department in the mid-1970s. Whether by fate, or, more likely, because of the city budget crisis then, which caused layoffs and a freeze on hiring cops, my life unfolded in a completely different direction. But I don't know whether I would have taken the job had it been offered. Looking back, I see I was much more involved in rebelling against tradition, family or otherwise, than in joining it. Still, more than twenty years later, when I see a beat cop walk by, or watch the news tape of the latest sensational crime or scandal, or listen, enraptured each time, to my brother and father's remembrances of the job, I am haunted by thoughts of how things might have been.

Though, because I never put on the uniform, I stood just outside their insular circle, I was very much a part of the cop society. And, in many ways this vantage point offered me a better view.

What lies ahead is a memoir of three generations of New York City cops in my family. My grandfather was a patrolman and traffic cop at the turn of the century, the time of the very birth of the modern department; my father was a policeman for twenty-three years, the last fourteen as a detective-lieutenant squad commander in possibly the most infamous of precincts—the 41st, Fort Apache. As an undercover cop and later a Bronx detective, my brother was involved in scores of cases that have been fodder for a myriad of cop books, movies, and TV shows. The place in which I grew up, Pearl River, became a bedroom community for hundreds of commuting city cops, and it indelibly dyed everything within its boundaries in the blue of the NYPD.

In the telling of this story, I take a risk, for in cop families "not airing your dirty laundry" is a sacrament taken somewhere between baptism and first holy communion. The "blue wall of silence," is as much in place in the cop home, where doors and windows are shut so "the neighbors won't hear," as it is in the precinct house. But the insular nature of my world has always left me screaming behind the gag. Cop stories are at root really just family stories, filled with secret conflicts, shame, desire, and humor, only dressed up with sirens and flashing lights. They deserve to be told, no matter the risk.

Partly, this book is a record of on-the-job tales—"war stories," as cops call them—taken from a trunk full of remembrances. Whether it was as a kid overhearing my father's conversations with his cop friends or his dinner table talks with my mother, or listening as my brother Frankie told his tales of peril and parable culled from the New York City streets, I found that these stories captured my imagination and transported me back through time to my father's office in the 41st Precinct squad room or to the backseat of the undercover taxicab my brother rode working the streets of Times Square.

But I don't rely on imagination, for, as my father is fond of saying, the drama of cops' war stories increases in direct proportion to their time away from the job, and the number of cocktails they've had. What follows is a researched social history of the New York City police department and the eras and events surrounding each of the cop members of my family. Though this is a family memoir, my approach is journalistic. I serve as both narrator and character. The perspective is uniquely mine and begins from my earliest memories.

One Saturday, when I was eight or nine, and my parents were out shopping at the Finast supermarket, I took it from my father's closet. I was surprised how heavy it was. The leather of the holster felt smooth and hard. It slipped out easily into my hand. The steel snub-nosed barrel and cylinder were cool against my palm. Currents of power and fright surged through me. But the fear I felt was not of the gun itself, but of the scolding I was sure to take if my father ever caught me. My curiosity, however, demanded to be satisfied.

I had watched his ritual a thousand times. At night, when he came home from work and stood in front of the hallway closet, my childhood imagination saw a Wild West gunslinger. I can still hear the slap his belt made as he whipped it off, his left hand at his side, holding the holster. I watched him—through the screen door as I stood on the stoop or peering over my comic book as I sat in the living room—while he snapped open the cylinder and let the bullets drop into his hand. I watched as he locked the bullets in a metal box, then wrapped the belt and holster together and placed them deep on the top shelf of his closet and shut the door.

I held the gun only a minute or two, aiming it at an imaginary bad guy, as I watched my reflection in the living room mirror, all the time listening for his car to pull into the driveway. I remember how the .38-caliber Police Special fit perfectly in my small hand.

CAMELOT

Pearl River

In short there's simply not a more congenial spot . . . than here in Camelot.   —Alan Jay Lerner, *Camelot*

1

My mother didn't want to move out of the Bronx. Period. She was more than content in the Fordham neighborhood in which we lived. When my father brought up the subject, my mother became quiet or began to talk about the weather or the nosy downstairs neighbors. She was a city kid, born and bred. All she had ever known was the Bronx. She liked that her friend Theresa lived one floor below. She liked that Alexander's was a few blocks away at Fordham Road and the Grand Concourse. In the Bronx, her first question to a new face at Devoe Park at the bottom of Sedgwick Avenue was "Are you from this parish?" St. Nicholas of Tolentine, gothic and cathedrallike, was more than just her church; it gave her her identity. For my mother, a move to Pearl River might as well have been a move to Russia. It was a foreign land—far too spread out, and far too far from the Bronx. "Do they even have Catholics there?" she had once asked my father, only half jokingly.

But by 1954, my father began to tell my mother that he was concerned for the safety of my older brothers, Frankie and Eugene, then nine and eleven. Neighborhood gangs, like the Scorpions, the Golden Guineas, and the Fordham Baldies, had begun to make their criminal presence felt. Though at that time, Fordham gangs were little more than juvenile delinquents, with most of their nefarious activities conducted between the factions (rumbles and the like), my father knew how quickly that could change. In the 41st Precinct, where he worked, just two miles or so south and east of Fordham, the seriousness of teenage gang crime was already in evidence. The Puerto Rican Lightnings had members just a few years older than Eugene. And, though he wouldn't broach the topic with my mother, who thought the Irish were the true chosen people, the Gents, a South Bronx Irish gang, had a division called the Junior Gents that *were* Eugene's age.

He had witnessed the handiwork of these pint-sized gang members, who gathered, sometimes thirty strong, in front of Eddie and Miriam's candy store on the corner of Hoe Avenue and West Farms Road. He saw the gaping wounds ripped in young flesh by car aerials (then the weapon of choice). One night, a young mother who lived over Eddie and Miriam's dumped a pot of cold water on the young toughs for making too much noise and keeping her baby awake. The Junior Gents retaliated by decapitating a stray cat, shoving a broomstick in the bloody corpse, and firing it like a lance though the woman's window. The Junior Gents were already using zip guns and marijuana. For most of those kids, heroin and revolvers were just around the corner.

Though his children's safety was undoubtedly of paramount importance, it wasn't my father's only motive for moving from the Bronx. Unlike my mother, he hadn't been born in New York City, but grew up in a small coal-mining town in eastern Pennsylvania. Though he moved to New York when he was only eighteen, and had, by 1954, been a city cop for twelve years, his allegiance to the Bronx wasn't anywhere close to my mother's. His dream was the garden-variety American version—a house, with a driveway and a backyard.

Even my mother had to admit that a home in the "country," as they called Pearl River at the time, would be a luxury of space. With four boys then (I was born in 1954), a move out of the cramped two-bedroom apartment at 2300 Sedgwick Avenue had become a necessity. But my mother's solution to the problem lay right across the street. She would take the stairs up to Tar Beach and look longingly at the newly erected apartment house, which advertised "studios," not the no-bedroom city apartments of today, but three-bedroom flats, with two—my God, two!—bathrooms. In the hopes of dissuading my father's intentions, my mother concocted a scheme with her friend Theresa to buy a coin-operated Laundromat, then a futuristic idea. My father humored her for a while, until it came time to fork over the down payment. He wasn't about to let her anchor him to the Bronx with a business. He wasn't going to gamble their savings. That money was going to be a down payment on a home.

Though my mom gave in to my father's wishes for a move out of the city, she didn't cave easily. During the spring of 1955, my parents took several car trips to Rockland County looking for houses. With each new house they considered, my mother would formulate some sort of excuse. It's right in front of a mountain, she said of one. The mountain, my father remembers, was little more than a hill. Another, in the neighboring town of Tappan, was in a community without a Catholic church or school—a sacrilege, she said. Others just gave her a bad feeling. When they looked at the house on the corner of Blauvelt Road and McKinley Street, my mother was caught in her own trap.

With my father walking ahead, angry and frustrated at her lack of cooperation, my mother chatted with the sales agent, who told her that this house was already promised to a doctor. But, the sales agent said, this was the model; there were other identical homes in the development that weren't taken. Mom saw this as an opportunity to prove that she wasn't being stubborn. After taking the tour of the house, she told my father that she liked it, and would be interested if this house, and only this house, was available. The builder, Mr. Lombardi, happened to be working in the yard that day, and my father went to speak to him. From the window in the kitchen, my mother smiled with approval at my father and then at Mr. Lombardi, all the time confident that the house was already sold.

In the yard, Mr. Lombardi told my father that the doctor had yet to come up with a binder for the home, and that if he really wanted it, it was his. In near despair, my mother watched as my father and Mr. Lombardi shook hands on the deal.

A little over three months later, on a blistering July day, the Seven Santini Brothers moving truck pulled in front of 2300 Sedgwick. As we drove over the George Washington Bridge, my mother cried; leaving the Bronx was a hurt she would never really get over. Yet, when the whole family walked (and carried me) into our new home, the first order of business was to hold hands and jump up and down listening to the beautiful silence of no one knocking back.

It was almost as if developers like Lombardi had civil servants in mind when they built their houses. They were ugly, cheap, and all looked the same. Asbestos-shingled Cape Cods and split-levels, carbon-copied twelve and fifteen at a clip, each with its own weedy and stony half-acre, sold on the average for $15,000. With as little as $500 down, and mortgages of thirty years obtained with the G.I. Bill (most of the buyers were World War II or Korea veterans), lifelong city apartment dwellers could be home owners. No more paying rent. No more trying to find the building super to fix the toilet. No more city buses blowing their horns below your bedroom window. With the completion in 1955 of the Tappan Zee Bridge over the Hudson River, and the extension of the New York State Thruway, cutting the commute from Rockland County to New York City to less than half an hour, people could keep their civil service jobs and still live like country lords.

It was a carrot hung from blue-collar heaven, and the houses sold like sheet sets at a white sale. Between 1950 and 1960 over 50,000 people moved to Rockland County.

In my memories from our early days in Pearl River, my father is standing somewhere in the background. Freshman lanky, but with a prodigious beer belly that made him look like a kid smuggling a basketball out of a gymnasium. He would pat it often and say: "Cost me plenty." His hair was coal black, thick and swept back. His face was long and his nose was just a size or two too wide for it. Most of the time his expression was dour, the corners of his mouth turned down. But when he did laugh it resonated with a deep baritone, and his stomach would shake.

The reason my father isn't in the forefront of my memories is simply because he wasn't around all that much. It wasn't that he spent all his off time in the bars, like some cops did. No, it was his job that kept him away. Often, the phone would ring at dinnertime or afterward and I'd listen to his all-business detective-boss voice. When he hung up the phone he would go to his closet, strap his gun back onto his belt, put on his suit jacket, and after a short muffled explanation to my mother, head out the door. Once in a while, I would answer the phone when one of those calls came for him. The gravelly voices on the other end would sometimes say: "Could I speak to your daddy?" Sometimes, disregarding my age, they would just ask for Lieutenant McDonald.

But even when my father was there, at home, he erected a wall between himself and his family. Each evening I'd watch for him to pull into the driveway. I didn't run to him and jump in his arms the way some kids did when their fathers came home from work, the way you'd see on television shows like *Father Knows Best*. Instead, I'd peer out of my bedroom window, or from the side lawn, where I played whiffleball, sometimes just by myself, pretending I was Ed Kranepool launching homers into the big pine tree on the corner of our property. My father's long legs would fold from the car and he would stand on the driveway for a moment and stretch his back. He wore tortoise-shell sunglasses, the kind you see in photographs of John F. Kennedy on his sailboat off Hyannisport. He would rub the back of his neck before climbing the brick steps to the house. Inside, he would fix himself a scotch and sit silently in his chair in the living room.

When I did hear him talk about his work, the words bubbled up uncontrolled, like gas from a corned-beef-sandwich lunch. From these utterances I knew his precinct was a "jungle," and that it was filled with "Mau-Maus." I knew that the word "junkies" was always preceded with the imprecation "goddamned." I knew, too, that he was "in the chorus," the euphemism he used for the police department, although this was at first confusing. "Why do policemen sing?" I asked my mother.

I somehow knew his job was important. But I came to this conclusion not because of anything he said, but because of what he wore. Meticulously hung in the vestibule closet, over his neatly positioned size eleven "David" wing-tip shoes (two pair, one black, one brown; stretched with shoe trees, polished regularly, and resoled and reheeled once a year), his suits had "weights" for summer and winter. Some of them came with two pairs of pants.

But it was his expression rather than his clothing or few words that told the full story. With each year, his face became more stoic until it looked as though it had been chipped from pale rock. The details of what went on each day and night at his job aside, the result of that struggle—even to a six-year-old—was obvious. The cops were losing.

2

Pearl River prior to the suburban explosion of the 1950s might well have been a country town in any number of places in rural New England. It was heavily wooded with birch, pine, and elm, dotted with cattail-filled marshes and undulating hills. There were orchards—apple and peach—and fields of corn, cabbage, and tomatoes naturally irrigated by tumbling streams. Even after we moved into the house on the corner of Blauvelt Road and McKinley Street, I can remember deer and red foxes scampering through the backyard, and, of course, raccoons who welcomed suburbia and the garbage that came with it with open paws. One of the favorite pastimes my friends and I had was to search for arrowheads in the woods of a section of the town called Naurashaun, which, three hundred years before, had been inhabited by the Lenni-Lenape Indians. Though we found plenty of rocks, we unearthed no trace of the tribe.

Throughout southern Rockland there were pre–Revolutionary War homes, and graveyards with crumbling and tilted tombstones, that dated back to the 1700s. George Washington's Continental Army had once made camp in Orangeburg, a town bordering Pearl River to the east. In 1781, Washington celebrated his victory over Cornwallis at Yorktown in Mabie's Tavern in the neighboring town of Tappan, not far from where, in a farmhouse owned by a family named Bogart, General Lafayette had once set up headquarters. Major Andre, the British spy, was tried and convicted of treason in a tavern in Tappan, now a restaurant called the 1776 House.

In 1890, an industrialist named Braunsdorf purchased a parcel of southern Rockland named Muddy Creek, after a lazy brook that wound through the area. He built a sewing-machine factory and then enticed the New York and New Jersey Rail Road, a subsidiary of the Erie line, to build a line of tracks nearby by erecting a train station, which still stands in the middle of what is now Pearl River. Early lore has it that railroad workers or local residents (or both) found pearls in freshwater oysters embedded in Muddy Creek. But more likely, Braunsdorf changed the name of the community to Pearl River as an early public relations move, to entice business and settlers to the growing community. Braunsdorf was a visionary. He built stores and the first post office in

Rockland County. He was also an inventor. If it weren't for Thomas A. Edison's idea some years later, Braunsdorf's electric arc light might have made him a household name.

In the fall of 1942, the Army Corps of Engineers, along with several local contractors, built a troop staging camp on farmland in Orangeburg. With its proximity to the Hudson River, and thereby to New York Harbor, Camp Shanks became one of the two largest GI embarkation facilities in the country (the other was a sister camp, Camp Kilmer, at New Brunswick, New Jersey). Through the barracks of Camp Shanks, 1.3 million U.S. soldiers passed on their way to Europe to fight the war. Thousands more were processed through the camp on their way home; most of these were frontline soldiers.

In the years after the war, stories in the *Journal-News*, the local paper, told about G.I.s from around the country who first saw Rockland County during their time at Camp Shanks, liked it, and returned to settle there. The camp was also used as a processing facility for German and Italian prisoners, both those on their way to internment in POW camps in the United States and those being repatriated back to their homelands. There was even a story in the paper of a German POW who first saw the lush, rolling hills of the county through the barred windows of Camp Shanks and returned to Rockland after the war, where he made his living as a Volkswagen mechanic.

One of the American soldiers who passed through Camp Shanks on his way to Europe but did not return was army lieutenant Vincent Skelly, my uncle. He was killed in action in Saint-Lô, France, a few weeks after the Normandy invasion.

In 1956, the 1,300 acres that made up Camp Shanks was sold to housing developers, and the land became part of the suburban explosion.

The multitudes of city cops who eventually moved to Pearl River actually began with just a small group of apostles. In 1955, there were only about a dozen city cops living in the area. Some of the earliest, along with my family, were Edward "Tink" Bentley and his brothers, Walter and Andrew, who were radio car partners on the West Side of Manhattan; Frank Eckart, also a cop on the West Side, who moonlighted as a lifeguard at Nanuet Lake, the swimming club to which we belonged; and Ed McElligott and Ray Sheridan, detective partners in the 48th Precinct in the Bronx, who bought homes right next to each other in Pearl River. The reason cops were such a small percentage of this initial migration was simple. For them, it was illegal to live in Rockland County.

Back in the Depression, the longtime Bronx borough president, James J. Lyons, had championed a law requiring municipal city workers, such as cops and firemen, to live within the five boroughs of New York City. His rallying cry was "Local jobs for local boys." Although exemptions to the law were passed in the late 1950s—and by then, for the most part, police brass tended to ignore the regulation (probably because more and more of the upper echelon of the NYPD was moving out of the city, too)—the Lyons Law was still very much in effect when my family moved to Pearl River. My father, like the other early cop settlers, had to "maintain a residence" in New York City. On tax forms and other official papers, he used the address of my mother's sister Ruth, who lived in Parkchester.

For my father, the move to Pearl River was something of a gamble and very uncharacteristic. He was a stickler about adhering to the rules of the police department. Once, as a patrolman, during the first days of World War II, he and a small squad of other rookie cops were assigned to guard the reservoir in Central Park as rumors swirled that the Japanese were planning to poison the city water supply. It was a late December night, and the temperature dove to near zero. There was a windowless pump station near the reservoir that was heated, but he refused to even warm himself for a minute, because his explicit orders were not to leave his post. He might have frozen to death had it not been for a grizzled old patrol sergeant who pulled him off the post and drove him back to the station house to thaw out. One of my father's favorite expressions was "play by the book," and he did, throughout his police career. Apparently, however, his desire to get out of the Bronx was so strong, he was willing to do so at the risk of his career—one that was filled with promise. In 1955, as a detective-lieutenant squad commander, my father had arguably the highest profile—and undoubtedly the highest rank—of all the city cops in Rockland. For the first few years we lived in Pearl River, he rarely drove his own car to work. Fearing being spotted by either a boss or a shoofly (an Internal Affairs investigator), my father took a lift with a Con Edison worker who lived in town and worked near his precinct in the Bronx. Perhaps there is no one better at hiding from investigators than cops, and my father was no exception. When a case made him miss his lift home, he would borrow a car from a used-car dealer near the station house. We never knew what kind of broken-down heap would pull in to the driveway. It could be an old round DeSoto or big-finned Chrysler. But he wasn't only fearful of shooflies and bosses. He was also worried about the native neighbors, who didn't exactly roll up the welcome wagon to the homes of any of the new arrivals from New York City. Though some native Rocklanders, especially the businessmen and merchants, were happy with the encroachment of suburbia, some saw it with the enthusiasm of a Parisian watching the Germans march through the Arc de Triomphe.

By the late 1950s, though it was still illegal for them to live in Rockland (exemptions in the Lyons Law allowed for cops and other city workers to live in counties that, like Westchester and Nassau, were contiguous with the city limits), the number of New York policemen in the county increased dramatically. Because of the clandestine nature of the situation, official records of how many city cops actually lived in Rockland were not kept. But to offer some insight, three of the twelve homes in the development where we lived were owned by city cops. Given the fact that there were hundreds of new housing developments throughout lower Rockland at the time, and although the ratio of cops to non-cops varied throughout, at the very least the original twelve had grown by twelvefold.

As each day the shadow of New York City crept closer to their bucolic way of life, the suburbanites feared that lurking in that darkness were all of the city's ills. Sometimes these suspicions boiled over into pure resentment. The people who lived across the street from us wouldn't let their children play with my older brothers, because Frankie and Eugene were "city kids." But nowhere was this animosity more in evidence than in the relationship between the local police and the city cops.

As it had been from its earliest existence, the New York City Police Department of the late 1950s was the most insular of societies. In a paramilitary organization, with overwhelmingly homogeneous ethnicity and culture (read: Irish, Catholic) the danger of the job and a common enemy (criminals) encouraged a locker room–like camaraderie. For the city cops living in Rockland County at this time, this brotherhood was intensified even further by their secretive living situation. They car-pooled and socialized together. They joined fraternal organizations like the Knights of Columbus. Their families—our families—went on vacations together to the Police Camp in the Catskills. For city cops, there was no good reason to venture outside their circle. In their minds, the outside world was a place they had little in common with, a place that did not operate under the same rules and codes. In those years, Rockland County was the outside world.

Before the Palisades Interstate Parkway was completed in 1958, offering an exit to Pearl River and Orangeburg, city cops would drive home from work on the winding two-lane country road Route 9W. Just off 9W in Tappan stood two taverns, Sullivan's and the Orangeburg Hotel. It was here that the two cop cultures first collided.

Perhaps, on the part of the Orangetown cops, there was a feeling of being outgunned—a pure machismo type of thing. By 1957, 1958, the twenty-four-man force of the Orangetown Police Department was outnumbered five to one by the big-city counterparts living in their jurisdiction. After day shifts and midnight tours, Sullivan's and the Orangeburg Hotel would be thick with the cigar smoke of city cops sitting shoulder to shoulder at the bar. As at Rick's Café Américain in *Casablanca*, nothing infuriates the locals more than when the saloons fall to the occupying army. What irritated the Orangetown cops even further was the use of the local ball fields.

For years before city cops came to the county, the high school field in the middle of Pearl River had been a favorite spot for Orangetown police and other native Rocklanders to play softball. The city cops practically took over the field. They had enough players for two teams to play against each other, with a third full team waiting to play the winners. It was after losing the softball fields that the Orangetown police had a meeting at which they decided not to extend any professional courtesy to the city cops. During this time, my father was pulled over for a broken taillight on one of the junk heaps he had borrowed from the used-car dealer. When he told the Orangetown cop he was a lieutenant on "the Job" in the city, the local officer was unimpressed. Though my father wasn't issued a ticket, the local cop gave him a stern warning (what any other citizen would be allowed), and promised the next time he saw him, he would write him up. Other city cops weren't as lucky. Their cars parked near the ball field routinely received tickets for the most inconsequential of offenses. Some were pulled over for minor traffic violations and given summonses. Certainly, in looking back, these indiscretions on the part of city cops—matters of softball fields and bars—seem trivial. But, perhaps, for the Orangetown cops, ball fields and bars represented resentments that ran much deeper.

City cops were better paid; the detectives wore better suits, and they worked in a job that was world renowned. In 1960, the pay for Orangetown cops was less than $5,000 yearly, far less than the city cops made, and that salary came without medical benefits or a pension. All of the Orangetown cops had to work second jobs. For them, the New York City cops were not only an occupying army, but their guaranteed twenty-year pension plans meant they were going to be in Rockland County forever. What's more, Orangetown cops were often the target of ridicule by the city cops. Then, there was essentially no crime in Rockland County, save the occasional drunk driver and teenage prankster. City cops joked that their country cousins shot a squirrel once in a while just to make sure their guns worked. But the rift between the two police departments didn't last forever. And, ironically, it was a scandal involving an ex–New York cop that marked the end of the division.

On Thursday, March 26, 1959, with hatchets and sledgehammers in hand, a task force of twenty-one law enforcement agents, including members of the New York State Police and the State Crime Commission, and agents from the Rockland County district attorney's office, broke through the front door of the Comfort Coal building in Piermont, executing a midnight gambling raid. What had tipped off the local authorities was the preponderance of "gangster cars," black Lincolns and Cadillacs, parked throughout the sleepy hamlet on specific nights of the week. Piermont, just a few miles from Pearl River, was like the town time forgot. So unusual was its Depression-era look, Woody Allen would years later use it as the backdrop in his period piece *The Purple Rose of Cairo*. In 1959, a black Lincoln parked anywhere in Piermont went about as unnoticed as a farm tractor pulling into an IRT subway station.

Once inside the building, the agents arrested forty men and confiscated some $6,000. Orangetown cops who had staked out the building for some weeks prior said that the gambling operation's weekend take reached $50,000 and more. The night of the raid, most of the gamblers were found sitting around plywood tables playing three-card monte and gin rummy. Though the accommodations were rustic, they were also quite genteel. On a plywood buffet table sat platters of fried chicken and sliced watermelon, and bottles of anisette. Most of those arrested had New York City addresses. The raid was conducted without notice to the local police chief, John J. Smith.

Smitty, as he was known, had been the police chief of Piermont for less than two months. Before his short tenure as chief, he was a New York City plainclothes policeman assigned to the 10th Division vice squad in Harlem. In April 1958, less than a year before the Piermont raid, the Tenth Division had been disbanded for ties with "KGs," police parlance for known gamblers. Smitty and others from his unit were packed off to the Bronx Park Precinct—in exile, to be sure. In August of that year, after Piermont residents had voted to form their own police department (they had been under the jurisdiction of the Orangetown police), the Piermont Village Board began conducting a search for a police chief. The job paid $5,500 a year and came with the responsibility of heading a force of four officers.

Just how Smitty became a candidate for the position I'm not sure. I do know, however, that his subsequent appointment was fought by the Rockland County Police Benevolent Association. They contended that Smitty, still a member of the New York City police department while he was under consideration for the Piermont job, was required to live in New York City, and so couldn't possibly have fulfilled the Piermont job's requirement of six months' Rockland County residency. Still, in January 1959, the state civil service commission approved Smitty's appointment, over the PBA's objections.

The night of the raid, Smitty resigned his post, but that bit of theatrics didn't solve his problems. Three months later, he was indicted by a Rockland County grand jury on gambling charges. At first, Smitty contended that he was not involved in any way with the gambling operation. But as time went by, and information was gathered—mainly from the gamblers themselves—it became known that Smitty was not only aware of the game, but was involved in its operation.

What frightened the local residents, fueled the investigation, and ultimately put Smitty in an untenable situation was not the size of the game, but the players involved. One of the men arrested that night was Michael "Big Mike" Pinetti, from East Harlem, Smitty's old beat. Pinetti was a real-life Nathan Detroit. He ran crap games and other gambling enterprises all over Manhattan. He also had close ties with Willie Moretti, a high-ranking member in what was then the Luciano crime family. For native Rocklanders, Pinetti was their worst fears made real, and in Smitty they saw the personification of the slick big-city cop who thought they were all rubes. Because of this, Smitty took the worst of the punishments handed down by the grand jury. While Pinetti was sentenced to two months in jail, the ex-chief was given one year. His crime was officially "neglect of public duty." But for most city cops, including my father, Smitty's crime was much more grievous: he had stained the reputation of all the cops who lived in Rockland, and, for that matter, of every good cop in the entire department. In my father's view, there was only one thing worse than a bad cop: a bad cop who made good cops look bad. But besides besmirching good reputations, Smitty's actions also drew a spotlight on the city cops living surreptitiously in Rockland County. Though none of the city cops had to leave their homes and move back to the Bronx, the last thing they wanted was publicity, which is exactly what the Piermont raid brought. For two solid months, Smitty was the headline in the local *Journal*

News. He even made, the day after the raid, page one of *The New York Times.*

Still, in some ways, Smitty's transgression helped heal the break between the Orangetown and New York City cops. For one thing, it took the wind out of the more blustery city cops. It turned out the Orangetown police didn't only shoot squirrels. They were trying to do their job and weren't as naive as their big-city counterparts thought them to be. And, on the part of the Orangetown cops, even for the most hostile of them, a year's jail sentence gained Smitty a certain amount of sympathy. Orangetown cops knew he was a father with a house full of children. They also knew that jail time, for a cop of any stripe, was an unthinkable punishment.

But perhaps what gained Smitty the most sympathy—in time, even from the city cops—was that it was just hard not to like him. In the years that followed the raid, Smitty's personality overshadowed his crime. He later became a bartender, working in a number of taverns in Pearl River. Smitty had the perfect temperament for behind the bar, gregarious and fast with a funny line. As each generation of Pearl River teenagers reached drinking age—many (myself included) New York City cops' children—Smitty kept watch over them like a defrocked priest in a Jimmy Cagney movie. So, too, did Orangetown cops flock to the other side of the bar from Smitty. There they confided to him that card and crap games had in fact existed in Piermont for years before he arrived, albeit in a more localized form, in the back of the barbershop and the grocery store.

But there was another reason why the rift between the two departments disappeared. As the number of city cops in Rockland County increased, they moved to houses across the street and down the block from Orangetown cops. When they became neighbors, a familiarity grew between the two police departments. They had plenty in common—the struggles of home ownership and putting children through school. Not too long after the Piermont raid, a popular New York policeman named Gately was killed on the way home from work when his car crashed on the Tappan Zee Bridge. His funeral was held at St. Margaret's in Pearl River, and the church overflowed with New York City cops. On the steps of the church stood a color guard sent by the Orangetown Police Department. If there was any animosity left on either side, it was dispelled that day.

3

Although he hung up his suit jacket each night, my father kept his tie on tight to his collar. At the dinner table, he would fold it inside his shirt. Right up until he undressed for bed, he wore his tie. I once told the mother of a friend of mine on the block that my father wore a tie in the shower. She laughed and asked where I got my sense of humor from, as if it was known that my father was devoid of one.

He wasn't. But he seemed the butt of the joke much more than the teller. My parents belonged to a card group that met every Friday night. For the most part, the players were city cops and their wives. When the game was held at our house, I would listen from my room to raucous laughter and banging on the table, part of a card game called Bernie, Bernie. I never heard my father's voice. When the gathering was held at houses other than ours, my father was always the first to leave. He earned the name "Mr. Coats" because he would gather his coat and my mother's and wait impatiently for her to hurry her good-byes.

In personality, my mother and father were polar opposites. Fiery and emotional, traits that showed in her intense blue-green eyes, my mother was as demonstrative as my father was self-contained. She had an explosive temper, inherited from her Irish-born mother and handed down to her sons. Most of her ire seemed to be directed at my father. My parents' arguments were always one-sided. My mother would rant at him: "Jesus, Mary, and Holy

Saint Joseph, once in while think about someone besides your-self." I suppose most of her anger toward him was residual, from the move out of the Bronx. But there were other underlying resentments—never mentioned even during the screaming.

Sometimes, in the middle of her tirades, my father would look up the stairs and see me standing there watching: "Let's go to Dairy Queen, Bri. I have the collirobbles," he'd say, using his term for the ripping pain in his stomach. In his Volkswagen on the way, he'd chew the end of an unlit cigar. I wanted to know why he didn't stick up for himself in arguments with my mom. But I didn't say anything. Neither did he.

They didn't argue all the time. And, although I can't remember many intimate moments between them—tender touches, or any-thing more than perfunctory kisses good-bye—there were some clues to the affection they had for each other. On my mother's birthday or Christmas, my father would go to the Pearl Shoppe, a quaint little store in Pearl River, and buy her a silk scarf or a pair of earrings. His gift would always be accompanied with a card, which was then displayed on the shelf under the bow window in the living room. He signed the card in the same manner every time: "Love, Franko"—which, no doubt, was her term of endear-ment for him. But I can't remember ever hearing my mother call him that. Most times, when they were together in the house, my mother would sit in her reclining chair doing a crossword puzzle, separated from my father by the oak table—and about a million miles—both of them silently facing the bow window like some mismatched pair of officers on the bridge of Jules Verne's *Nau-tilus*, burrowing through the soundless sea.

My mother tenaciously held on to her Bronxness, and she had lit-tle to do with anyone in Rockland County who could not recall the opulence that once was the Grand Concourse. As it hap-pened, by 1960, she was surrounded by people who could. The development on McKinley Street was almost wholly made up of

families from the Bronx, and they wore their old neighborhoods—and parishes—like name tags at a sales convention: Highbridge, Kingsbridge, and Throgs Neck; Sacred Heart, St. John's,
and St. Francis, to name a few. Some old Bronx habits lived
through the suburban transition. People sat on their front stoops
in the summer, though now separated by lawns and driveways.
Fathers played stickball on the weekends, with the three-sewer
home run rule surviving the move. We even had Bronx-like block
parties. Still, for my mother, these familiarities were nothing
more than cheap imitations, and she desperately missed her
Bronx friends and old home.

In Pearl River, the friendships my mother did make were with
the wives of other city cops. Like their husbands, they kept to
themselves. My mother belonged to the sister organization of the
Knights of Columbus, the Columbiettes, whose members were
mostly cop wives. Most of these women had young, growing
families, and accordingly, a great deal of their time was spent in
St. Margaret's School–related activities. In our early years in Pearl
River, before I was old enough to go to school, my mother would
take me along to the Columbiette meeting room in the basement
of the K of C hall. The din of conversation in that room was
sharp with nasal Bronx accents. The ashtrays were filled with
white-filtered cigarettes, all with deep red lipstick stains.

In those years, I formed a special bond with my mother; it happens when you're the youngest. My older brothers were all in
school: Tommy at St. Margaret's; Frankie at Pearl River High
School; and Eugene away at the State University of New York
Maritime College at Fort Schuyler, Queens. Together we'd go on
shopping trips to Alexander's in Fordham or to meet her best
friend, Nora, at the Automat on Fordham Road. They would sit,
drink coffee, and talk for hours and I would eat lemon meringue
pie and tour the little compartments looking at the treats behind
the glass doors. For me, these trips were like secret missions, a

glimpse into my mother's real happiness. Even at five or six, I knew that my mother flowered against the gray backdrop of the Bronx.

During the summer, on weekdays, my mother sat in a circle of beach chairs with the other cop wives at Nanuet Lake. On the weekend, their husbands, our fathers, had their own circle. With their white skin, and outfits of bathing suits, knee-high black nylon socks, and brogan shoes, you could have picked them out from the window of an airliner. All of my friends at the lake were the sons and daughters of New York cops: Michael Skennion, Gerard Sheridan, the Baumann girls, and others. Even on our vacations we were surrounded by cop families.

The Police Camp in the Catskills had been given to the New York City police department in the early 1920s by David Kaplan, a wealthy New York financier. Once Kaplan's country estate, the land consisted of 600 acres of dense wood and clearings veined with crystal streams that spilled down the side of the mountain. When the NYPD took it over, they called it the Police Recreation Farm, and used it for the rehabilitation of policemen and members of their families who had taken ill with consumption or pneumonia. But mostly it was used for cops who needed the fresh mountain air to dry out.

By the mid 1920s, the center was already being used more for recreation than rehabilitation. The police commissioner at the time, Richard E. Enright, ordered policemen, including the Riot Battalion, to help in building sewers, a reservoir, and bungalows, to modernize the camp for pleasure use.

By the early sixties, there was a waiting list to reserve a week at the camp, which lodged a hundred cop families in bungalows or in the main hotel, Kaplan's old large and sprawling house, built at the highest vantage, with a wraparound porch and a vista of lush green magnificence.

The last time we went to the camp was in 1960. On that trip it was just me, Tommy and my mother. My father had to work, as did my brothers Frankie and Eugene. One night after dinner, I played flashlight tag with some friends in the darkness that engulfed the grounds surrounding the main hotel. I could hear the clink of cocktail glasses and loud cop conversation from the front porch. I heard my mother telling a story of ordering oysters that night at dinner. All of the waiters at the camp were the sons of cops, and most of them became cops themselves. One even became the police commissioner—Robert J. McGuire, who had worked at the camp in the 1950s. My mother said that the young man who was taking care of her table returned with a message from the chef, who said that if she wanted oysters she should go to Sheepshead Bay. I can still remember the laughter from her story floating on the still summer night air. That night, the sky was littered with sparkling stars. My friends and I lay on the grass and picked out the constellations. To us, that everything we did involved other cops' families was the most natural thing in the world—our orbit in a solar system held in place by the gravity of the New York City Police Department.

In November 1960, my mother was absolutely aglow when John F. Kennedy was elected president. But even my parents' political affiliations kept them at odds. My father voted for Nixon, and he wasn't alone among the New York cops living in Rockland. The attachment of the New York City police department to the Democratic party, a partnership that dated back to the very beginning of Tammany Hall, didn't survive the move to suburbia. The saying went: "As soon as a cop buys a power lawn mower he becomes a staunch Republican."

Because it was such a loaded subject for both, my parents made a deal early on in Kennedy's term that political discussions were verboten. Still, my mother couldn't help but remind him every now and then who had won the election. But, in time, even my father softened toward JFK. I can remember his laughter wafting up the stairs from the rec room as he sat watching the young president's beguiling press conferences. But perhaps the most obvious area in which Kennedy's presidency affected my father, and every other New York City detective, was fashion. Since the inception of the detective bureau, its members had always been identified by the hats they wore. My father's was one of the more popular styles, a plain Dobbs fedora. But other detectives wore homburgs, even porkpies (the hat that Gene Hackman's movie character, Popeye Doyle, wears in *The French Connection*). Detectives in Manhattan's 14th, 16th, and 18th Detective Squads, especially those near the Theater District, were known for flipping up the front brim of their fedoras, a style that Mickey Spillane's Mike Hammer made famous. But with Kennedy's thick, uncovered locks, detectives' hats became a relic, like the bobby-style helmets the cops at the turn of the century wore. Luckily for my father, he had a Kennedy-like head of hair. There were plenty of detectives who didn't, and from that point on, their baldness was exposed for the world to see.

The Kennedy years marked the end of the successful transition to America's suburban way of life. City cops in Pearl River measured this success in the most modest, practical ways. Through the miracle of immigrant Italian masonry and cheap wood paneling, built-in garages were turned into rec rooms. Cement was poured for patios and redwood decks were affixed to the backs of houses. For the most part, city cops weren't the handiest of groups. Most, having grown up in apartments, hadn't picked up a hammer in their whole lives, unless it was to hit someone over the head with it. Hadler's, a hardware store in town, became a popular meeting spot for city cops who imposed upon the proprietor, George Hadler, for instructions on basic home-improvement projects—simple electrical wiring and how to mix cement.

Like most of that Depression, World War II generation, they also measured success in the opportunities given to their children. Bragging rights came along with the enrollment of cops' kids in private high schools in northern New Jersey, such as Don Bosco and Bergen Catholic, which my brother Eugene attended. Later, colleges such as Fordham University and NYU provided the same chest-thumping platform.

But ultimately, success was measured purely along civil service lines, and rank was the great divider. Even as a young kid, I knew the chain of command: patrolman, sergeant, lieutenant, captain, deputy inspector, full inspector, and so on, and I knew the subtle differences between them: Patrolmen's kids wore hand-me-down clothing and inherited their older siblings' bicycles. Lieutenants' kids got their own bikes and shopped at Robert Hall for new Easter suits or dresses each year. Perhaps the biggest jump was from lieutenant to captain.

One of my father's friends in town was James Skennion. After his first wife died, Mr. Skennion married a New York City police-woman, whom everyone called Mary, including her stepchildren, Jimmy and my friend Michael. If you had to pick a poster family for New York cops living in Pearl River, the Skennion family would be it. They lived in a fine brick home with a built-in pool on a cul-de-sac. Mr. Skennion was an affable man who talked out of the side of his mouth, the side that didn't hold the cigar. Whenever I saw him—at Nanuet Lake, or at pool parties held at his home for his cop friends' families—he would tousle my hair and in a growl like a friendly lion ask, "How are you, lad." But aside from his built-in pool and good-natured way, what made Mr. Skennion quite possibly the most popular of the cop fathers was his job.

One of the few memories I have of being alone with my father was the day he brought me to a Yankee game. We didn't even need tickets: My father showed his badge to get us in the stadium, and Mr. Skennion, as captain in charge of the detail at Yankee Stadium, arranged for our seats behind home plate. We stopped in his office in the bowels of the stadium before the game. While we were there, a tall black man dressed in a suit walked in the door. Mr. Skennion greeted the man with a roar of hello and a slap on the back and then turned to me: "Lad, I'd like you to meet Big Ellie," he said. "Big Ellie who?" I replied. That I didn't know Elston Howard, the then All-Star catcher for the Yankees, was cause for a big laugh all around. "You must be a Mets fan," the catcher said, smiling. Actually, I was. I had Mets pennants in my bedroom, and my brother Eugene had, the year earlier, in 1962, taken me to the Polo Grounds to watch them play, an event that instantly formed me as a fan for life. In spite of my allegiance to the crosstown team, Elston Howard signed a baseball for me, and I decided right then and there that being a captain was much more important than a lieutenant.

By 1963, there were over a thousand city-cop families living in Rockland County. Though this number represented a fraction of the then 28,000 members of the NYPD, by no means did 1963 mark the end of cops moving out of the city. The number of commuting city cops increased by hundreds, thousands, over the ensuing years.

And as more and more city cops moved to Rockland, and as those cops moved up the ranks of the police department, a political power base developed. This was an arena in which my father was well versed—put him in a room filled with cigar smoke and a politician or two, and he was at his best. He had spent a good part of his police career involved in the Detective Endowment Association, a line organization and quasi union of New York City detectives.

As members of the Knights of Columbus the city cops had lobbied several county politicians, including a state senator named Joseph Nowicki, for exemptions to the Lyons Law. To concentrate their political punch even further, city cops splintered off from the Knights of Columbus and formed a chapter of the Ancient Order of Hibernians, an Irish fraternal organization. The charter membership of the Pearl River chapter of the AOH read like a verse from "McNamara's Band": Sheridan, Dunn, Moran,

O'Brien, and McDonald. My father was the first president of the chapter, and wrote the bylaws on the typewriter on his desk in the 41st Precinct squad room.

There is nothing like a parade to draw the attention of politicians. In 1962, along with my father, Ray Sheridan, the Bronx detective who lived next to his partner, organized the first St. Patrick's Day parade in Rockland, which was held in New City, the county seat. Except for a few logistical problems (the small streets in New City and not being fully prepared for the crowds) the parade was a resounding success, with thousands of people watching. The event empowered city cops in the AOH as a political entity. That same year the "Lyons Law" was repealed.

In March 1963, on the Sunday after St. Patrick's Day, the AOH parade, having been moved to the wide streets of Pearl River, marched down Middletown Road and turned onto Central Avenue, led by Finbar Divine of the New York City police department's Emerald Society Pipe Band. Six foot four, with a waxed handlebar mustache soaring from his face like the wings of a black hawk in full flight, his chest thrust forward, pumping his five-foot-long crosier, his noble chin an icebreaker slicing through the cold March winds, he fronted the bagpipes wailing "Garry-Owens." Behind the band, little boys and girls, dressed in Catholic school uniforms, the girls' knees rosy from the cold, followed, as though Finbar were a fearless giant leading them through the safe green fields of Pearl River. It mattered little that twenty-two miles south a coming funnel cloud was forming that would spiral crime rates to the city's all-time high. It didn't matter that the move of white policemen from the city they were charged with protecting exacerbated a racial division that was already exploding in riots. No. For my father, and the other city cops who proudly watched, the parade was a manifestation of their dreams. It was the same dream that, fifty odd years earlier, my grandfather had

had when he moved his family to a neighborhood in Brooklyn—then suburban itself—filled with cops who commuted on the newly built subway. It was a dream my brother Frankie, surrounded by cop culture and infused with familial instinct, would inherit, and struggle to keep alive. Along the route, New York City cop parents: fathers wearing green tam o'shanters, faces red from an earlier-than-usual scotch, mothers with Kelly green scarves and guilty eyes hiding truths of unhappy homes or too much St. Patrick's celebration the night before, clapped and smiled, secure in the knowledge that this their town was as insular and magical as Brigadoon. Or better yet, with Kennedy in the White House, Camelot.

4

The following summer, 1963, was the last time all of my brothers lived in the house in Pearl River with my parents. Eugene was on summer break from the Maritime College; Frankie was working two jobs—construction and the Honey Wagon, as my father called the garbage truck Frankie hung off early each morning; Tommy, then thirteen, was playing Babe Ruth League baseball; and me, nine years old. Most of my memories of those years were of Frankie. My other two brothers were important presences, but Eugene was much older and a mystery to me, defined more by his absence than any quirks of character, while Tommy was just enough older than me to consider me a pain in his ass. When we were leaving the house to go out and play, my mother would yell those words to Tommy that would make me shiver: "Take your brother with you." For Tommy, this was the greatest of burdens, and he never shied away from letting me know it. Frankie, however, was a different story.

Under the pine trees, I would watch him wash his car, a Malibu Super Sport with baby moon hubcaps. When I tried to help, he would spray me with the hose or grab me by my hands and spin me until I walked like my uncle Joe coming home from the American Legion Hall. At night, we'd shoot sock basketballs into a hamper placed on my desk, a nickel a game. Having practiced all day, I'd beat him most of the time, firing caroms off two walls, using the shade on the window as a backboard. But I'd play him double or nothing, until he got even (most times I'd miss on purpose). I knew his rituals by heart. Getting ready for a date with his girlfriend, Carol, he'd press his chino pants to a razor-sharp crease and hang them by the cuffs from the top drawer of his bureau. He paid me a quarter to buff his loafers until they shined like the Malibu, but I would gladly have done them for nothing. He'd spend an hour in the shower, then wipe a hole in the fogged-up bathroom mirror, and spend forever shaping his hair with Georgia Peach—the front into a pompadour, the back into a ducktail. Though not handsome in the classic sense, he had rough good looks with intense eyes like his mother's, and a single deep dimple in his chin that looked as though, as a baby, he had fallen asleep on the point of a pencil. For hours after he left, the bathroom would be thick with the sweet fragrance of Old Spice aftershave.

One night that summer, when my parents had gone out for the evening, Frankie had a party at the house. From my bedroom, I heard some loud shouting and came out to see what was happening. My brother was standing in the living room facing a teenager with broad athletic shoulders. His name was Bobby, and he was screaming in Frankie's face, the argument over their girlfriends. Frankie glared at Bobby. When my brother became angry, all other emotion was displaced, his eyes glazed, his outward demeanor would seem calm, almost serene. Plenty were fooled. For Frankie was like a shark feigning indifference to his prey. But I knew what was about to happen.

I had watched, peeking out the kitchen window, his fights with Eugene on the side lawn. At one time, Eugene, two years older, always had the better of Frankie, who couldn't seem to infiltrate his older brother's superior reach. Still, no matter how bad a beating he took, even with tears streaming down his cheeks, his lips fattened and bloody, or his shoulder pinned to the ground by Eugene's knees, Frankie would not give up. "You punch like a girl," he would say defiantly. But as they grew older, as Frankie developed a barrel chest and bulging arms, not even Eugene would take him on. By the time he was in his late teens, even my father tiptoed around his anger. The night he graduated from high school he was involved in an accident while driving my mother's car. I saw the flashing lights of the police car in our driveway from my bedroom window, then saw my father, wearing only his boxer shorts and sleeveless "guinea" T-shirt, as he called it, talking to the cop on the front steps. At first, the conversation was muffled. Something about Frankie running a stop sign and smashing the car into a utility pole. The young Orangetown policeman knew my father was a detective-lieutenant in the Bronx. By this time, the local police treated city cops, especially those with rank, with a mixture of envy and respect. The patrolman stood on the steps holding his hat behind his back. He told my father that though Frankie had been drinking, no charges would be filed. My father thanked him, but his tone was commanding, dismissive.

When the patrolman left, the screaming started. At first, Frankie sat on the couch, his head down, as my father lit into him. The car, a two-tone white and aquamarine Chevy Bel Air, had been totaled. Carol had suffered a broken arm. As my father riddled him with white-hot words, I saw it begin. As always, the first sign came in my brother's eyes: a stare focused on a spot on the floor somewhere near his feet. I saw my father's eyes go wide. He, too, knew Frankie's anger, and at that moment looked afraid. Had it not been for my mother, awake now, dressed in a nightgown and having closed the doors so the neighbors wouldn't hear, wedging herself between them, Frankie would undoubtedly have done something he would have felt very sorry about. Instead, he turned away and with frightening fury punched the kitchen wall, caving in the plaster. My father stood there, more shocked than angry, as Frankie slowly walked out the front door.

At the party that night, the punch was a lightning-quick left hand that literally lifted Bobby off the ground. He slammed against the wall, the snap of his head breaking the thermostat. There was a gasp among the others in the living room. Frankie himself seemed taken aback by the viciousness of the blow. He quickly turned and walked out of the house and onto the front lawn. I ran down the stairs and went to him. He blew the smoke from a Lucky out in a stream, as if trying to exhale a demon that lived within him. His face now was soft, his eyes repentant. He put his arm around me and we walked under the big pine on the corner of the property. Though I was frightened of many things then, I was not afraid of my brother's anger. Of course, when I was a child, it was never directed at me. But more than that, I understood it. Like the anger of the Incredible Hulk in my Marvel comic books, Frankie's rage was a superpower, one he didn't ask for or want. And each time it arose, and changed his very physicality, it extracted from him an emotional price. Only I knew that the aftermath of one of his explosions was when Frankie's soul was most exposed. More than any other time, it was here where my hero worship began.

On November 22, 1963, my father drove from the 41st Precinct to meet Eugene in lower Manhattan. My oldest brother had broken his arm in a touch football game and was having the cast removed. That day, Frankie, home from the Brooklyn Navy Yard—having enlisted in the Navy a few months before—drove with his friend Artie Norton to pick up tuxedoes for Artie's wedding. Tommy and I were in class at St. Margaret's when the news came. Sister Marie Gabriel announced it over the loudspeaker on the wall at the head of the classroom.

We were let out of school early, and when I arrived home, my mother was sitting in the living room holding her head in her hands. I went to her and touched her lightly on the shoulder; for a moment, she looked at me without recognition, her eyes red spiderwebs, with heavy dark circles underneath. Then, as if the realization of who I was at once descended upon her, she grabbed me and pulled me to her chest, her action giving way to the deepest of sobs. Eleven years earlier, two years before I was born, she had lost a child, my sister, Mary Clare, just four years old. The unspeakable grief of that loss, buried in the Gate of Heaven cemetery and the years that had passed, had been again released by the tragic events in Dallas. For my mother, all hope was lost, sealed in a coffin and accompanied down Pennsylvania Avenue by a single riderless horse.

My father was called into work that evening, the brass of the NYPD fearing chaos in the streets, an overreaction. There would be no chaos. For the South Bronx, like the rest of the country, stood silently numb that night, as if it had been engulfed by the most frigid air—the big policeman, as my father called the coldest of winter crime-free nights.

The Camelot of Pearl River, too, began to die that day. The innocent facade, slowly at first, started to peel like cheap wood panel. Our town was not magical, nor was it insulated from the eruptive events of the country in the coming years: the assassinations, the threat of nuclear war, the war in Vietnam, and the coming plague of drug abuse that would spread like an airborne virus, float over the moat of the Hudson River, and settle like a fine toxic dust on the neatly kept back lawns.

Often, during those next few years, the last of my father's police career, I would be awakened at two or three in the morning by the click of his pipe tapping against the glass ashtray. Silently, I would creep to the door and peer down into the darkness of the living room to see him sitting again in his wing chair, the smoke from his pipe rising, metallic blue in the shaft of light from the lamp on the table, surrounding him like a ghostly wagon train keeping the demon Indians at bay. Next to him was a half-empty glass of buttermilk, drunk to coat the internal bleeding. "Goddamned scotch," I'd hear him mumble, a self-admonishment for the three he would allow himself when he came home from work. The scotch was needed, and not the culprit. Not the only one, anyway. The stabbing pain in his stomach was from the knife wounds, and bullet wounds, and every kind of wound a human can suffer. By 1963, there were almost two murders a week in the 41st Precinct, better known as Fort Apache. And each killing ripped open his stomach a little wider. And each, it seemed, took him farther away from me.

The next day, as a result of military concerns that the assassination had national security implications, Frankie was put on active duty and sent to Key West for advanced training, then on to Jacksonville, Florida. From the window of his bedroom, the one with the flower box of geraniums, the one that I would be given, I watched him on the steps saying good-bye to my father and mother. My mother pushed the tears in her eyes away with her palm; my father stiffly shook my brother's hand. Just before Frankie ducked into the backseat of his friend's car, he looked up at me and waved. I started to cry.

TAMMANY

Thomas Skelly

There is more law at the end of the policeman's nightstick
than in all the decisions of the Supreme Court.
—Alexander "Clubber" Williams

1

My maternal grandfather, Tom Skelly, was born on the Upper East Side of Manhattan in 1868. His parents, Jane Wheeler and Matthew Skelly, emigrated from Ireland during the great potato famine of the 1850s. Like most of the famine refugees, they arrived in the new land with practically nothing. But, as a young boy, my grandfather didn't experience the hardships his parents endured, nor did he know the squalor of the tenements on the Lower East Side, the home of the second wave of Irish immigrants in the 1890s. He had the great good fortune to be American born, and with that came the inherent right to the bounty that was and is this country. Because of that stroke of luck, combined with the fact that his father worked his skinny Irish ass off building a small horse-drawn trucking company, my grandfather grew up in a family that was relatively financially secure.

Beginning with just one rig, my great-grandfather built the business; eventually he owned a half-dozen rigs, with as many drivers working for him. He tended to hire "off-the-boat" Irish, and on their backs, and with his own sweat, he became successful enough to afford a private home in the "suburbs" of East Sixty-first Street and Third Avenue. It wasn't Fifth Avenue, but it wasn't bad. And it was a world away from the tenements.

But in 1878, my great-grandfather fell off a rig, dead of a heart attack. Perhaps my grandfather would have never become a policeman had his father lived a few years more, until Tom was old enough to run the family business. The New York City police department of his time was a vehicle of societal acceptance for Irish immigrants. The department was nearly 50 percent immigrants, the overwhelming majority of them Irish. Unlike other jobs Irish filled—masonry and construction—the police department, with its uniform and tight brotherhood, gave them a sense of belonging and purpose, perhaps even a little superiority. But my great-grandfather had already reached a level of acceptance with his business, and my grandfather was an American. Certainly, there was discrimination, even toward American-born Irish. But it was not nearly as harsh as it was toward recent Irish immigrants, those who met with the now often talked about sign "No Irish need apply."

My great-grandmother tried to run the trucking business for a while, but, according to my mother, the drivers stole from her, and she was forced to give it up. She took the little money she had left and opened a candy store on Second Avenue and Eighty-fifth Street. There, in an apartment above the store, she lived with her three children. In the 1880 census, my great-grandmother is listed as a white female, forty-eight years old and widowed, her occupation "storekeeper." Her daughter Mary is seventeen, single and working as a drip maker (candles? or drapes?). Her sons, Thomas and Joseph, are twelve and eight.

My great-grandmother's life had gone from bad to good to bad again. She had survived the potato famine and the crossing. She worked as hard as her husband, not only raising a family, but working on the rigs herself. Four of her children had died, including young Matthew, two years older than my grandfather, who died at ten, just two months after Matthew Senior passed away. But while her husband was alive, she had enjoyed her new land and her fine home. Her letters back to Ireland enticed much of her clan to follow her to America, where dreams were a reality, not peat fire variety the way they were in Ireland. Then, the day her husband died, all of it was snatched away.

In his youth, my grandfather Tom went to the "Brothers' school," as my mother called Catholic school, a local grammar and high school. In his late teens and early twenties, he drove a rig for his sister Mary's husband, Larry Redmond, who was in the trucking business for a while. He also worked on and off as a stevedore along the riverfront.

At the age of twenty-five, sometime in 1893, Tom Skelly joined the New York City police department, then called the Metropolitan Police. The exact date of his entry into service is somewhat of a mystery. City records give several dates, including March 15, July 10, and November 15, 1893, and March 27, 1905, the last undoubtedly wrong because that date would have made him ineligible for the pension he received when he retired in 1919. What is perfectly clear is the dishonesty of the organization he joined.

So corrupt was the department of my grandfather's time, the *Mail and Express*, a newspaper of the day, called it "a ghastly sinkhole of official impropriety." *The Brooklyn Daily Eagle* spoke of it as even more infamous, calling it "the most corrupt, brutal, incompetent organization in the world." The going rate for a badge then was $300, a veritable fortune considering the average weekly wage in the tenement community, where most of the Irish-born cops lived, was around $5. Those who didn't have the financial resources to pay for the badge outright borrowed the money from the local Tammany Hall politician, to be paid back with interest. Tammany Hall was the crooked Democratic political machine that ran New York City for the last half of the nineteenth century and into the twentieth. For most of those years, the police department operated as Tammany's graft collection agency. The system worked from the bottom up. Patrolmen who were in the pocket of the Hall looked the other way as wardmen collected graft from businesses like barrooms and gambling halls. There was a saying in the police department then that summed up the duties of a patrolman: "Hear, see, say nothing. Eat, drink, pay nothing." The captain of the precinct then would take his slice, kicking back a small percentage to his collector; the local Tammany boss would then take his, with the rest filtering back to the Hall itself. It was a lucrative business. One published report of the day estimated the graft collected in a Sixth Avenue precinct called the Tenderloin at $75,000 to $100,000 a month. Within the department, promotions were bought: $3,000 for precinct detective, as much as $15,000 for the position of precinct captain. Captains ruled like feudal lords.

I have no way of knowing whether my grandfather paid for the then square badge of the police department. I do know, however, that such a practice was the rule rather than the exception. Tom did have to fill out an application and take an entrance examination. But these tasks were perfunctory and had little to do with whether or not you were appointed. In memoirs published in a 1905 *Cosmopolitan Magazine*, a retired police captain listed some of the questions asked on his entrance exam: "What direction is Sydney from the South Pole?" "What is a straight line?" "What poet is called the 'Bard of Avon'?"

If my grandfather did have an angel, it would have been someone like Whispering Larry Delmore, the illiterate Yorkville Tammany heavyweight, who could sign his name only with an "X"; or Mike Cosgrove who owned a saloon on East Eighty-seventh Street, right next to the Algonquin Club, Tammany headquarters in Yorkville. Cosgrove, first a ward heeler, and later mentor to Senator Robert F. Wagner, had ties to Big Tim Sullivan, who oversaw Tammany interests in the gambling halls on the Bowery and was the unofficial political boss of all the districts south of Fourteenth Street. (He later became a state senator and congressman, but those jobs actually carried less weight than his former position.) If Mike Cosgrove opened the door to the police department for my grandfather, then it follows that Tom would have been assigned to a precinct within Sullivan's domain.

He was. City records say that my grandfather was first assigned to the 10th Precinct, which lay south of Houston Street and east of the Bowery. This district was populated mainly by Germans and Polish Jews, and the individual neighborhoods were named accordingly: "Jewtown" and "Little Germany." The Jewish quarter was centered at Hester and Essex Streets. There, the five-story tenements—where at night families would sleep lined up next to each other in one-room apartments—were, during the day, transformed into individual factories called "sweater shops." Women worked sewing machines making knee pants, coats, and other garments. On the sidewalks, in front of small stores, men in long black coats and beards would outbargain each other to compete for customers, the clicking of passing horse hooves keeping beat to the haggling in Yiddish. An outdoor shopping bazaar, called the Pig Market (undoubtedly an ethnic joke), lay at the corner of Hester and Ludlow Streets. There, hats, suspenders, pants, poultry, fruits, eyeglasses, baked goods, and cigars were sold, the best bargains to be had on Friday, just before the Sabbath.

As a patrolman, my grandfather was assigned a beat, a few square blocks that was walked clockwise, with the right shoulder nearer the buildings. Roundsmen (later renamed sergeants) walked in the opposite direction, their left shoulders to the building, so they would come upon the patrolman doing his rounds. During the nighttime, a patrolman's duty was mostly to check the locks on doors and windows, move vagrants and drunks along, and look in on the open businesses, mostly bars and gambling halls in my grandfather's precinct, to make sure nothing was amiss.

Throughout his precinct the fumes of breweries and illegal stills mixed with the smell of fish and onion that emanated from the Jewish tenements—and the horse manure that covered most of the streets. There were perhaps 500 bars east of the Bowery and south of Fourteenth Street then, and most of them made their own whiskey.

At night, the streets were rife with small-time criminals and fences. In the parlance of the day, the 10th Precinct was "the crooked ward"; the Bowery, lined with bawdy saloons, gambling joints, and whorehouses, was called Thieves' Highway. Playing the numbers, then called policy betting, was the most prevalent form of gambling. But dogfights, cockfights, and boxing matches were also popular, along with procuring the services of transvestites and other prostitutes of every age. The whiskey in the Bowery was most times laced with camphor or other toxic additives. Cops called some of the saloons "sleeping cars," a reference to the fact that disreputable barkeeps administered "knockout drops," chloral hydrate, to some patrons, and then robbed them while they were unconscious, according to *Low Life* by Luc Sante. One hall on the Bowery, McGurk's, became infamous and a tourist attraction for headquartering a suicide craze. McGurk's clientele was partly longtime prostitutes from the strip. These down-and-outers, too old and ugly to make a living at their trade, would find final solace in McGurk's by drinking carbolic acid, then the transportation mode of choice to the next world. McGurk made no attempt at concealing the morbid allure of his saloon. On the contrary, above his doorway an electric sign—the first on the Bowery—garishly blared "McGurk's Suicide Hall." In 1899, seven suicide attempts were made at McGurk's, six of them successful. McGurk himself was even known to offer impromptu eulogies over his just-former customers' bodies. But suicides were not confined only to McGurk's. The term "the Dutch act" was coined because of the frequent suicides in the German quarters of the 10th Precinct ("Dutch" being a term for German, i.e., "Deutsch").

2

In my grandfather's day, the captain of the 10th Precinct was one William Devery. Perhaps there has never been a cop as powerful and corrupt as Devery. His ties to the political machine were as thick as the blocks of the very hall of Tammany itself. His father, a mason, helped in the construction of the Tammany building on Fourteenth Street. As a child, Devery would deliver his father's lunch pail. Like my grandfather, he was a born and bred New Yorker. There, however, any similarity between the two ended.

A bear of a man, weighing 250 pounds, Devery was known for his white-hot temper, colorful personality, and blatant and unrepentant corruption. While my grandfather would sit in the cheap bleacher seats at the old Polo Grounds to watch his beloved Giants play, Captain Devery and his partner, the gambler and bookmaker Frank Farrell, owned the New York Highlanders, a team later sold to Colonel Jacob Ruppert and renamed the New York Yankees. Devery's own fortune was once estimated at $300,000, more even than the aristocrat Teddy Roosevelt had.

Devery would rise to the highest rank in the department, chief of police, after a Tammany coup broke Republican control of the police board. Yet even at that lofty perch, he would operate his network of police protection each night from a West Side street corner. A steady stream of gambling bosses, pimps, and criminals of every imaginable type would report—with envelopes stuffed with cash—to him personally. When the *Mail and Express* printed a menu of prices police charged for protection, including $50 a month for pool-hall gambling houses, $25 a month for rumrunners, 80 percent of thefts, and $3,000 a year for an illegal abortionist to ply his trade, one of Devery's inner circle suggested that Devery assign a detective to find out where the leaks where coming from. Devery responded in his usual irreverent way: "A detective? We need a plumber!"

As is the case today, cops, especially corrupt ones, made great copy. Lincoln Steffens, then a police-beat reporter, referred to Devery once as a "lovely villain." One of Devery's duties as chief of police was to preside over departmental trials, which often he did drunk. The defendant was usually one of his minions brought up on charges of corruption. Devery was known to advise them from the bench. One of his favorite sermons—"When ye're caught with the goods, don't say nothin' "—was perhaps the foundation of the NYPD's blue wall of silence. To Devery, the sin wasn't the crime itself, but getting caught.

By all accounts, my grandfather had an easygoing, mild temperament. My mother says that he was soft-spoken, with a dry wit. She remembers one story he told about a cop who had to write a report of a horse that died on Kosciuszko Street. The cop couldn't spell the location, so he dragged the animal around to Smith Street.

My grandfather thought of himself as something of a boulevardier. He would dress in a fine tweed suit, wear a flower in his lapel, and frequent the dance halls around the city. Before he was married, he dated a number of women he met at those halls. But, as is often the case with Irishmen, even Irish Americans, he remained the devoted son. He lived with his mother, above the candy store, until he was married at twenty-eight. His gentle nature, however, was not the best of fits for the head-breaking ways of the police department in those days. Probably the cop of that era best known for ruthlessness was Alexander "Clubber" Williams.

Born in Canada of Irish descent in 1839, Williams worked as a shipbuilder in Key West and Japan and as a ship's carpenter and longshoreman in New York before he joined the police department in 1866. A towering, powerfully built man, Williams immediately earned a reputation for taking on the toughest characters in his precincts. His first day on the job, in a Brooklyn precinct, he entered a saloon to arrest two known criminals. When they resisted, he threw both of them through the saloon's plate-glass front window. His reputation served him well, and he quickly rose through the ranks of the department. In 1876, he was assigned the captain's post at the 29th Precinct, the Tenderloin, a name that Williams himself bestowed upon it. Of all the precincts then in the city, the Tenderloin, filled with every conceivable establishment of vice (along with legitimate entertainment like the Metropolitan Opera House and the Broadway theaters) was by far the most lucrative for corruption. Upon learning he was to be transferred there, Williams remarked, "All my life I've never had anything but chuck steak; now I'm going to get me some tenderloin." Even as captain, Williams was known to prowl the street, holding his nightstick over his shoulder, ready to administer a beating to anyone he deemed deserving. And no one was exempt. Augustine E. Costello, a newspaperman and author, who wrote a flattering ode to the police department called *Our Police Protectors* but also published Clubber Williams's famous tenderloin remark, was beaten senseless in the 29th Precinct house after Clubber arrested him without charge.

Though Williams became a kind of poster boy for the rough cop of the day, he was by no means the only one. Jacob Riis, a photographer and journalist who became famous for his exposés of tenement life, reported an example of an average cop's handiwork. A crowd of onlookers had gathered to watch a building fire. A beat cop approached and attempted to disperse the crowd by singling out a particularly interested citizen and cracking him full force across the back with his nightstick. The man, stout, with a full beard, buckled in pain and quickly obeyed. Riis, who was watching at a close distance, approached the policeman and informed him that he had just clubbed the former president of the United States, Ulysses S. Grant.

During his term as police board president, a position later

called commissioner, Teddy Roosevelt often made midnight excursions to the seedier precincts in the hope of exposing police corruption and dereliction of duty. Usually accompanying him were Riis and Lincoln Steffens. One of Roosevelt's favorite destinations was the 10th Precinct. One night, in the 10th, he came upon a cop in close conversation with a prostitute. When the commissioner asked the cop what he thought he was doing, the officer threatened to "fan" him with his billy club. When Roosevelt identified himself, the officer turned and ran at full gallop down the street, with the prostitute in hot pursuit.

Still, the public at large seemed complacent about police brutality. Each year in May, the department held a parade down Broadway. Behind a full brass band, thousands of cops—sometimes as much as a third of the entire force—marched in uniform, led, in Devery's day, by the fat chief on horseback. Along the route, tens of thousands would watch and shout, "The finest!" as the parade passed. Their laudatory cheers became part of the city's nomenclature. Even today, the NYPD is often referred to as New York's Finest. The only problem was, back then some of the criminals cheered as loud as the honest citizens.

In 1894, a partisan Republican commission headed by Clarence Lexow, a New York state senator from Rockland County, was formed to investigate election abuses by Tammany but evolved into a scrutiny of police corruption. The commission was established after several sermons—more like searing attacks—on the department and its vice-fueled graft by the Reverend Charles Parkhurst. Parkhurst, the minister of the staid (and mostly Republican) Madison Square Presbyterian Church, was also the president of the New York Society of Prevention of Crime, an organization devoted to closing whorehouses and other lurid establishments in the city. The Reverend's homilies made front-page news (Parkhurst himself had notified the press that his speeches would be newsworthy), and swelled antipolice sentiment among the more powerful and rich New York City Republicans. The police fired

back by demanding Parkhurst provide evidence of police impro-
prieties, and that he deliver such evidence in front of a grand jury
made up of Tammany sympathizers. Parkhurst set out to do exactly that. He hired a private detective named Charles Gardner to
personally guide him through the underbelly of the New York
night. What Parkhurst witnessed repulsed him. One establishment offered the services of male prostitutes to homosexuals; another featured gambling on matches between wild dogs and rat
packs. All of the vice-laden institutions Parkhurst witnessed operated with seemingly little concern for anonymity. He presented
his proof to a grand jury, which, because of the attending publicity, was more independent than the one first formed, and forced
the transfer of all but one of the precinct captains in the districts
he had toured. Those transfers, however, did nothing to change
things—and, in fact, were a boon to the replacements, because it
was customary for vice operations to pay $500 to new precinct
commanders.

Though in some circles Parkhurst was elevated to the exalted
level of a "saintly" reformer, among the denizens of the night, and
even the regular working class, Parkhurst was a joke. Many of
these saw his crusade against the police and vice as more an ethnic
attack on German and Irish immigrants than the righteous battle
against evil that the reverend professed to be waging. The police
department and Tammany, whose constituency was made up
wholly of immigrants and the children of immigrants, used their
leverage with the lower classes in a publicity war against Parkhurst. Before the grand jury assembled, Devery arrested Gardner,
Parkhurst's detective, for procuring the services of prostitutes and
attempting to bribe a madam. According to police testimony,
Gardner was seen playing "leapfrog" with a prostitute during one
of Parkhurst's tours, with the good Reverend looking on. The
story was quickly entered into folklore of the street, but with one
little change. This variation of the ditty "Ta-Ra-Ra-Boom-De-
Ay" was a big hit in the dives of the Tenderloin:

Dr. Parkhurst on the floor
Playing leapfrog with a whore,
Ta-ra-ra-boom-de-ay,
Ta-ra-ra-boom-de-ay.

The later Lexow Committee's findings, however, wouldn't be as lenient as the grand jury's, and as a result of the commission many members of the New York City police department's upper echelon, including William Devery, were fired. Some even faced jail time. Still, none of these punishments stood on appeal, and two years later, in 1896, Devery was reinstated.

To my knowledge, my grandfather didn't commit many sins as a young policeman, at least not sins of the magnitude of Devery and his lot. There are no records of departmental disciplinary actions taken against him. (Though the police department was permeated with corruption, it did go through the motions, as exemplified by Devery's court, to give the appearance that it policed itself. "Clubber" Williams, for example, was brought up on departmental charges 358 times, even fined 224 times. Each of these actions, however, was strictly ornamental, and the fines were minuscule compared to the amount Williams was making off the streets.) Nor was my grandfather involved in any sensational arrests. In fact the most dramatic event that happened to him in his early years on the beat had nothing to do with the police department at all. It was an event, however, that changed his life forever.

3

As he stood at the altar in 1895, he might not have realized it, but my grandfather was marrying not only the Erin beauty beside him but her family as well, and, for that matter, the whole of Ireland. His new bride might have immigrated to America a few years before, but as far as she was concerned, she brought the Old Sod with her.

Julia Murphy was born on St. Patrick's Day, 1875, in County Kildare, Ireland. When she was fifteen, she emigrated to the United States, following her older sister, Mary, who had come over a few years before. Often, older brothers or sisters would make the voyage from Ireland to America first to set things up, then send for their younger siblings. From what my mother says, her Aunt Mary was independent and strong-willed, characteristics that helped her to survive in the new land. By the time Julia arrived, Mary was already "forelady" in a millinery company on East Ninth Street.

Mary was an artist, and one of her duties was to go to the stores on Fourteenth Street and Broadway to sketch the expensive hats in the windows. Back downtown, milliners would make cheaper versions. According to my mother, artists ran in the Murphy family. A sister, Nora, who stayed in Ireland, was an art teacher and something of a Bohemian. During the summer, she would travel to the south of Ireland. There, our family lore says, she became friendly with George Bernard Shaw.

Julia had made the voyage with her sister Bessie. Mary had arranged jobs for them both: Bessie was to be a seamstress in a company called Swartz that made uniform pants (policemen were among their most frequent customers), and Julia would have a place in the millinery company where Mary worked. The three sisters lived together in an apartment on East Seventh Street. Like most new immigrants, they needed to pool their wages to afford housing, and they needed to be within walking distance of their jobs.

Julia, it seems, hated New York. It was far too crowded and smelly, with foreigners speaking languages she had never heard and dressing in ways that she had never seen. What's more, even at fifteen, she found herself fighting off the advances of lascivious men almost every day. Julia was both blessed and cursed with astounding beauty. Her neck was long and graceful, her features perfect, her face softly angular, her eyes hypnotically dark.

Mary protected her younger sister with ferocity. During the day, at work, she kept a watchful eye on her, and at night she forbade her to leave the cramped and stuffy apartment. Perhaps because of her confinement and uncomfortable feelings in her new environment, Julia became more and more unhappy. When she was seventeen, Mary arranged a job for her, away from New York, as a chambermaid for a wealthy family in Bar Harbor, Maine. In the summer of 1892, Julia packed her suitcase, said a tearful goodbye to her sisters, and boarded a train north. But the change in scenery did little to perk up her spirits, and she found that she couldn't run from her beauty. The family in Maine had a Filipino houseguest who stayed most of the first summer Julia worked there. He would leave amorous notes under lamps and cushions for her to find as she cleaned. Several times, Julia found herself alone with the houseguest in close quarters—in hallways or in the pantry—and narrowly escaped his advances. She complained to the head housekeeper, who at first disregarded her tale as the fantasy of a young girl—that is, until she found one of the houseguest's notes. One day soon after, the housekeeper, a bull of an Irishwoman with burning red cheeks, confronted the man. "You keep your yellow hands to yourself," she warned him. And from then on the Filipino left Julia alone.

For Julia, Maine was only a little better than New York. And it was still not Ireland, for which she was desperately homesick. What's more, she missed her sisters terribly. After only a year and a half, she returned to New York and again lived with Mary.

If there was any solace in New York for Julia, it was the number of Irish who lived there. And when she returned, now nearly nineteen, she began to socialize at church gatherings and Irish ladies'-society dances. Though Mary looked upon Julia's newfound independence with a jaundiced eye, her younger sister had matured while she was away, and a rebellious streak, not unlike Mary's own, had awakened.

One of Julia's favorite dances was held at Webster Hall, not far from Mary's apartment, on Thursday nights. The dance was called maid's night out, because of the preponderance of single domestic servants who attended. Though, at one time, social functions such as these were restricted to native-born Irish (and were usually run by Irish county societies like the Limerickmen, Meathmen, and Wexfordmen), by Julia's day the doors were open to first-generation Irish-Americans. Still, the overwhelming majority of those who frequented the dances were Irish born. The music was gay, even raucous, with virtuoso step-dancers, and set dances consisting of four couples whirling around the floor. But there were also the more intimate partner dances, called couple dances or two-hand dances, to a waltz or a polka.

Julia was extremely popular, and seldom did a set go by that she wasn't escorted onto the floor. One night, a man with a jaunty mustache and a mischievous glint in his eye approached her and asked for a dance. As he spoke, she was quite surprised that he didn't have an Irish brogue. And on the dance floor, she was impressed with his mastery and grace, and a bit amused when he whispered in her ear if he could call on her at home.

"Well, now. That depends," she said, eyeing him coyly. "What is it that you do for work?"

"I'm a policeman," came the answer.

"Thomas Skelly the policeman, is it?" Julia said capriciously.

In 1896, my grandfather was transferred to the 13th Precinct. The 13th bordered the 10th, extending east to the East River. The characteristics of the two precincts were pretty much the same except, as you neared the river, the population in the tenements became even denser. Germans and Jews still dominated the inland neighborhoods, but the buildings along the river were heavily Irish. The smell of lager beer and fish and onions gave way to that of boiled cabbage, and, of course, there was still the odor of distilled whiskey. The transfer also came along with a raise in pay: Tom's salary was now $1,150 a year. He and Julia could have afforded an apartment in just about any section of Manhattan save Fifth Avenue and its environs. But Julia was not willing to give up her family, even if seeing them only meant a short ride downtown.

In her defense, being a cop's wife in those years meant spending much of your time alone. Cops then worked nine-hour shifts, and most often were required to remain "on reserve" in the station house for an additional six hours. Usually, patrolmen were given one day and one night off in eight-day rotations, and their time off hardly ever fell the same way two weeks in a row. It was commonplace for cops to work thirty-six hours straight, and not unusual for them to sleep on a cot in the dormitory of the precinct house for four or five nights running.

In October 1896, Julia gave birth to the Skellys' first child, Walter. Born prematurely and nursed in the cold, drafty tenement, Walter didn't have much of a chance. He died one year, three months, and twenty-seven days after he was born. Walter had contracted bronchopneumonia and, according to his death certificate, had convulsed for five days before he expired.

Devastated after the death of her child, Julia gave in to her husband's urgings that the tenements were no place to begin a family. She agreed to move uptown, to 106 East Eighty-ninth Street. One year later, in 1899, my grandfather was transferred to the 28th Precinct in Yorkville. He was now living and working where he had grown up. He knew the shopkeepers and the neighborhood folk. The new apartment was airy and bright, in a fine building not too far from Park Avenue. Julia gave birth to two healthy babies, Marion, called Mazzie, in 1898, and Tom Junior in 1900. And even though Julia's sisters and other family members made the journey uptown far too often for his liking, my grandfather had every reason to believe his life was in perfect order.

4

The side-wheel steamboat called the *General Slocum* had been hired for Wednesday, June 15, 1904, by St. Mark's Evangelical Lutheran Church on Sixth Street between First and Second Avenues, the spiritual center of a densely populated German community called Weiss Garten (White Garden). The outing involved a short cruise to the north shore of Long Island, where a picnic was to be held. At nine o'clock that morning 1,300 church-goers, mostly women and children, boarded the vessel at the Third Street pier. According to newspaper reports of the day, the children's laughter could be heard for blocks.

Named after a Civil War officer who went on to become a congressman, the *General Slocum* with its great paddles was a familiar sight on the river. The captain, William Van Schaick, had the year before been given an award for safely transporting 35 million passengers. The June 15, 1904, fire started in a forward hold called the lamp room, in which were stored a barrel of kerosene, a barrel of benzene, and glassware packed in hay. Investigators believed that a kerosene lamp exploded in the hold, setting the hay ablaze and then igniting the kerosene. The fire is believed to have started as far south as Fifty-fifth Street and was burning out of control by the time the boat had steamed abeam Blackwell's Light, on a dot of an island across from Eighty-sixth Street. The engineer and mates on the steamer futilely fought the blaze as worn fire hoses burst from the water pressure. What's more, the captain was not notified for seven precious minutes. During that time the *General Slocum* sailed into the treacherous currents of Hell Gate, sealing the fate of many aboard. When finally notified, Van Schaick made the disastrous decision to try and make North Brother Island, a two-and-a-half-mile-square patch of land in the arm of the East River that leads to the Long

Island Sound. During the mile-and-a-half-long trip through the racing waters, the *General Slocum* burned like a bonfire. Passengers who jumped into the water were swallowed by the currents. The canvas of their life preservers was ripped and worn, the corking inside crumbled like stale bread. But an even worse fate awaited those who chose to stay aboard.

As the alarm sounded in the Eighty-eighth Street station house, my grandfather and two dozen other patrolmen, including Thomas Cooney, scrambled into wagons that headed north along the Manhattan shoreline. Tugboats and other vessels shuttled the police to North Brother Island. The river tug my grandfather and Cooney boarded was called the *Wade*. As it neared the burning wreckage, Cooney dove into the river. Newspaper reports said that he single-handedly rescued ten people from the gurgling water, swimming back again and again to the tug with hysterical survivors clutching him around the neck. My mother said that Tom stayed on the tug, pulling aboard those whom Cooney and others saved from the river. Meanwhile, the steamer was an inferno. From the deck of the *Wade* my grandfather and crew members watched helplessly as people were burned alive. At one point, a deck buckled and snapped, catapulting passengers into the river, some with their clothing ablaze, like fiery human arrows.

With confusion and death all around him, my grandfather didn't notice that his partner, Cooney, had been swallowed by the water. No one on the *Wade* did. Only when the tug, filled with survivors barely clinging to life, headed back toward North Brother Island, did my grandfather realize that Cooney was missing. Frantically, he and the mates searched the tug, and the black waters strewn with bodies and burning debris, but Cooney was nowhere to be found.

Much later that afternoon, his body, along with hundreds of others, was pulled from the water.

All that night of the *General Slocum* disaster, and throughout the following day, river vessels and horse-drawn hearses shuttled the bodies to the Twenty-sixth Street Pier in Manhattan. Relatives lined up for blocks to identify the bodies laid out in rows on the pier. That Friday there were hundreds of services in thirty-seven different churches, including 114 at St. Mark's Evangelical Lutheran alone. For days afterward, police officers and volunteers on river vessels searched for the dead. Each day, the gruesome body count in the newspapers rose, finally reaching over one thousand.

Captain Van Schaick faced criminal charges. He was found negligent in his duty and sent to Sing Sing prison after being sentenced to ten years. Blinded in the accident, the captain was pardoned by President William Howard Taft after serving three and a half years. The disaster shattered the community of Weiss Garten. In the following years most of the residents, unable to live with the horrible memory of the *General Slocum*, moved out of the Lower East Side, a great number of them settling in the Yorkville section, which remained a German enclave for the next seventy years.

I imagine my grandfather was a hero the day of the *General Slocum* disaster. I can imagine his heroism a lot easier than I can imagine him. He left no letters, scrapbooks, or even photographs. I did locate a photograph of him in the archives of the Museum of the City of New York. The group shot, streaked and faded with time, was taken in 1912, in front of the 13th Precinct, which housed Traffic Squad B, his assignment at the time. The bottom part of his face, just below his mouth, is hidden by the high, rounded police hat on the officer in front of him. All the men look pretty much the same: Most have bushy handlebar mustaches; all wear a dark frock coat with a double line of copper buttons. My grandfather's mustache is the most neatly trimmed, and it turns slightly upward at the corners of his mouth. He wears a thin, almost imperceptible smile. There seems to be a glint in his eye.

Almost one hundred years ago, he lived and worked in the same neighborhood I live in now: Yorkville. The old Eighty-eighth Street precinct house—now an upscale redbrick building filled with young professionals who pay thousands a month in rent—stood on the next block behind my apartment; his beat could have brought him right past my front stoop. Once in a while, mostly at night, I walk to his old precinct's address, 432 East Eighty-eighth Street, and close my eyes and pretend that I've been transported back in time. And, if the street is quiet enough, I can almost see the cops mustered out in front, each of them wearing bobby-style hats and navy blue coats. In my mind's eye, I can see Tom Skelly, my grandfather, his finger pulling on the end of his dapper mustache as he whispers an amusing story to the cop standing next to him.

Two blocks from the station house are Carl Schurz Park and a promenade that overlooks the East River. At night, the lights from Gracie Mansion, the mayor's home, cast jagged shadows across the walkway from the trees and fence that surround the mansion. The river is a wide ribbon of oily blackness on which gracefully slide weighty tankers nudged by tugs. The grace of these big ships belies the ferocious currents beneath. A tidal river, the East flows alternately in both directions with an amazing force. A cop from the NYPD's scuba unit once told me that on a simulated rescue maneuver he jumped in the river at Fourteenth Street and was swept north to Ninety-sixth Street, over four miles away, in less than ten minutes. The swirling currents at the confluence of the East and Harlem Rivers are some of the most dangerous in the United States. There, off the shore of Wards Island, once was a favored dumping spot for mob hit men, their victims bound with masking tape in the trunks of Ford Galaxies and Chevy Novas, their final resting place waiting soundlessly at the bottom of the river.

When I think of my grandfather on the tug that day, and of Cooney's ultimate sacrifice, a welling begins at the bottom of my lungs. The feeling is a familiar one to me. Throughout my life, every time I read a story about hero cops or see sad news footage of them, I experience it. The written history of the New York City police department has always been punctuated with scandal, brutality, and the most criminal of actions, perhaps more in some eras than others, but still as consistent as commas. But throughout those pages of its history, the police department has also been as consistent in incredible heroism. When I look at photographs of the soot-covered policemen holding the crumpled, blackened bodies of the seamstresses who died in the 1911 Triangle Shirtwaist Factory fire; or listen to Police Officer Stephen McDonald, paralyzed in a wheelchair and hooked to a respirator, forgive the young black man whose bullet put him there; or watch the news footage of the World Trade Center bombing and the blue shirts carrying people to safety; or see any news story of the funeral of a cop killed in the line of duty—the images of the grieving widow and children—my soul clenches. But, until now, I have always kept those feelings to myself.

5

Though the mayoral election of 1901 (Seth Low, a former mayor of Brooklyn and president of Columbia University, was elected mostly on his promise to reform the police department) brought sweeping changes, and finally the end of William Devery's reign, the NYPD of the early part of the twentieth century was still rife with corruption. Tammany politico-cum-gangsters like Big Tim Sullivan were still very much in charge. In an April 2, 1902, telegram to *The New York Times*, the Reverend Parkhurst described the situation this way: "We had supposed that the administration was going to reform the police. It looks as though the police were going to reform the administration."

In early 1905, my grandfather was offered the position of door-man at a Tammany-run betting shop. It might have come as a re-ward for his taking part in the rescue on the river. Though the post meant working throughout most of the night, and though he would be surrounded by hard and sordid characters, it was a lu-crative job. Not only would he continue drawing a salary from the police department, he would also be paid as much, if not more, by the gambling establishment.

In all respects, that year should have been a banner one for my grandfather. He now had over five years at the 28th Precinct, and, no doubt, had settled into a familiar routine. As a result of the *General Slocum* tragedy, he had proved his mettle as a policeman, and was well respected in his precinct. He had moved his family to a bigger apartment, around the corner from Eighty-ninth Street, on Lexington Avenue. And, to top it off, the Giants won the 1905 World Series, beating the Philadelphia Athletics on the strength of three shutouts by Christy Mathewson. Things were moving along just fine. That was, until he turned down the door-man position.

As a young father then, Tom Skelly had matured out of his boulevardier days. At night he would sit in his parlor, wearing a velvet smoking jacket (the annual Christmas gift from Julia and the children), a Camel cigarette burning on an ashtray next to him, reading the sports section of the *Evening World* to see how his Giants had fared that afternoon. Unlike his father, who was endowed with an immigrant's motivation to succeed in the new land, my grandfather was content with a policeman's salary—it was quite enough to keep his family warm and healthy, with a few dollars left over for a night or two a week at the local tavern. He was of the first generation of New York's civil servants, a forerun-ner of generations to come who would live within the financial bounds and constrictions of their careers, trading any dreams of riches—at least of honest ones—for job security and a pension.

Years later, he told my mother that he turned the offer down because he simply didn't think policemen should be involved with gambling. But he also knew quite well that once he was on the Tammany payroll there was no turning back. Though many cops filled their pockets with graft, many more lost any vestige of a pension while in the clutches of the Hall. For cops who fell from favor but retained their jobs, though, the fate might have been even worse.

By one news account of the day, after arresting the keeper of a Tammany-protected saloon for opening on Sunday, a patrolman was transferred, or "railroaded," six times in four months. According to *The Police Establishment*, by William Turner, a patrolman named Jeremiah Moran, who had refused to contribute to various Tammany-held organizations, was, in the space of one year, transferred from 126th Street in Manhattan to Astoria, Queens, then to Flushing, and finally to the recesses of Whitestone in the Bronx. Turner wrote, "Moran no longer bothered to unpack." It was not at all uncommon for cops to pay a "protection fee" of $25 a year to guard against being transferred, but even that was of little help if you were on the bad side of the Hall. In refusing to toe the Tammany line, my grandfather must have known he had taken quite a risk. Perhaps, having lived in Yorkville his whole life, he thought that his deep roots in the neighborhood would provide protection against any Tammany repercussions. It didn't.

Almost immediately after he turned down the offer, he was sent to the 3rd Precinct on Greenwich Street in Greenwich Village. His commute to the Lower West Side, the opposite corner of the island of Manhattan from where he lived, was, on good days, an hour by trolley car. Add two hours a day for travel to the already inhuman hours cops then worked, and my grandfather hardly ever saw his wife and children's faces. But Tammany's wrath didn't end there. By the time Tom's twenty-six-year police career was over, he would work in seven different precincts: the 10th, 13th, 28th, 3rd, 2nd, Traffic A, and Traffic B. What's more, he would stay at the same salary, then $1,400 annually, for the next sixteen years. It was 1918, a year before he retired, by the time he received his next raise—$50 a year.

My grandfather endured these hardships because he had no other option. At the time of his Greenwich Village transfer, he had already served twelve years in the department, just eight years short of retirement and pension. He was also nearing forty. For a man that age, in those times, starting over would be just about impossible.

Just as my grandfather became accustomed to the long trip to Greenwich Village, he was transferred again, this time to the precinct that operated out of City Hall—still not an easy commute from the Upper East Side. But, by the time he was sent to the City Hall Precinct, technology had jumped one step ahead of even the malevolent minds of Tammany. In 1904, the Interborough Rapid Transit subway opened, making the commute to City Hall from Brooklyn a breeze. In 1905, my grandfather moved his family to Brooklyn.

The house he bought was on Fifty-fifth Street, some distance from the brand-new subway station, but easily accessible to it by trolley car. Though his finances were such that he had to take a considerable mortgage on his purchase, the house had an apartment on the first floor, and the rental income would help considerably with the payments.

As the Tappan Zee Bridge and Palisades Parkway would do fifty years later, the subway kindled a migration of cops who worked in lower Manhattan, to Brooklyn neighborhoods like the one in which my grandfather settled. The trend also mirrored the Pearl River phenomenon in other ways. It was the forerunner to the later American dream, of houses with backyards and, for cops, insulation and isolation from the stress and seediness of the places where they worked. My grandfather's next-door and down-the-block neighbors were both assigned to the City Hall Precinct, and the three of them (whenever they worked the same shifts) would ride the newfangled contraption together as it rattled its way underneath the East River.

The move to Brooklyn, my mother says, brightened my grandfather's view of his job, and his life. Not only was he now a home owner, but he also had distanced himself—despite the subway—from his wife's family. Throughout the time they lived in Yorkville, Julia had held open their apartment doors to her relatives newly arrived from Ireland. My grandfather had once remarked to his wife: "Do the Irish even know what a hotel is?" My mother's oldest sister, Mazzie, often said that my grandfather's first order of business in Brooklyn was to hang the pictures of his wife's family—which covered the walls of the apartment in Yorkville—in the bathroom of the new home. My grandfather delighted in needling his wife about her heritage. Sometimes, after a few drinks, he would sing:

My name is O'Brien, I'm from Harlem,
I'm an Irishman as you can see,
I can sing like a thrush or a starlin', or the little bird up in the tree,
They tell me to go over to England,
And pay a short visit to France,
And there to bring out my new fashion,
And call it the high-water pants. . . .

Still, my grandfather was careful to take his raillery only so far. Julia had the quintessential Irish temper, and ultimately, at home, she was the boss. The pictures didn't hang in the bathroom for long.

Julia also took responsibility for finding a tenant for the apartment, which she did, only a week or so after her family moved in upstairs. My grandfather came home from work that day to find his wife sitting with a young couple in the backyard having tea. My mother says he wasn't thrilled with Julia's choice of tenants. The couple's name was Baruch, and they were Jewish.

During the early years of the twentieth century, hundreds of thousands of Jews emigrated to the United States from Eastern Europe. This tidal wave of people had followed a similar flow of Irish a few years before. This dynamic caused a natural animosity between the two ethnic groups. Language barriers and suspicion of different customs and beliefs formed walls behind which Jews and Irish (along with Germans and Italians) huddled tightly in isolation from each other. For the Irish cops, this division was farther exacerbated by the distrust the Jews had for the new land's legal system (perhaps for good reason). In the Jewish wards of the 10th and 13th Precincts, people believed fervently in policing themselves. Criminal justice was handed out not in city courts but by elders in temple. But as the influx of Jews continued, their criminal element spilled from the insular community to the city at large. In 1908, Police Commissioner Theodore A. Bingham wrote in *The North American Review* that fully half the criminals in New York were Jewish. His remarks were considered inflammatory and out of proportion by the Jewish community, but undoubtedly there was a burgeoning Jewish criminal problem. Ruthless Jewish gangs like the Eastmans, named after their leader, Edward "Monk" Eastman (born Osterman), prowled the Lower East Side. Though Big Tim Sullivan was still the overall crime boss of the East Side, and Eastman and other gangs paid the appropriate homage to him, Sullivan fully realized that Jewish gangs were a growing force to be reckoned with. He even took to wearing a yarmulke and attending Jewish services as an act of gangland diplomacy.

The Baruchs, however, were far from being criminals. The downstairs apartment was often filled with the graceful notes of classical music played on a Victrola or the muted sounds of the piano playing. They were educated and sophisticated to a level that Julia—and later, even my grandfather—admired. They were also family oriented. While they lived in my grandfather's house, the

Baruchs raised a son named André, who grew up to become a radio personality and star in early television.

Julia didn't give a second thought to renting the apartment to Jews. As far as she was concerned, it mattered little what ethnicity her tenants were, as long as the rent was on time and they were clean and quiet. As in all of their family squabbles—though my grandfather would grouse for a while—Julia would ultimately have her way.

In 1910, my grandfather was transferred again, this time from the 2nd Precinct to Traffic Sub Division A. He would spend the last nine years of his police career as a traffic cop. By all accounts, he was perfectly content with his new assignment. He didn't have to walk a beat in the crime-infested tenement neighborhoods. He didn't have to sleep on the lumpy cots in the station house. In the Traffic Division, he wouldn't have to answer to crooked captains or Tammany bosses. But perhaps most important, he wouldn't have to witness graft among his brethren in the rank and file.

In the police code of the day, William Devery's code, a canon that would survive throughout the history of the NYPD, the worst offense any cop could commit—even an honest cop—was to inform on other policemen. In one published report from my grandfather's day (reprinted in *The Blue Parade* by Tom Repetto), an honest policeman was asked whether, if he had witnessed a cop take a bribe, he would report it. The honest cop answered: "I wasn't born in Ireland, but my father and mother were, and thank God! none of my name were ever informers either in the old country or in this. I would be ashamed to look my children in the face if I turned informer. . . . My father was ninety years of age when he died and he used to tell us children of the fate that followed informers in Ireland—the devil would sometimes claim their bodies even before they got to the graveyard and to the tenth generation ill-luck, misfortune and a curse went with them. . . . Show me a 'squealer' . . . and I will show you a fella who had a heart of a coward and a disgrace to the police."

Though Tom enjoyed a joke at the expense of his Irish in-laws, his devotion to his mother and reverence toward his father's work ethic imbued him with the deepest respect for the Irish and the hardships they endured. And, aside from their lighthearted bickering, and along with her beauty, it was his wife's strong Irish will that drew him to her. He supported Julia when she began to collect nickels and dimes, kept in a coffee can in the cabinet over the stove, for Irish Freedom, an organization that funded the Irish struggles against the English, and he never tired of Julia telling the story of her father being jailed by the English for harboring Fenian rebels. Though my grandfather had every reason to resent the Irish Tammany regime, this animosity did not filter down to the cops with whom he worked day in and day out, even when his refusal to toe the Tammany line meant shunning by some in his ranks. For my grandfather, an assignment to the traffic squad was an oasis, as far from the Tammany graft machine as he could get and still be able to wear the blue uniform of the police department.

The traffic squad also meant steady workdays and regular days off. His schedule was eight a.m. to five p.m. Monday through Friday, and half a day every other Saturday. His free Saturday afternoons were frequently spent at the Polo Grounds. In the teens and twenties, baseball games rarely took longer than two hours, not like the three- and four-hour marathons of today. Players would run on and off the field like they had dinner reservations. My grandfather would usually be on the train by five o'clock and home for dinner.

This is not to say that it was a cushy job. To be a traffic cop in 1910 was to be in the midst of insanity. The streets were a riotous mix of skittish horses and unreliable early automobiles. There were no crosswalks, no traffic lights, no traffic signals at all. In 1912, 38,000 automobiles were registered in New York; they were still the exception rather than the rule. The biggest problem with automobiles in that day was an epidemic of runaways—cars that, left idling because of the difficulty in starting them, had slipped into gear. But trying to control horse-drawn traffic was harder by far than any problem even today's automobile traffic poses. Tom Skelly's first traffic post, on lower Broadway, was a main trucking and passenger route to downtown Manhattan. A traffic cop standing in the middle of the street staring at a team heading toward him, full gallop, was, to say the least, in a precarious situation. Only two years before he arrived in traffic were the first rudimentary regulations put into effect, requiring drivers to raise the whip to signal a stop, and keeping slower traffic to the right. In 1905, special legislation, with the backing of the courts, empowered traffic cops, and drivers started to take them seriously. Before then, traffic violations were considered a nuisance by the courts and were most times dismissed. Often magistrates would administer stern warnings to traffic cops not to clog their schedules with such trivialities. Disputes between horse-drawn truck drivers were commonplace, and fault in an accident was sorted out with fists on the street. Some years earlier, as police board president, Teddy Roosevelt had introduced a twenty-nine-member bicycle unit, known as the Scorcher Squad, to apprehend speeding horse-drawn trucks and carriages. The squad made over 1,300 arrests in its first year.

Besides vehicular traffic, the other serious concern was pedestrians. In those years, crossing a busy thoroughfare was a life-or-death proposition. For a while, traffic cops gave preferential treatment to pretty girls and important people. Because of this, an order was imposed "that under no conditions would traffic men take hold of any person by the arm for the purpose of escorting him or her across the street, except a blind person." Cops were then issued semaphore disks marked "Stop" and "Go" to control traffic.

My grandfather's last command was Traffic Sub Division B, where he stayed for six years. The fixed post was on Thirteenth

Street and Fourth Avenue, just a block south of Tammany Hall; his career had come full circle.

Though Tammany's influence with the police department would continue until Mayor Fiorello La Guardia's tenure thirty years later, the Hall's foundation had already begun to crack. One by one, the reigning lords of corruption left the police department. After his police career, and, without Tammany's backing, a failed attempt at a political one, William Devery lived in opulence in a townhouse on East Tenth Street and kept himself busy with significant real-estate interests in the beachfront community of Rockaway. Clubber Williams, too, lived well after his police career, spending most of his time in his Cos Cob estate, or in leisurely cruising on Long Island Sound on his steam-powered yacht. Big Tim Sullivan, however, wasn't so lucky. In 1912, while a congressman, he was committed to a private asylum for a mental breakdown. Some time later, he escaped the asylum and was run over by a train—a gruesome event that led to suspicions of foul play, which were never confirmed. For ten days his body lay in the morgue at Bellevue before a policeman recognized the former Tammany king of the Bowery underground.

The Thirteenth Street traffic post was on the main thoroughfare for wealthy bankers and financiers heading from their homes on Park or Fifth Avenue to Wall Street. My grandfather became friendly with a number of these princes of finance; at Christmastime the chauffeurs would stop the limousines, and gloved hands would appear out of back windows with envelopes for him, a few dollars in each. By today's standards this would be thought of as graft. But then, giving the beat or traffic cop a Christmas envelope was no different from giving a holiday gift to the postman or doorman. One Christmas, an executive of F.A.O. Schwarz on East Fourteenth Street gave Tom a wooden elephant on wheels. The toy was the high point of his children's Christmas that year, and, for years after, made the rounds, handed down from sibling to sibling.

By the late teens, my grandfather had witnessed a complete

changeover from horse-drawn transportation to automobiles. In the spring of 1919, a Wall Street banker he had become friendly with had his chauffeur pull the car over at Grandfather's post. The banker asked him if he planned to be a traffic cop the rest of his life. Tom considered the man's words carefully. He had been a policeman then for twenty-six years. For most of that time, he had struggled within a corrupt system, and was treated by it vindictively. Still, he had always found pride in wearing the uniform of the NYPD. As a little girl, after the family moved from Brooklyn to the Bronx, my mother waited at the central rail station for him to come home. "He always looked so spit-and-polished," she said. "His shoes had a glossy shine, and his gloves were so white. He would hold my hand as we walked together back to the apartment. Everyone seemed so friendly to him. People in the neighborhood would wave at him and say hello. People looked up to him, and respected him for being a policeman."

In June 1919, at the age of fifty-one, my grandfather took his wealthy friend up on his offer, and went to work as a bank guard for the Bank of New York on Fifth Avenue. The staid environment of banking was quite a change from the rough world of the police department. If there was corruption in the banking business, and undoubtedly there was, it was on a level that my grandfather would not be privy to, nor would it affect his life. He spent his next fifteen years wearing the bank guard's uniform, standing erect on the glimmering tile floor in the cavernous bank office, and smiling at the customers—men in high collars, women wearing fashionable bonnets. At night he would come home, now at the regular, respectable hour of just after four p.m., take off his still-shiny shoes, and rub his feet. Twenty-six years of walking a beat, directing traffic, and standing at a bank guard's post could be counted in bunions, calluses, and ingrown toenails.

For a while Tom owned a car, an Essex, and sometimes on weekends he would drive to Long Island to visit some of his old chums from the police department who had moved there when they retired. He stayed faithful to his Giants, and once in a while would attend a game. But as he grew older, his Sunday afternoons at the Polo Grounds became more and more infrequent.

Thomas Francis Skelly, my grandfather, died on June 6, 1935, at the age of sixty-seven. The wake was held, as wakes often were back then, in the parlor of his Bronx home. Some of his old neighbors from Yorkville came to pay their respects, as did several of the cops he had worked with over the years. Julia prepared ham and cabbage and bought plenty of booze—for in her hands, of course, it was an Irish wake. Gone was all my grandmother's youthful beauty. The years had left her heavy with jowls, and she had great, sad eyes. My mother remembers that her uncle Joe, my grandfather's younger brother, arrived at the wake carrying a giant arrangement of white carnations in the shape of a cross. She seldom saw her uncle. He was a big man, much bigger than his older brother, with a full, bushy mustache and great big hands. He, too, was a cop, but he was a first grade detective and worked in the "Silk Stocking District" of Park and Fifth Avenues. All my mother knew about him was that he owned a boat, which he kept on Long Island; that he lived in a nice apartment on the East Side; and that he was married to a German lady.

At the wake, he came to my mother and held her for a moment in his big hands. His eyes welled with grief, or remorse, or both, and his voice shook in a soft, deep timbre: "Your father was an honest cop" were the only words he said to her.

In late October 1997, I received an envelope from the New York City police department, finally a response to my many inquiries about my grandfather. Inside was the entire official record of Tom Skelly's police career—one sheet of paper, his pension certificate. On it are printed his date of entry into service, July 10, 1893; his retirement date, June 21, 1919; his badge number, 2790; and his annual pension, $825. Listed are the names and birth years of his wife and five children: Julia, 1875; Marion, 1898; Tom Junior, 1900;

Ruth, 1907; Eleanor, my mother, 1910; and Vincent, 1914. The certificate is stamped in large, hollow block letters, "DEAD"—his police career summed up in a few dry facts. Having lived with two more generations of New York City cops, and having been surrounded by hundreds of them my entire life, I wasn't surprised by the recorded indifference.

THE SQUAD COMMANDER

Frank McDonald, Sr.

1

I am driving with my father across Route 84 in Pennsylvania toward Archbald, to see, in his words, where it all began. Eighty years old now, my father hasn't been there in many years, and in that time an extension to the highway has been built. When we took our exit the roads were unfamiliar to him. "Jaysus," he said, affecting his father's Irish brogue, as he did often when talking about his childhood. "You'd think I'd know the way. I sure as hell knew the way out of here."

I reassure him that his memory is not at fault, but progress. We pull into a gas station to ask directions to the Red Hill cut, the road through the mountains to the town where he grew up. When I ask the attendant at the station the way to Archbald his face breaks into a grin: "What do you want to go there for?" he says.

A coal-mining hamlet carved out of the anthracite-rich hills of northeastern Pennsylvania, Archbald had been built out of the sweat and stubbornness of miners at a time, the mid to late 1800s, when coal ran this country. The town lived by the union: first the

Knights of Labor, and later the United Mine Workers of America, which fought in legendary labor disputes, often went on strike, and eventually gained better working conditions and wages for its members. But it was the union's greed that led to the demise of the mining industry, and ultimately, to the decimation of Archbald. Strikes during the First World War necessitated the use of alternative fuels—most prominently, petroleum products. By the Great Depression, Archbald, and its coal-mining industry, were choking on the dust of poverty and despair.

As a child, I went with my family to Archbald once or twice, on trips to the Pocono Mountains. I laughed at the size of the house on Cemetery Street where my father lived with his younger brother, Joseph, and his mother and father. It seemed a quarter the size of our house in Pearl River, and lay on a plot of land no bigger than a throw rug. My father said the house was originally a one-room school, and had been converted into a home with a tiny parlor and a small kitchen downstairs, three bedrooms upstairs. Two of the bedrooms were so small, he explained, that you couldn't stand up in them, as they followed the contour of the steeply pitched roof.

I yawned at the stories of the Depression my father told on these trips or at the dinner table: The soup meat his mother would buy on Saturday, and how she would miraculously stretch it into meals for most of the week. Or how his house was heated only by an open hearth in the kitchen. You might as well have slept out of doors, he said, for all the heat in the bedrooms. And the house didn't have indoor plumbing until he was in high school. As children, he and his brother would bathe in a galvanized tub in the kitchen, the water heated on the hearth. My father said he remembers Pete, my grandfather, coming home from the mines and soaking his feet in the tub, his long johns pushed up to his knees and down to the middle of his ass as Mary, my grandmother, scrubbed the black soot from his back with a stiff brush. As my father and Joe grew older, they would shower at the shifting shanty, a communal shower room where the miners washed the black coal dust from their bodies after work. The shanty was a half-mile from home, and the brothers would make the trek carrying a towel and a bar of lard soap.

I never knew my paternal grandparents, Pete and Mary. They were both dead long before I was born. There were pictures of them in the house, though. In one, Pete is tall and gaunt, wearing round-framed glasses, looking like the man holding the pitchfork on the Kellogg's Cornflakes box. His ears are very large and shaped like a Chihuahua's. His nose is thin at the bridge, but flares wide at the nostrils. Though his mouth is turned down at the corners, it gives the impression that he is smiling, or rather, keeping something amusing to himself. There is also something mischievous in his coal-black eyes.

Mary is a very large woman, with great heavy breasts covered in a frilly blouse with puffy sleeves. She wears her hair neatly piled in a bun, which crowns a round, sweet face. Her lips are slightly pursed and her smile seems a little sad. I imagine her rising each morning at five a.m., stoking the fire, removing the socks, work shirts and long johns hung over the hearth to dry, then cooking breakfast, making Pete his lunch, and walking, stooped slightly forward from the weight she carries, the three quarters of a mile to St. Thomas Aquinas Church for six o'clock mass. I also imagine her rocking Pete, home from a two-week drunk, like a baby, weaning him off the horrors with a bottle of warm ale, stroking his matted hair and saying: "There, there. All done now, Pete. All done."

According to family lore, Pete's immigration from Ireland to the United States in 1883 had little to do with the poverty and oppression that afflicted most of the legions of Irish who arrived on these shores in the nineteenth century. Pete's father, Jerome McDonald, was a shopkeeper in Carrickmacross, County Monaghan, on the northern border of what is now the Republic of Ireland. He was also an exclusive distributor of Lipton tea—as you might well imagine, an enormously important commodity there. Pete's six brothers and sisters who remained in Ireland were all well educated and would never experience the hardship that Pete endured in the United States.

Now by modern standards, the events of that morning at Ballymackney school in Carrickmacross, which Pete and his younger brother Owen attended, would not have dictated the geographical relocation that Pete planned that evening as he stuffed his cloth bag with a few shirts, a change of underwear, and the statue of the Virgin Mary his mother had given him for his Holy Communion. But in the Ireland of those days, punching the schoolmaster, a person held in the utmost esteem—as important as any county official—was an offense of the highest order. And even though the schoolmaster, Snoodles McNally, wasn't a popular man and possessed a temperament that was irascible at best and especially rancid when he took a drink, which was most of the time, the townspeople would have never forgotten the incident, and a stigma would have been attached to Pete. He would forever be the boy who gave Snoodles McNally what-for.

The story goes that Pete had come to the aid of his younger brother, who was receiving a savage beating from the schoolmaster. But whether the punch, righteous as it may have been, was the only reason Pete decided, at that precise point, to come to America is not completely clear. More likely, the landing of Pete's straight right hand squarely on Snoodles McNally's nose was the crowning event of a series of indiscretions. By all family accounts, Pete was the most rebellious of the Carrickmacross McDonald clan, and because of these shenanigans, he was not his father's favorite. Whatever the precipitating reasons, that very evening, carrying his few belongings, Pete found his way to the port of Dundalk with just enough fare (his own savings and some money from his mother) for the voyage to America.

Pete entered himself on the ship's passenger list as a twenty-one-year-old laborer, which was a lie on both counts. The ship was filled with hundreds of other Irish. He passed the time of the voyage, which first stopped at Liverpool, then went on to New York, listening to the other passengers' tales of hopes and plans, and these undoubtedly lifted Pete's dampened spirits.

He wasn't completely alone when he arrived in America. Friends of the family, and a cousin or two from his mother's side, had made the voyage before him. But Pete once told my father that when he stood alone in Castle Garden at the southern tip of Manhattan, then the immigrants' portal to the new land, he cried for his mother and his home.

Pete might well have become a policeman, my father once told me, had he stayed in New York. Several of his cousins were then members of the police force. But at sixteen, he was far too young for police work, and lying about his age was likely to be more difficult there than it was on shipboard, where nobody cared as long as he paid his way. So one of his cousins found him a job as a gardener. By the time Pete was twenty-one, old enough to be a cop, he was far from New York.

His first job in America was at the Johnson estate in the Riverdale section of the Bronx. Wealthy landowners, the Johnsons held title to most of Riverdale and parts of Manhattan. Pete spent his time grooming the vast lawns and gardens of the estate; he lived in the caretaker's shack with several other gardeners. His three years at the Johnson estate were more of an adventure than a means of survival. Though he was paid little, he had a warm home, hot meals each day, and good company.

There he met an Irish-American girl by the name of Mooney who was visiting the Johnson estate with her family. Though she was far above his station, the Mooney girl was charmed by Pete—his Irish guile and youthful sun-browned body, lithe and muscular from the hard work on the grounds. She invited him to visit her at her home in Mount Vernon. The very next weekend, and on many subsequent weekends, Pete did exactly that.

Fulfillment of his teenage hormonal urges did not come without a price. The trip to Mount Vernon included the crossing of the Harlem River in a rowboat and then a ten-mile walk. But according to stories handed down by Pete himself, the journey was well worth it, as Miss Mooney's liberal standards left him absent of want and girls like her in that day were hard to find. On the way home, his story went, Pete would, more often than not, "borrow" a horse from an unwitting Mount Vernon farmer.

Soon Pete became restless at the Johnson estate. He took a job across and up the Hudson River, in a rock quarry in Haverstraw, New York. Miss Mooney, merely the first of Pete's many conquests, was quickly discarded, and Pete began what would be his life's work, tunneling into the earth and breaking rocks. It was while he was working the quarry that Pete first heard of the job opportunities in the Pennsylvania coal mines. Less than a year later, he was off to Archbald.

As Pete labored under English foremen and bosses, he cursed his dumb luck at having traveled 3,000 miles from his famously beleaguered homeland only to be oppressed by the Brits in Archbald, Pennsylvania. Though Irish were among the earliest settlers of Archbald, in the 1840s, it was English and Welshmen who owned the land. Miners back in the old country, the English and Welsh first discovered and mined the anthracite coal in the Lackawanna Valley, where Archbald lay. A miner's life is a hard one whether conducted in the British Isles or America; although conditions here were somewhat easier and resources were more plentiful, the English landowners gained power while the Irish broke their backs; thus an old world dynamic was imported to these shores.

But this was America, not England. And the natural contempt the raw Irish laborers, like Pete, felt toward the English foremen and bosses of the Pennsylvania coal mines was the genesis of the United Mine Workers Union, in which Pete remained active for the rest of his life. Though his education did not extend beyond primary school, he was still far more literate than most of the Irish who worked the mines. Because of his writing skills, he was elected the first recording secretary of the local union chapter under the first United Mine Workers Union president, John Mitchell. In the dimly lit clapboard houses of the union men, where meetings were held, Pete, his round-rimmed glasses reflecting the low light, would keep the minutes of the meetings in a strong, looping script. Pete also wrote long, lyrical letters home for the illiterate Irish coal miners, happily offering this service for the opportunity to exercise a creativity that welled within him.

In 1902, the year of the great mineworkers' strike, Pete became a naturalized citizen. That winter, led by John Mitchell, 147,000 members of the United Mine Workers walked out demanding pay increases, an eight-hour workday, and other concessions from the mine owners. As the strike—and the winter—wore on, the entire country felt its effects. Large industry and basic services such as home heating and travel on locomotives were significantly reduced by the short supply of hard coal. In Archbald and nearby Eynon there were frequent union demonstrations, even riots. During one of these, the National Guard fired into the crowd, seriously wounding a man. Meanwhile, fearing an explosion of civil disorder, President Theodore Roosevelt appointed a commission to arbitrate the dispute. The union's team of lawyers was headed by Clarence Darrow. Knowing that the strike had captured the attention of the country, and sensing that public opinion lay with the miners, Darrow staunchly held his ground, refusing to give up any of the miners' demands. In an eight-hour closing argument worthy of a Hollywood screenplay, Darrow said the strike was "one of the important contests that have marked the progress of human liberty since the world began." Darrow told the commission that the mine operators were fighting for "slavery . . . for the rule of man over man, for despotism, for darkness, for the past." Darrow's eloquence was handsomely rewarded. In March 1903, the commission granted the miners almost everything they had wanted. Darrow, of course, would go on to further acclaim in a storied career as a lawyer. In 1925, he defended the right to teach Darwin's theory of evolution in the Scopes trial. But by then, his victory for the miners twenty-two years earlier was barely a memory in Archbald.

It was 1916 when Pete waited at the altar of St. Thomas Aquinas Church for Mary Sweeny to walk down the aisle. By then he was forty-four, his hands gnarled and rough as rock, his lungs, like the houses, trees, and streets of Archbald, coated with coal dust and the rest of his insides stewed in Irish whiskey.

Mary Sweeny, fifteen years younger, no doubt married Pete to escape her surroundings. She grew up the youngest of twelve siblings in a boardinghouse and bar that her father ran in Simpson, Pennsylvania. It was no place for a woman to visit, never mind live and work. And, by all accounts, Mary's childhood was horrible. Her father was a tyrannical drunk who beat her mercilessly, sometimes in front of drunken coal miners who would urge him on. She was a heavy girl, nearly obese by young womanhood. The coal miners called her names and told jokes about her weight, loudly enough for her to hear. Her father worked her like a coal miner's mule. She spent her days scrubbing and wringing out the miners' coal-caked shirts and pants and their shit-stained underclothing, sweeping and mopping their rooms, making sure there was brown paper in the horrid foulness of the outhouse. Still, she was good-natured, known to hum to herself as she cooked dinner for the dozen miners and the dozen members of her family. And she started every day at mass, where, perhaps, she prayed for a better life. For better or worse, her prayers were answered in the form of Pete, a sometime lodger and frequent drinker at the boardinghouse, who proposed on one knee in the kitchen.

Pete's drinking caused as much hardship in my father's family as did the Depression. Though he wasn't drunk all the time—in fact, he took the pledge on several occasions and stayed sober for long stretches, sometimes as long as a few years—it seemed he never missed an opportunity to sabotage his career or his family's fortunes by going on a binge. Coal miners were paid by the pound of coal they produced; the richer the chamber, the more money they would earn. Each time Pete worked his way up to a fine chamber, a punishment for being drunk and missing work would send him to the most infertile reaches of the mine. Once, after being dry for two years in the Temperance Society, the A.A. of its day, Pete was in line for promotion to foreman at more than double his miner's pay, only to have the promotion taken away when he went out on a two-week drunk to celebrate.

Partly the allure of the drink for Pete was that it dulled the pain of his job and released him—albeit temporarily—from the residual guilt of running away from his homeland and the fresh guilt of not being able to provide for his family during mining strikes and the Depression. I now wonder how he felt, what Irish demons roamed his thoughts, as he waited on line at the local parish for government surplus cheese or at the borough building for the relief check. But outside influences can never completely justify a drinking problem. For Pete, and in varying degrees for generations of my family, it is more an inside job—a hole in the Irish soul in the shape of a shot glass, one that has a cracked bottom and can never be filled no matter how much whiskey is poured into it.

The biggest career disappointment caused by Pete's drinking came in union politics, where his most fervent aspirations lay. He was passed over time and again when he ran for higher office. He was popular with the workers in a joker's role. But that same reputation held them back from casting their vote for him in the serious atmosphere of the unions.

Despite the trouble produced by Pete's periodic inebriation, Mary stayed the doting, loving wife. "He has the heart of a poet," she'd say. And so he did. In the barrooms of Archbald, Pete would stand and recite "The Diamond D," an ode to a coal miner, or, though he never took a lesson, sit at the piano and play a raucous drinking song or a sweet and haunting Irish lullaby. And even three sheets to the wind, Pete was able to make people laugh. My father remembers one day during the Depression when Mary sent my uncle Joe to fetch Pete from Moran's, a speakeasy in a private house not too far from Cemetery Street. When Joe walked into the barroom, Pete was dead drunk, his face on a table. As Joe shook him awake, Pete looked at his son through whiskey-blurred eyes, and though he'd never owned a vehicle more extravagant than a bicycle, said, loud enough for the whole bar to hear: "Did you bring the car, Joe?"

For my father, Pete's drinking was the source of ridicule and humiliation by Archbald's small-town gossips. It was hard for my father to hate Pete, though. When his father was sober, Frank saw in him an intelligent, caring man. Pete's eyes, my father said often, had a sparkle, a life force that engaged those in his presence and drew them in with a sorcerer's spell. Pete's sober personality had the beauty and glimmer of an icicle hanging from the porch of his home, but it was only a matter of time before whiskey, like a quick rise in temperature, dislodged it to fall and shatter before his family's eyes. Waiting for the crash steeled my father's feelings. But it was a certain deadness in his mother's eyes, a never-talked-about unhappiness, that bothered him the most. Often, when Pete was out on one of his roundelays, as Mary called his drunks, Frank would sit next to his mother on the tiny gray porch (all porches in Archbald were then painted battleship gray) of their home. She would stroke his hair and look longingly at the surrounding mountains of Archbald. "Someday," she'd say, "I'd like to follie the Red Hill Road and see what lay on the other side of those hills." In her whole life, she had never traveled farther than twenty miles from Simpson, the town where she was born. She would gaze down at my father, who sat at her feet, and again up at the mountains, but her eyes would ultimately always settle on Cemetery Street, in anxious wait for the sight of her husband staggering home.

"Promise me you'll never drink, Frank," Mary asked of my father once.

On our recent trip, I stood with my father on that same porch. He knocked on the door, but no one was home. The house, though still small, had been re-sided and there was a small flower garden in front. Indeed, all the homes in Archbald are now brightly painted and vinyl-sided, with neatly kept lawns and gardens. The last of the coal breakers, those towering structures that incessantly spewed coal dust day and night, has been closed for some twenty years, and Archbald is now a bedroom community for the growing high-tech firms in nearby Scranton and Carbondale. As we drove the streets of his childhood, my father pointed out where Moran's, the speakeasy, once stood; and where now stands a large ranch-style house. We went to the shifting shanty, which still stands, but in disrepair: crumbling brick walls, the inside draped with cob-webs. Our last stop was the cemetery, only steps from the porch where my father once sat with his mother. We stood over the un-marked plot where both his parents are buried. The afternoon had turned crisp and a chilly wind rustled up Cemetery Street. I waited quietly, watching him from the corner of my eye, his head bowed, his eyes closed. When he finally raised his head and looked toward me, I saw that his eyes were moist with tears. I pre-tended not to notice. Clumsily, I went to him and draped my arm around his back. "Come on, Pop," I said. "It's getting late."

2

In 1935, right after he graduated from high school, my father left Archbald for the same reason the immigrants left Ireland: there was no future there. Pete spent most of a relief check for his ticket to New York. On the porch they said their good-byes, Mary crying and Pete stiff and sober: "Good luck, boy" were the only words his father could muster. A few blocks from his home, in front of the Alco barbershop, my father boarded the trolley to Scranton, Pennsylvania, then a train to Hoboken, New Jersey, and last a ferry across the Hudson River to West Twenty-third Street in Manhattan. When he arrived in New York he had one suitcase, one fried-bologna sandwich (one having been eaten on the trip), and $2.

In New York, he lived with his aunt Mary, her son Frank McCabe and an Irish cousin with the same name as my father—Frank McDonald. With three Franks living together, they called my father by his middle name, Jerome. Aunt Mary's apartment was on Thirty-sixth Street and Second Avenue, a railroad flat. My father slept on a lumpy couch under a window that looked out onto Second Avenue and a small park across the way. Because he slept in the living room, where most of the household activity was centered, he was always the last to bed. Some nights, if Mary was entertaining a relative or neighbor, Frank would struggle to keep awake in a chair, silently praying that his aunt wouldn't offer her guests another cup of tea. Even when he did get the room to himself, he lay awake, listening to the cars and the shouts of the city night outside, so unfamiliar compared to the quiet of Archbald.

Frank McCabe found him a job as a clerk for a company called the National Credit Office, a subsidiary of Dun & Bradstreet, a credit investigation firm. The first day on the job, he was sent to make collections on West Thirty-seventh Street, in the Garment District. There were more people on that one street than he had ever seen in his life. The buildings were a towering maze of elevators and room numbers that left him wandering and wondering whether he would ever finish his rounds. It took him most of the day to complete an assignment that should have been done in an hour. When he finally returned to the office, his boss told him that he had better become more familiar with the city, or else look for another job. Each day, Frank became more seasoned, making mental notes of building numbers and shortcuts, until he knew every back alley and service elevator on the street. His pay was $12 a week, $8 of which he gave his aunt for room and board.

For fun, he'd go to the cinemas in Times Square or play basketball in the park across Second Avenue. He had played basketball in high school, even a few semipro games in his senior year. On the court, he made his first friends in New York. One of them was a wiry young man named Billy Graham, who had a thick East Side New York accent, and whose father owned a saloon on Thirty-sixth Street. Frank and Billy would battle under the backboards each evening, a classic struggle of my father's height and expertise against Graham's scrappy, street-fighter tenacity. One night, the two sat on a bench in the park and talked about their plans for the future. Graham had his all mapped out. He was going to become a professional fighter. He had already fought a few local club fights and had shown some promise. "I'm going to be the champion of the world some day," he told my father. When Graham asked about Frank's plans, my father said: "I'm thinking of taking the police exam."

"Well, you'll always have shiny shoes and a paycheck, Jerome," Graham said.

My father took the entrance examination for the police department on April 4, 1939. It was the largest police civil service examination in the history of New York City. My father was one of 30,000 applicants. The Depression had made civil service attractive to people of the most diverse ethnic and social backgrounds ever. For the first time, universities and colleges such as NYU, St. John's, Fordham, and City College all offered classes in police procedure. The mayor of New York, Fiorello La Guardia, began a campaign for what he called the professional police force. Extra credit would be given on final exam grades for people with college experience. "In the Police Department we need chemists, mechanics, accountants, electricians and engineers. We need them every day for the efficient and well-balanced work of the department," the mayor said in a speech one day. Three fourths of the 30,000 applicants had some college credits. Of the 1,200 who were ultimately appointed to the police department, nearly 1,000 had college experience; of those, 289 had law degrees.

Although a graduate of what he called a soup school, Archbald High ("soup" was a reference to the free lunch that came with the limited educational environment), my father was a pretty fair student, and he retained his scholar's habits well into adulthood.

He loved going to the library, and when he wasn't playing basketball, he spent hours picking volumes from the shelves and reading until the librarian would shake his shoulder and say she was closing up. In preparation for the civil service exam, three nights a week he attended Delahanty's, a prep school for the police test. Most of the other evenings he shunned the basketball court and pored over the police textbook with questions from past exams.

The test was held in Commerce High School on the Lower East Side of Manhattan. My father was one of the first to arrive, his pencils sharp, a good hot lunch, fixed by Aunt Mary, in his stomach. The testing room, a gymnasium, was filled with wooden desks and chairs. Frank fidgeted with his eraser and looked around the room, sure that everyone else was smarter than he, although he noticed one or two who seemed at least as nervous. The monitor handed out the test pamphlet. On it was printed, "The Municipal Civil Service Commission," along with a note that warned: "This is a difficult test." Frank opened the pamphlet, scanned the first page, and noticed a question that made him wonder if he had studied the right books:

Suppose that while you are patrolling your post you observe a woman, clad only in what seems to be a sheet, strolling along Madison Avenue. The woman is leading a doe by a chain. A

crowd is beginning to collect around the woman. You should (select from the following):
(a) Take the woman and the doe to the precinct. (b) Telephone the ASPCA to take the doe and disperse the crowd. (c) Summon another patrolman to take care of the doe, then compel the woman to return to her home. (d) Remove your coat to cover the woman and then compel the woman and the doe to return to her home. (e) Pay no attention to the incident because it is probably a publicity stunt.

He took a deep breath and thought for a moment, and then the absurdity of the question dawned on him: No doubt a publicity stunt, he thought. He marked "e," and moved on. Unlike prior civil service tests for patrolmen, which rewarded those who could memorize the most cram information, the 1939 test aimed to measure commonsensical judgment and reasoning, along with testing applicants in traditional academic areas like mathematics and word definitions. With each question Frank answered, his confidence grew. Three and a half hours was allotted for the test, and after three hours, during which he went over his answers to the one hundred multiple-choice questions twice, he was finished. He took the trolley back to Aunt Mary's, confident that he'd done his best. Though he knew the odds against him, nearly thirty to one, he thought he had a chance.

It would be five weeks before the test results were announced. During that time Frank worked for the NCO in their main office, as he had now been promoted to file clerk. He no longer had to navigate the buildings and the mass of people in the Garment District; rather, he worked in a clerk room, clothespinning credit slips to an elaborate set of wires and pulleys—the interoffice communication mode of the day.

In the meantime, he moved with Aunt Mary to the Bronx; the apartment house on Second Avenue was being razed to build the Midtown Tunnel. Just the two of them lived in an apartment on

Loring Place. Frank McCabe had moved out, and Irish Frank had been kicked out for doing too much carousing in the Bronx bars.

As the weeks went by, each day after work, my father would stop at Delahanty's to see if the results had been posted. Sometimes he would stay at the school to play basketball; other times he went with his friends from the credit office to the movies. As the days went by, he became more and more anxious about his results. More than just the security of a civil service job now fueled his desire to become a policeman. He watched the cops walk into Delahanty's in uniform, cops studying for the sergeant's test or higher, and he saw in them a certain confidence, almost an arrogance. Their swagger was intoxicating. He saw the uniform as armor. If he was wearing it, no one would laugh at him as they had at his father.

Finally, the results of the test were posted. The question concerning the woman and the doe had been inspired by the real-life experience of a patrolman on a Madison Avenue beat, who encountered the pair a few weeks before the test. It was a publicity stunt for the World's Fair, which was being held in New York at the time. My father had marked the right answer. More important, he had also marked most of the other questions with the right answer. My father's name was on the list of those who had passed.

Although he knew he'd passed, he still wouldn't know how he'd placed on the list until the official notice arrived at Loring Place a few days later.

For a few moments, my father held the letter from the civil service commission in his hands, unopened.

"Go ahead, Jerome," his Aunt Mary urged. "I'm sure it's only the best of news."

He scanned the letter for the all-important number. It was 804; he had made the top 1,200 with room to spare.

3

In those days, if young Frank McDonald's head had glowed, he could have been a lamppost. At six feet three inches, he weighed 158 pounds, and that was with a Manhattan telephone directory under each arm. He was in fairly good shape from playing basketball and living the life he'd promised his mother, no drinking or smoking. But he was seven pounds under the police department weight requirement for his height.

In my grandfather's Tammany days, though there were also height-for-weight requirements, cops who didn't fit into the envelope got around the regulations in the most inventive ways. In one published memoir of that time, a fat cop wrote that he put a wad of chewing gum on the counterweight of the scale when the doctor wasn't looking. But with Mayor La Guardia's election, Tammany and its disregard for rules were all but dead. (Tammany Hall actually died as a result of yet another scandal. Judge Samuel Seabury directed what was first an investigation into organized crime's influence with New York magistrate's court judges, but the inquiry evolved to target a city contract payoff scheme to then mayor James J. Walker. Jimmy Walker, the darling of Tammany, decided discretion was the better part of valor and in 1932 resigned, but did so with his usual panache. With photographers' flashbulbs exploding around him, the dapper Walker waved good-bye as he walked up the gangplank to a ship sailing to Europe. With him sailed the last of Tammany's significance in New York City; in 1933, La Guardia was elected mayor.)

Colorful, honest, and forceful, La Guardia was the perfect mayor for the times. As the Depression demoralized the common man, "the Little Flower," as La Guardia was called, aggressively reorganized city government, vigorously battled corruption and gambling, and exerted his considerable influence with Franklin

Delano Roosevelt to get the city millions in federal funds to build highways, hospitals, and airports. By 1939, he had turned his attention to the NYPD. His aim was to build a super police force. With a majority of college men on the list to be appointed, the mayor now wanted the brawn to go along with the brains.

The physical exams for what would become known as the Class of 1,200 were given at the NYU gymnasium and athletic fields in the University Heights section of the Bronx. They were presided over by a panel of athletic directors and coaches from city colleges and universities: the football coach at City College, the track coach of NYU.

Frank McDonald passed the physical exam with the proviso that he gain seven pounds within a month or be dropped from the list. For the next thirty days he drank milk by the gallon and ate everything in sight: chocolate cakes by the dozens and the hearty, potato-laden meals his Aunt Mary made. But despite the enormous caloric intake, by month's end he had gained only four pounds. When the day came to be reweighed, he sat in City Hall Park, across from the civil service building, and ate ten bananas. Almost bursting, he went into an Automat and drank as much water as he could hold. The lengths people went to pass that year's police department entrance physical were extraordinary. As my father walked into the civil service building, a cab stopped and two men emerged, carrying a third man strapped to a board. He had been stretching on it for two weeks to make the height requirement. This may seem preposterous, but desperate attempts to make the grade—including that of the man on the board— were reported in numerous newspapers. (My father says that the man on the board made the requirement and years later rose to the rank of a deputy chief inspector.) When my father stepped on the scale, it registered the minimum—exactly 165 pounds. That day, he made himself a promise that he would never eat another banana as long as he lived.

* * *

The police academy training was held in a precinct in Brooklyn and presided over by a drill-instructor type named John Murray. The recruits called him Father John because of his patrician looks and no-nonsense demeanor. At the Academy, Frank McDonald learned how to shoot a pistol, what to expect on the streets of New York, and how to defend himself with a billy club and his hands. One of the rituals was boxing matches between the recruits. One day, my father was pitted against a young recruit named Mike Codd. When they entered the ring, the first punch Codd threw landed well below my father's belt, and he collapsed on the canvas. Just like that, the fight was over. When he regained his breath, my father staggered over to Codd and whispered: "If you ever do that again, I'll knock your teeth out." One night, years later at a function honoring Mike Codd as the new police commissioner, my father reminded him of the story.

The competition was stiff in the Academy, and although there was a line drawn between the college men and those, like my father, who had only high school educations, the Depression was a great equalizer. No matter who you were or where you came from, all the recruits were working for a common goal: the job. For Father John, a college degree meant little as far as police work went. And the academy instructor relished dispersing the college men to remote precincts when recruits were sent out in the "field" with patrolmen.

On September 4, 1941, the day he graduated from the Academy, my father was assigned to the 28th Precinct. The salary was $1,500 yearly, only $50 more than the rate my grandfather Tom Skelly had retired at twenty-two years earlier. Still, my father felt flush. He had just left the credit company, where he'd been making $18 a week; before that, he and his family had depended on public assistance. When he donned his uniform, a baggy fit over his gangly frame, strapped on his service revolver, and reported for work that first morning, the sergeant at the desk said: "Welcome to Harlem, son," and smiled. Harlem or hell, my father thought, it was a step up from Archbald.

When he received his first paycheck from the police department he sent two train tickets to Archbald, for his mother and father to come visit in New York. My father said that when he met his mother at the Twenty-third Street ferry port, her eyes were the size of tea saucers. She had never been on a train before, nor had she been on a boat of any kind, and how must she have felt, my father wondered, when she saw the sight of Manhattan rising to the heavens before her?

My father rented a room at McAlaster's boardinghouse on the beach at Ninety-sixth Street in Rockaway, and there, he and his parents had a big seafood dinner before he was off to the city to work. The next morning he went to McAlaster's again to meet them for breakfast. There, his mother still wore an amazed expression. She said that the storm the night before was one of the worst she'd ever heard, and that it kept her up most the night. There hadn't been any storm, my father remembered. His mother had never heard an ocean before. She thought the waves crashing against the shore were the roll of thunder.

My mother had listened to the Rockaway waves years before my father ever set foot there. A four-mile barrier beach on a peninsula that juts from the southern shore of Queens, Rockaway became known as the Irish Riviera, thanks to investors and developers like the infamous William Devery. The silky sand beach, dotted with colorful umbrellas and filled with the laughter of youth, fronted a boardwalk lined with graceful rooming houses, small hotels, and Irish bars. But for my mother, the allure of Rockaway was more than the gaiety of sight and sound. She had once fallen in love, deeply in love, there. And this, too, was long before she met my father.

She was nineteen and had gone on a week-long holiday to

Rockaway Beach with some friends and her sister Maz. While there, she met a boy, a lifeguard by the name of Timothy Carey. Each day she spread a towel on the sand beneath his chair, at night they walked the noisy streets holding hands.

I have a picture of my mother at a beach about that time—1929 or 1930. In the photograph, she stands with her older sister and two friends, the Lindinger girls. She wears a loose-fitting one-piece bathing suit, and her legs are slender and athletic. Her long, curly hair is swept back over her shoulder. Her eyes have a devilishly seductive look.

When Julia found out about the lifeguard, she forbade my mother to see him. Julia was protective of all her children, but Eleanor was her youngest daughter, and she wasn't about to give her up at the age of nineteen. Desperate, lovesick, my mother went to her father for support. But by then he had had his fill of arguments with Julia, most of which he lost. He refused to take his daughter's side, and my mother never forgot his failure to stand up for her.

Eleanor and her lifeguard lover decided to elope. She knew she would be the talk of the neighborhood. She also knew that Julia would be furious and disown her. Yet her heart leaped as she stood on the platform of Grand Central Station with her lover holding her arm and two tickets for Ocean City, Maryland.

They would marry in Ocean City; Tim would find work as a lifeguard, and she as a secretary. Made shortsighted by desire, they didn't even think as far ahead as the coming winter, when my mother's new husband would be out of a job.

But, at some point during the train ride, her thoughts went to her parents. The idea of never speaking to her mother again made her sick to her stomach. By the time she arrived in Ocean City those feelings were just too painful to ignore. She took the next train back to New York and cried the whole way.

Eleanor didn't try to keep in touch with the lifeguard after that, and she kept the hurt and her resentment toward her parents inside. The lifeguard undoubtedly spent that summer in Ocean City. The following year my mother did take a trip back out to Rockaway and ask about him, but she was told by the other lifeguards that Tim hadn't returned for his job that summer.

Years later, when my father was a young desk sergeant in Harlem, a somewhat older than average patrolman was transferred to his precinct. His name was Tim Carey, and it seemed vaguely familiar to my father (my mother having once told him the story of her young love). When Patrolman Carey reported to the desk, my father asked him if he had ever worked in Rockaway as a lifeguard. The patrolman enthusiastically answered that indeed he had, undoubtedly thinking my father knew him from there. When he "turned out" assignments to the patrolmen for that tour, a midnight–to–8 a.m. shift on a February night, my father gave the newcomer a "fixer" (a stationary post) at the edge of the Polo Grounds, on 155th Street and Eighth Avenue—"the North Pole," as the cops from the precinct called it. Patrolman Carey never had the slightest clue what he had done to deserve such an assignment.

When my mother met my father she was nearly thirty, eight years older than he, and somewhat scandalously single, given the place and time: the insular Irish neighborhood of Fordham in the early 1940s. Once, when I asked about her late-in-life marriage, she paused, looked across the living room at my father sitting in his chair, wrinkled her nose, and said in a giggling whisper: "Maybe I should have waited a little longer."

Although she lived with Julia up until she married my father, my mother was stubbornly independent and undoubtedly had her own plans for the future. Times were changing for women. Although many girls of her era still thought marriage the ultimate goal, even in these just pre-war-industry times, it was becoming increasingly acceptable for women—albeit with a very low glass ceiling—to build their own careers. Eleanor worked in a stenography pool for the Mutual Insurance Company in downtown Manhattan, having learned her trade at Grace Institute, then a well-known secretarial school. She had gone to Grace after only one year at Theodore Roosevelt High School, and against the wishes of her father. She often told me, in a pat motherly way, that her happiest moments came when her children were born. But, had her life gone in a different direction, she might have been just as happy being a single career woman. Her best friend in the world, Nora Banks, was single her whole life.

Like my grandparents Tom and Julia, my parents met at a dance. It was held at the YMCA on Lexington Avenue in Manhattan in June 1941, while my father was still in the police academy. Frank went there that night at the urging of a friend from the credit office, Bill Kelly, who had promised him that there would be plenty of girls from the big insurance companies in attendance, all of whom were great dancers.

When my father approached the girl in the pillbox hat—a Fordham neighborhood girl, he knew, because Fordham girls, the single ones with their own money, dressed to the nines—he affected his father's brogue and said: "Are you doing any dancing a'tall, a'tall?"

My father says that my mother blushed and accepted his offer. My mother, however, says that she had her suspicions of him right off. He seemed a bit young to her, he was about as wide as a mop handle, and she thought his confidence was just an act. She did dance with him, but there her doubts about him grew even stronger—he didn't even know how to do the Lindy. When he told her he was from a place called Archbald, she nearly—her "big-city girl" attitude in full bloom—walked away.

For his part, my father didn't waver. Still riding the high from passing the police exam and entering the Academy, he tried to impress her by whispering: "You know, I'm a police officer."

"So what," my mother said. "So was my father, and my uncle, too."

Later on that night, my father asked the Fordham girl out for a cup of coffee. He had hoped it would be only the two of them, but on agreeing to go, my mother invited all of her friends to come along. As luck would have it, they sat next to each other in the crowded booth in a coffee shop on Third Avenue. Perhaps it was there that she began to see something appealing in the country boy. She giggled with her girlfriends when someone said that my father had ears like two open doors on a taxicab. She liked that he didn't seem sensitive about the needle the girls were giving him, and when they were getting ready to leave, and my father asked if he could see her again, she flashed a demure smile and said positively, "Maybe."

My mother declined several times when Frank first began asking her out. My father wasn't the only suitor she had, and besides, she was deeply involved in her job and a bevy of causes, like the America First antiwar movement. She often attended rallies at places like Madison Square Garden to listen to Charles Lindbergh and others speak against America's involvement in the war in Europe. But my father remained persistent. And one night, my mother invited him to her house for dinner. As with the lifeguard years before, Julia wasn't so thrilled with my father. Perhaps it was because he was a policeman: resentment still festered from the department's treatment of her husband. More likely, it was because Julia was afraid my mother would become seriously involved. By then her other children were married, and her youngest son, Vincent, had enlisted in the army. It was only Julia and my mother living in the apartment. If my mother were to get married, Julia would be all alone, a point she made often to my mother with more than just innuendo. This Irish guilt, a skewed sense of filial responsibility, was, undoubtedly, another reason my mother stayed single so long.

Julia spent most of that meal in sullen silence—that is, until after dinner, when my father asked if there would be any dessert. Julia scolded him for being rude and stormed out of the kitchen in a huff. My father thought that he had permanently damaged any chance of getting Julia's blessing on his relationship with her daughter.

One of their first real go-out-for-dinner dates was on December 7, 1941. As they sat enjoying a luau buffet at Mayer's Parkway Inn in the Bronx, there was a commotion near the bandstand. An "extra" edition of the *Journal Tribune* had been delivered, and the Hawaiian band members had gathered around to read about the attack on Pearl Harbor. As the news spread through the dining room, a combination of fear and anger gripped my father. His younger brother Joe was in the army, stationed at Shoffield Barracks at Pearl Harbor. My father slammed his hand on the table and announced his intention to enlist the next morning. My mother, who also had a brother in the army, calmed my father down.

"Let's first find out how Joe is before you go off to save him," she said. My uncle Joe did survive Pearl Harbor; my father took my mother's advice and didn't enlist. Instead, he stayed in the police department (New York City policemen were offered an exemption to the draft), and the following June they were married. That summer, they rented a small apartment in a house on Ninety-sixth Street in Rockaway. Though the world was turned upside down by the war, for the newlyweds, the summer of 1942 was a kind of extended honeymoon. My mom spent her days at the beach, while my father commuted into the city to work. At night he would come home exhausted and fall asleep next to his new bride, listening to the ocean waves crashing against the shore and dreaming of the staged explosions in Madison Square Garden.

As a rookie policeman during wartime, my father was assigned to go from apartment house to apartment house trying to enlist people in the air raid warden program initiated by Mayor La Guardia. The mayor was so afraid of an air attack on New York (perhaps rightly so) that he recreated the Battle of Britain in

Madison Square Garden. My father and a thousand other rookie cops play-acted the city's emergency response plans.

In Rockaway, my mother befriended a woman staying at the same apartment house. Ruth Mackey's husband was also a policeman. My father and Charlie Mackey were introduced by their wives, and though Mackey was much farther along in his career— he ran the NYPD's celebrated bomb squad—he took to the young patrolman. The two spent many happy evenings chatting about police work on the porch, with its view of the laundry lines that hung between the Rockaway bungalows.

"The flags of Ireland," Mackey once said of the laundry.

When the summer ended and my parents moved to the Bronx, my father kept up contact with Mackey, often visiting him at his office in the police headquarters annex at 400 Broome Street.

Besides running the bomb squad, Charlie Mackey had another talent, one he was loath to advertise. In those days, a warrant wasn't needed for wiretaps. In fact, there was little regulation of wire taps at all. Private organizations sprung up offering the service to anyone—and on any phone—for a price. Police used them frequently in investigations, mostly of illegal gambling enterprises. Most of the time, in those days, wiretaps had to be installed in the basement of the same building where the phone to be tapped was located. The placing of a wiretap required not only technical expertise, but burglarlike cunning to get in and out of basements undetected. Among those who knew him, Charlie Mackey was thought of as the best wire man in the department. Many years later, that expertise would almost place him in the middle of one of the most infamous events ever to occur in our nation's capital.

In the early seventies, well after he had retired from the police department, Mackey was approached by a retired cop he knew was working for the government in Washington, D.C. The ex-cop told him that he had a wire job for him in the Capital that would involve very little work and would pay handsomely. It was a bugging job, the acquaintance said, not a wiretap, and a one-shot deal. As a seasoned ex-detective, Mackey was skeptical from the outset. He told the acquaintance he'd have to think about it and get back to him. Mackey didn't bother calling back, but the ex-cop was persistent, calling him on several other occasions. "It's only a hotel room," the ex-cop pleaded. Mackey had to admit the offer was tantalizing, and he could have certainly put the money to use. But, finally, he followed his initial instinct and told the contact that he was just not interested. Over the next several months, Mackey realized he had made the right decision. The article that caught his attention was in *The New York Times*. It was about a burglary at Democratic party headquarters, in the Watergate Hotel.

In the parlance of cops, Charlie Mackey became my father's rabbi. But the first favor Mackey arranged for my father, as it happened, was not in the police department. During one of their porch chats the summer after the Japanese bombed Pearl Harbor, Mackey told my father that he had a nephew who was a captain in the Office of Naval Intelligence. He said that they were looking for cops, especially New York City cops, to work in the division stationed at the Brooklyn Navy Yard. A few weeks later, my father went to 50 Church Street, the headquarters of the Third Naval District. Policemen admitted into the ONI were automatically made navy third-class petty officers. Thanks to Mackey—and his nephew—not only was my father given this rank when he joined the ONI, he also spent the first year and a half of his military service in Brooklyn, close enough to commute home.

In December 1942, my father began his wartime naval career. By then, my mother was almost six months pregnant with their first child, my brother Eugene. Although she was never in favor of the war, with her brother, Vincent, a lieutenant in the army, and my father's brother Joe in the South Pacific, she proudly taped a flag with blue stars on the apartment door, indicating family members involved in heavy fighting.

On March 2, 1943, Eugene was born. Even Julia congratulated

my father on a job well done. That night he had his first drink, a weak scotch and soda, which went right to his head.

Less than a week later, he received a telegram from Pete.

My father was granted leave from the ONI when he learned of his mother's illness. When he arrived in Archbald she was lying on a bed in the living room of the home on Cemetery Street. She had had a stroke, and was barely conscious when my father walked in the room. He leaned close to her, held her hand, and whispered to her that she was now a grandmother. Mary weakly squeezed my father's hand to let him know she understood. His leave was only for two days, and my father stayed that night in his old home. The next day he took the train back to New York.

Less than a week later, he received another telegram from Pete saying that Mary was dying. He arrived at Peckville Hospital the next day, just in time to hold his mother's hand once more before she passed away. Pete sat in the hospital room, propped up against a wall, so drunk he had no idea what had just transpired. Of all Pete's benders my father had been witness to, this one hurt him the deepest. Still, the next day he weaned his father off the horrors with a bottle of warm ale, as he had seen his mother do countless times, so Pete would be at least half presentable at the wake and funeral.

Two weeks after Mary died, Pete showed up at the door at 2300, dressed in his Sunday suit and holding a busted suitcase. "The people in Archbald said I should come live with my son," he said.

My mother wasn't altogether thrilled.

In the late winter of 1944, my father received orders to report to San Francisco, from where he would be sent to the 7th Fleet in the South Pacific. But the head of the San Francisco Office of Naval Intelligence, a man named William Quinn who was a former chief of police of San Francisco, changed the order; my father and two other New York City cops were assigned to him. My father fought the remaining year of the war on the shores of Treasure Island in San Francisco Bay, locking up sailors who stole from footlockers and chasing down AWOL cases.

The week after the D-Day invasion, my mother's brother, Vincent, was killed in action by a sniper as he tried to carry a wounded soldier to safety.

My father's brother Joe was at this time engaged in combat on several islands in the South Pacific. My father had no contact with him for months—in fact, Joe wasn't notified of his own mother's death until a month after it happened, when he finally received the crumpled letter from my father. Through the Red Cross, and his contacts in Naval Intelligence, my father had tried to arrange a leave for Joe to attend his mother's funeral. But Joe was involved in such heavy fighting, a leave was out of the question.

(Joe ultimately did return home after the war. He was placed in the Fort Devins army hospital near Worcester, Massachusetts, for treatment of shell shock and hepatitis. After having survived the bombing of Pearl Harbor, after four years in the armpit of the Pacific theater—four years of witnessing the most unspeakable horrors—and after six months in an army hospital, he returned to Archbald to live with a friend's family. At the train station, the only familiar face there to greet him was that of an old Irish railroad worker, who asked: "Have you been out of town, M'Donald?")

The day my father returned to New York after his discharge, he called my mother from Grand Central Station, expecting to hear shrieks of joy and a voice overcome with emotion. What he heard was an order to pick up some milk on the way home. Often, during wartime rationing, an enlisted man in uniform was the only person able to obtain such precious commodities. My mother had given birth to two wartime babies: Eugene, undoubtedly conceived during that first summer in Rockaway, and Frankie, during my father's weekend leaves from the Brooklyn Navy Yard. For my mother, there was no time for sentimental reunions. For my father, there was a lot of catching up to do in the world of dirty diapers and early-morning feedings.

4

On January 1, 1946, a bitter cold night, Frank McDonald was back in a police uniform in the 28th Precinct in Harlem. As he began his tour that night, a beat on a cold, quiet street, a man stumbled toward him and collapsed at his feet. Having just served nearly four years in the navy during World War II, my father hadn't witnessed so much as one shot fired in action. Now, not twenty minutes after he arrived in Harlem, there was a man lying on the street in front of him dying from a gunshot wound. The next day my father paid a visit to his rabbi on Broome Street.

Mackey knew a Brooklyn captain in plainclothes named John Martin, and was sure he could get my father assigned to him. Though my father wanted out of Harlem in the worst way, it wasn't only Harlem that impelled him to seek out his rabbi. My father's experience in the navy had given him a taste of what it was like to hold rank, and he brought this gathering ambition back to the police department. Unlike my grandfather Tom, Frank McDonald wasn't about to remain a patrolman the rest of his career. Still, he was leery of the plainclothes division, which had been rife with scandal and corruption from its inception.

There is a popular misconception that plainclothes policemen are part of the Detective Bureau or its more modern version, the Detective Division. Plainclothesmen were not detectives. (There is no longer a plainclothes division. In the years after the 1972 Knapp Commission investigation it was disbanded. Charge of investigations into gambling, vice, and narcotics was given over to a newly formed unit called the Organized Crime Control Bureau [OCCB].) In the organizational chart of the New York City police

department, plainclothesmen were under the auspices of the uni-
formed arm. The genesis of the plainclothes division perhaps
dates back to the wardmen, the bagmen for the crooked precinct
captains of the nineteenth century. Often wardmen dressed in civilian clothing so as not to draw attention to their graft-collecting
activities. By the 1940s, the plainclothes division, which dealt exclusively in investigations into gambling and vice, was a cesspool
of corruption. A joke circulated in the police department after
one of the many gambling scandals tied to the plainclothes division: St. Peter is at the Pearly Gates when twelve plainclothesmen
appear before him. Peter goes in to see God and says, "I have a
problem; there are twelve plainclothesmen at the Pearly Gates
looking to come in all at once." And God says, "Well, just treat
them like anyone else—find out one by one if they're worthy of
heaven, and if they are, let them in. And, Peter," God says, "come
back and tell me how it works out." Peter leaves but returns almost immediately. "They're gone," he says to God. "The plainclothesmen?" God asks. "The Pearly Gates," Peter says.

My father's instincts told him to turn down his rabbi's offer, but
it was hard for him to say no to Mackey, who had already steered
him in the right direction once. Not knowing what to do, my father asked if he could sleep on it.

"Sure, Frank," Mackey said in a soothing voice. "Take your
time."

That night, he went home and asked my mother what she
thought. A city kid, the daughter of a cop, and now the wife of a
cop, my mother was more savvy than my father in many ways, at
least back then, even when it came to his job. Though she clearly
remembered the unfair treatment her father received after he
turned down the Tammany offer to be a doorman, she said: "Say
thanks, but no thanks, Frank. Something else will come along."

Something did. The next day, when my father went back to
Mackey's office, he told his rabbi that he was passing on plainclothes. Mackey smiled. "I thought you might," he said. He then

told my father that he also knew of an opening in the detective district captain's office in Harlem, and if my father wanted, he would make a call.

Two weeks later Frank McDonald was a detective, assigned to the 6th Detective District headquarters in Harlem, as secretary to the district captain. My father held this position for nearly four years and was secretary to several district captains, of whom Hughie Sheridan was the most memorable. Tall, silver-haired, and elegant, Sheridan looked more like an ambassador than a policeman. He went to a Harlem barber each day for a shave, and his hair was always neatly coiffed. He wore immaculate Savile Row suits and Turnbull & Asser dress shirts. He drank old scotch at the Artists and Writers club. "Top drawer, Frank," he would say to my father. "Always buy top drawer." (Though my father never could afford Savile Row, he did follow Sheridan's advice as much as he could, buying Hickey Freeman suits, Stanley Blacker blazers, and such.)

Sheridan liked my father, and the feeling was mutual. They shared a love of reading and, as a good clerical man—a fast typist with a flair for writing that brought life to the dull reports and letters of the office—my father was an asset to his boss, and Sheridan knew it.

While he was working at the district office, my father became the delegate from Harlem to the Detective Endowment Association. He was a natural politician. Towering, his weight finally catching up with his height, with midnight-black hair parted just to the right of middle and thick enough to comb back with an open hand, he had the kind of presence that made even a roomful of detectives stop and take notice. He was a voracious reader, which endowed him with a professorial vocabulary. And he also had experience, of sorts, in politics. In his senior year at Archbald High School he'd run for class president and been elected; his dominion comprised all of forty-eight students.

Frank's first year in the police union, the president of the DEA was a legendary Runyonesque character named Denis "Dinny" Mahoney. Because my father was the delegate from Harlem, Dinny, who grew up on West 118th Street, and whose closest police friends worked in the Harlem precincts, took a special shine to him. In the realm of police politics, Mahoney's blessing was like that of a pope.

Officially, Mahoney was assigned as a detective to the pickpocket squad, but it was said that he spent most of his working hours in the saloons along the Great White Way. He was a familiar figure at Billy Rose's raucous Diamond Horseshoe, and one of the few who could hold his own matching wits with Texas Guinan, the razor-tongued nightclub impresario. By all accounts, Mahoney was as brightly lit as the theater district itself. Chipmunk-cheeked, with a sharp pointed nose and small gleaming eyes, he acted as if he owned Broadway. He often wore a tuxedo, even a Prince Albert coat, and a variety of rakish hats including a white homburg and a silk plug that earned him the nickname Silk Hat Dinny. In the early 1920s, a news account of Mahoney's election to the ceremonial post of mayor of Harlem ran in the *New York Globe*:

> Perhaps there are no flags flying to the breeze in Harlem. Perhaps there is no blare of trumpets to mark the joyous occasion. But what of it? Harlem is still furiously celebrating, in its solid mental way, the election of one of its favorite sons as the Mayor of all one can survey uptown.
>
> Yes, mates, it was a real old fashioned election that catapulted "Silk Hat Dinny" into the mayoralty office. The new Mayor of Harlem is a detective-sergeant in real life and is connected with the One Hundredth Street police station.

The biggest event of the year for the DEA was their annual dinner-dance, held at the Hotel Astor in Times Square. The Harlem "mayor" was in charge of booking the entertainment.

There wasn't a theatrical agent on Broadway who could have done a better job. Mahoney grew up with the comedian Milton Berle on 118th Street. In those days, Berle's *Texaco Star Theatre* was the highest-rated show on television. Each year, as a favor to Dinny Mahoney, Berle served as emcee for the dinner-dance. But Uncle Miltie was only the beginning of the talent Mahoney paraded onto the Astor's bandstand: Benny Goodman's band would provide the swing, Jack Benny or Jackie Gleason the laughs, and Bing Crosby the voice.

One night, in 1942, just a week or so before the big dance, Dinny was sitting with a couple of his cronies at a table in Leon and Eddy's, a famous Broadway watering hole, when he noticed a great commotion at the door. The stir was caused by the entrance of a skinny kid in a tuxedo, with slicked-back black hair.

"Who's that?" Mahoney asked of one of his cronies.

"Frank Sinatra," came the reply.

Mahoney summoned Sinatra over to his table with a wink and a sideways tilt of his head. The next week, instead of singing to the horde of bobby-soxers at the Paramount Theatre, Sinatra was cradling the microphone at the DEA dinner-dance.

Needless to say, the ticket for the dance was the hottest in town. Along with just about every one of the city's VIPs, 600 New York City detectives and their wives, most of the men in tuxedos, all of the women in gowns, packed the huge ballroom and balconies of the Astor, while being entertained by the biggest names in show business. Mayor William O'Dwyer wouldn't have thought of missing the event; neither would any other top politician or New York businessman—all thanks to the connections of Dinny Mahoney.

For my father, those days of the DEA were heady times, a fulfillment of his Academy dreams. The stringbean of a boy from Archbald, all assholes and elbows, as he would say, was now mingling with the powerful and famous of New York. In his new surroundings he developed a certain confidence and cockiness. Detectives, he found, were treated with a respect he had not known as a patrolman and certainly not as a coal miner's kid. And the respect came not only from policemen, but from the city at large. Then, to be a detective in New York was to be something special, and while he drove Milton Berle or Sugar Ray Robinson home after the dinner-dance Frank would wonder what his friends back in Archbald would say if they could see him.

In September of 1948, while my father was still working for Hughie Sheridan, my mother gave birth to her third child. By all accounts, Mary Clare was a perfectly healthy baby. She had curly hair like her mother's, cornflower-blue eyes, and a rosy complexion. She hardly ever cried, but cooed, chortled, and smiled most of the time. Although she would never admit this, my mother was absolutely thrilled to have a baby girl come into her life, and not another boy. She stretched the family budget on pink baby suits and nightclothes. She'd bundle Mary Clare in blankets and a woolen bonnet and bustle her downstairs to visit Theresa or lay her in the stroller and proudly parade down Sedgwick Avenue to show her off to the other young mothers gathered in Devoe Park.

Late one night, when Mary Clare was just four and a half months old, my mother was awakened by a soft but deep cough coming from the baby's crib, next to her bed. The child had spat up a dark gray fluid, which covered her face and the front of her nightclothes. My mother was alarmed. Though she had seen plenty of every imaginable kind of regurgitation with her other children, she had never seen anything the color of what now covered her daughter. Early the next morning, without even calling to make an appointment, my mother dressed Mary Clare, now wheezing and coughing harder, in warm clothing, wrapped her in blankets, and rushed to the family physician. Though the office was busy that morning, a cold January day in the midst of the flu season, the doctor made time to examine the baby. With a waiting room filled with sick patients, the doctor quickly wrote out a prescription for a sulfa drug, the penicillin of its day, and told my mother to fill it as soon as possible.

My mother hurried to the druggist on the corner of Sedgwick Avenue and Fordham Road holding Mary Clare, still wrapped in blankets, and handed the prescription over the counter. Doc Applebaum, a diminutive man with a balding head and wire-rimmed glasses, had been the family druggist since my mother and father moved into 2300. He greeted my mother by her first name and asked about Mary Clare's condition. He knew all the neighborhood folk and had a genuine concern for each of them. As he started to fill the prescription, he raised his head over the counter and asked my mother, in a mildly perplexed tone, if she was sure the doctor knew the medication was for Mary Clare.

Yes, my mother said, she was sure. She told him that she had just then come from the doctor's office.

"It seems an awfully large dosage for an infant," he said.

For a moment, Doc Applebaum's words worried Eleanor. But Mary Clare had been wheezing and coughing with greater discomfort, and she wanted to bring her home to the warmth of the apartment. Besides, Theresa was watching Eugene and Frankie, and she had enough on her hands with her own baby in diapers. Again my mother told the druggist she was sure, and Doc Applebaum filled the prescription.

Eleanor rushed home, past Shultz's candy store and the dry cleaner, past Tony the greengrocers' and up the incline of Sedgwick Avenue. As she passed the alleyway to the carriage room she barely noticed the boys of the building holding their secret meeting. The bell in the tower of St. Nicholas of Tolentine rang as it did every hour, but my mother didn't notice. Up the steps of 2300 and through the large foyer she held Mary Clare ever tighter to her chest. The words of Doc Applebaum resonated in her thoughts.

In the elevator rising to the fifth floor, she decided to call the doctor, just to be sure the prescription was correct. Inside the apartment, she laid Mary Clare in the crib in her bedroom, being sure to change the blanket in which she had wrapped the baby for the trip to the doctor's office with a fresh one from the shelf over the radiator, built to keep the baby's bedclothes warm and dry. She then walked to the hallway where the telephone sat on a small round table and called the doctor, whose number she knew by heart. The nurse who answered said the doctor was too busy to come to the phone, but she would relay my mother's question. Over the phone, my mother could hear what sounded like agitated voices in the background—something about druggists doing doctors' jobs, and such. The nurse returned to the line and said the prescription was right and that the doctor said she should start Mary Clare on the medication as soon as possible.

The sulfa drug did little to improve Mary Clare's symptoms. Two days after her doctor's appointment, my parents brought Mary Clare to the hospital. There she was diagnosed as having double pneumonia and chickenpox, a viral disease for which sulfa drugs are useless. Though the infant mortality rate in those years from such a condition was extraordinarily high, Mary Clare survived after an extended hospital stay. But soon after, my mother became convinced that there was something very wrong with her child. At first, she thought it was just the illness working its way out of her system. But as the days folded into weeks, Mary Clare's complexion, once a healthy pink, took on an ashen cast. She seemed listless and unaware of her surroundings. There is a family snapshot of my father holding Mary Clare before she became ill. It was taken on the sidewalk near Devoe Park. He is tall and slender, dressed in a raincoat, wearing a fedora; his expression is the very essence of smiling proud papa. Mary Clare is wearing a wide-brimmed bonnet and a sweet small smile, perfectly safe in his arms. One night, a few weeks after she became sick, Frank came home and lifted Mary Clare from the crib. There was no recognition in his baby's eyes. She didn't reach and grab at his nose as she liked to do in the past. She didn't cry and reach for her mother. It was as though he was holding a lifeless doll in his arms.

Each morning my mother would wake from her fitful sleep and rush to the crib, expecting each day to be greeted with the smile she had once known. But each day the same dull eyes looked back at her. The baby would have spat up most of what she ate. The crib was smeared with thick, gooey vomit. Each night my mother knelt on the hardwood floor next to her bed and prayed to the Virgin Mary for a miracle. But as the weeks went by, Mary Clare slipped farther and farther away.

Six weeks after she became ill, my parents took Mary Clare to be examined at the New York Medical Center. There, the worst of their fears were realized.

The doctor's diagnosis was that Mary Clare had developed brain damage as a result of the viral infection. A year later, with most of the hope for a miracle drained from my mother, Mary Clare was admitted to Willowbrook State School, a hospital on Staten Island for severely mentally retarded children. The entry that day on her medical chart read like this:

April 12, 1950:
Mother, who was upset, but appeared intelligent and reliable, returned to the school (hospital) today and gave the following information: Patient is third of three children, two brothers, 7 and 5 years respectively. Pregnancy and birth normal. Developed apparently well up to 4½ mos. of age. Was able to turn over, to hold her head up. Vision and hearing keen. At that age child contracted pneumonia and subsequently chickenpox. Following these conditions, child regressed obviously. She lost interest in her environment and did not recognize her parents anymore. At 6 mos. of age, diagnosis of post-infectious encephalopathy was made at Medical Center. At present, child sits only when propped up, hearing impaired, vision unchanged, does not speak.

Each day, my mother drove to Staten Island to be with Mary Clare. Most days Frankie would go with her. Eugene had started school at St. Nicholas of Tolentine and would go to his grandmother's or Theresa's for lunch. Understandably, my mother was sullen and moody. At night she'd sit on the floral-patterned couch and smoke cigarettes. When my father came home—he was out with his detective friends more and more frequently—my mother would lash into him. The trip to Staten Island each day was too much of a strain on her. She seemed to argue with her husband all the time now.

On July 12, 1950, my parents went to Willowbrook together to take Mary Clare back to the Bronx. In an archaic tangle of bureaucratic red tape, Willowbrook required, in order for Mary Clare to be certified by the state, that the child be readmitted after a "home stay" of two weeks. On the Staten Island Ferry, Mary Clare began to shake violently as she lay in my mother's arms in the backseat of the car. The convulsion lasted over ten minutes. Afraid to jeopardize the state certification, my father drove all the way to Morrisania Hospital in the Bronx, with my mother clutching Mary Clare, trying to keep the extreme tremors from happening again.

After Mary Clare was released from Morrisania Hospital and brought back to Willowbrook, my father rented a cottage on Staten Island. My mother stayed there with Eugene and Frankie for the rest of the summer and into the fall. My father would visit only on the weekends. During the week, at night, he stayed alone at 2300.

For my father, in those days, the prospect of running a detective squad seemed about as realistic as being appointed the next police commissioner. You just didn't walk into a job like that. Squad commanders were crowned, not promoted. He would see them glide into division headquarters, dressed like mobsters: the finest homburgs, topcoats with felt collars, pinkie rings. They ate dinner at the Stork Club, were given the best tables at the Copacabana and Colony. They were gods. They knew everyone and answered to no one, and were treated with impunity and respect. They called everybody "kid," no matter their age or position. Just maybe, after ten or fifteen years in the bureau, maybe then, if he was lucky, he would get a shot at a squad. But not at only thirty-two, he thought, not even if he was the only horse in the race. But a funny thing happened in the starting gate.

In July 1948, Dinny Mahoney had died of what was called in one obituary a "complicated illness." The infirmity, no doubt, had its inception in Broadway scotch and Cuban cigars. In 1949, my father took and passed the sergeant's exam, and was on a list waiting for appointment. He had studied for the test mostly at night, with a friend and DEA cohort named Joe Harley, sometimes in one of the empty rooms in the chief of detective's office at police headquarters, where Harley worked. With Eugene just barely out of diapers and Frankie still wearing them, and then with the arrival of Mary Clare, the apartment at 2300 was a chaos of whines and cries and runny noses and smelly diapers. And even though Pete had since moved in around the corner with my uncle Joe (who had moved to the Bronx a few years before), the apartment was no place to memorize police procedure and sergeant's responsibilities. Though my mother understood how important the promotion was—with three children now, there was not much left at the end of the pay period—she couldn't help but resent her husband's absences from home.

In 1950, as Mary Clare was being admitted to Willowbrook, Joe Harley ran for the DEA presidency, with my father on his ticket as overall secretary. They won in a landslide victory. Their friendship became stronger as they worked side by side on the monumental task of filling Dinny's shoes. Harley was a quiet, even-tempered man, stout in stature, with handsome dark-Irish features and black hair combed back on the sides. Though he and my father lacked Mahoney's jaunty style—and his connections—

the DEA functions remained successful under their watch. Milton Berle was still stalwart at the dinner-dance, and my father was able to arrange for the Ink Spots, Mel Tormé, and others to perform. He and Harley worked long hours, sometimes late into the night, lobbying for extended benefits for police officers. Once a month, they would hold a dinner at the Belvedere Room at the Astor and invite congressmen and state senators. It was during these dinner meetings, the "rubber chicken circuit," as it was called, that the DEA first began to prevail upon politicians to vote for Social Security benefits for municipal employees (they were not, under the federal social security law, eligible in those years).

Harley's clerical job with the chief of detectives made him privy to the decisions and workings of the top echelon of the Detective Division. In 1950, the office in which Harley worked was a place under siege.

In September of that year, under the orders of Kings County District Attorney Miles F. McDonald (no relation), a major bookmaker named Harry Gross was arrested. The arrest was a result of an investigation into alleged police graft in connection with Brooklyn gambling. Gross rocked the city with allegations that he paid to the police $1 million of his $20 million yearly take for protection of his rackets. Those rackets included twenty-seven horse-betting rooms, dozens of sports bookmaking locations, and untold numbers of card games, crap games, and policy (numbers) operations.

But even more remarkable than the sums Harry Gross said he paid the police were the ranks of the police he said he was paying. Though the names of these ranking officers would not be officially tied to the scandal until two years later (when Gross testified in front of a Brooklyn grand jury), the very week after the bookmaker was arrested, Police Commissioner William P. O'Brien, Deputy Commissioner Frank C. Bals, and Chief of the Department William T. Whalen all resigned. And on August 31, 1950, as

Jimmy Walker had done eighteen years earlier, the mayor of New York City abdicated his office. Though William O'Dwyer had suffered a heart attack a few months earlier and was never officially implicated in the scandal, there were those who believed the mayor as guilty as any of his subordinates, and thought his leaving office was more an escape than a resignation.

When the rumblings of the Harry Gross scandal were first felt through the department, months before O'Dwyer resigned, my father, Joe Harley, and other officers of the police line organizations were summoned to city hall for a meeting with the mayor. A meeting between O'Dwyer and the police union officials was not unusual. The mayor had a close relationship with the police, having walked a beat himself as a young cop in Brooklyn. Most of the top echelon of the police department were his personal friends. Some of these friendships, like the one with Chief Whalen, dated back to when both men were rookies in the Police Academy. But even the rank and file thought of O'Dwyer as one of their own. My father called him the Bohola Boy, in reference to the town in County Mayo, Ireland, where he was born.

Family ties aside, O'Dwyer's good relationship with the police unions—a voting block, then some 20,000 strong, with wives and other voting-age relatives—was also good politics, even if it did hark back to the dark days of Tammany Hall.

From 1898, when the five boroughs were consolidated into the municipality of New York City, until the time of Jimmy Walker's resignation in 1932, the relationship between the mayor's office and the police department had by turns been one of allegiance or enmity. Most of this shifting had been dictated by political affiliation, most prominently Tammany Hall and Republican reformers. La Guardia was the first mayor of New York to have a hands-on relationship with the police department without totally being an indentured servant to a political machine. Though the old Tammany tiger had been defanged by La Guardia's election,

O'Dwyer's relationship with the cops was in many ways a revival of the Hall.

During the 1946 mayoral campaign, Judge Jonah J. Goldstein, one of O'Dwyer's opponents that year, addressed a meeting of the Patrolmen's Benevolent Association. During his speech, Goldstein said that he would conduct a "relentless barrage of police investigations" to drive out any underworld influences in the police department—a thinly disguised attack on O'Dwyer. In 1940 and 1941, O'Dwyer had been the Brooklyn district attorney, where he was lionized by the press as the second coming of Eliot Ness. While holding the D.A.'s office—for just two short years—O'Dwyer successfully headed more than eighty murder investigations. Most of these killings were by "Murder Incorporated," the Brooklyn dock mob. O'Dwyer's key witness in these investigations was Abe "Kid Twist" Reles, a Brooklyn thug and sometime associate of Murder Inc. A conscienceless killer himself, Reles had been convicted of stabbing to death a parking attendant who hadn't retrieved his car quickly enough. It seemed that once Reles started talking he couldn't stop. He implicated politicians and policemen as providing protection for the Brooklyn mob, and named Albert Anastasia as the "lord high executioner" of Murder Inc. But not one politician or policeman was subjected to the D.A.'s investigation. And when pressure from the public and the press forced O'Dwyer to act against Anastasia—who, for some inexplicable reason, seemed to have been granted immunity by the D.A.—Reles conveniently fell out of a fourteen-story window at the Half Moon Hotel in Coney Island, despite the fact that he was there under the protection of six policemen including O'Dwyer's friend Captain Frank Bals, later the deputy commissioner. Without Reles as a witness, the investigation into Murder Inc. was over, and no charges were brought against Anastasia.

When Judge Goldstein finished his speech he received a hearty ovation from the audience of patrolmen. But as soon as he walked out the door, the PBA voted unanimously to back O'Dwyer for mayor.

From the looks of O'Dwyer during that meeting with my father and the other line organization officials, it was obvious that the mayor was agitated over the state of his police department and all the newspaper talk of scandal. O'Dwyer was a towering man with a great white head of hair and a florid Irish complexion. But on the day of the meeting, his face was a road map of bursting capillaries. At one point he slammed the oaken desk in his office, sending a pipe stand flying.

"There is more money to be made in concrete than there is in cops!" my father remembers the mayor yelling.

At that moment, a thought flashed through Frank's mind, of Charlie Mackey and his offer to send my father to the plainclothes division in Brooklyn, the very nexus of the rumors of scandal that now swirled. With scores of cops losing their jobs because of the scandal, and with Mary Clare sick at home, my father exhaled in relief that he had decided to talk the offer over with his wife. When he went for a late lunch with Harley and some of the other line organization officers, my father clucked and shook his head in agreement with the rest at the table when someone said: "A few otherwise fine policemen take a couple of bucks from a Jew policyman and the whole department has its knickers in a twist. Even a good man like O'Dwyer is hiding like a hen in a fox house." But inside, my father's thoughts were all about his wife and her advice.

On December 18, 1950, my father was officially promoted to sergeant. The ceremony was held at city hall; Mother went in a stylish dress with a lace collar and wore a wide-brimmed hat. In the picture taken that night, she is holding on to my father's arm. She has a thin smile as she looks at him. He wears his new sergeant's stripes; his uniform is too snug around the middle, and he has started to gain a double chin.

Vincent Impellitteri, who as City Council president gained the acting mayoralty when O'Dwyer resigned, gave a speech that night. Fifty-two sergeants, along with a dozen lieutenants, two captains, two deputy inspectors, and two full inspectors, were promoted that day. Chief of Detectives August Flath was promoted to William T. Whalen's old position as chief of the department. But, besides my father's own, the promotion that would affect his career most was the one given to the man who became the new chief of detectives.

Like most of his fellow cops, my father was in awe of Conrad Rothengast. A native New Yorker with a brusque demeanor and a Prussian general's posture, the new chief of detectives had come up the hard way, serving in every civil service rank in the police department. He had even been busted from the Detective Bureau once, early in his career, and had worked his way back. The demotion was more a result of politics than a disciplinary matter. Rothengast had been a protégé of Richard Enright, the police commissioner from 1918 to 1925, when John F. Hylan was mayor. He worked directly for Enright in what was then known as the Commissioner's Squad, a precursor of the Internal Affairs Division. When Hylan lost the election to Tammany candidate Jimmy Walker in 1925, the new mayor appointed "King" George McLaughlin police commissioner. Boisterous and controversial, McLaughlin got his nickname because of his monstrous ego and lavish lifestyle. When he left the department he was presented with a solid gold detective shield encrusted with diamonds and rubies and inscribed "With appreciation, from the heroes of the bureau." On his appointment to commissioner, McLaughlin made it his first order of business to clean house. Rothengast was sent packing to the Bronx to walk a beat. From first-grade detective to patrolman is quite a tumble, but the event taught Rothengast a valuable lesson: Civil service was the safest road to advancement in the police department. He passed the sergeant's exam in 1928, the lieutenant's three years later, and the captain's in 1937. It was the kind of rise in rank my father admired and dreamed of—and tried to emulate.

After my father's promotion to sergeant, he was assigned briefly to the 32nd Precinct. Though he was now out of the Detective Bureau, and had to step down from his post as secretary of the DEA, my father remained close to Joe Harley, who now worked for Rothengast. As a sergeant, my father got his first taste of being a boss, and he liked it. He also found out he was good at it. He took comprehensive notes of his rounds supervising the patrolmen. He didn't take any nonsense, even though most of the men he supervised were older than he. One night, he found one of these old-timers drunk at his post. The cop's beat was a particularly crime-infested block and the drunken cop was a hazard not only to the people it was his job to protect but to himself. My father wrote the cop up—not a popular decision with some of the man's fellow patrolmen. But others, including the lieutenant and captain of the precinct, respected my father for it. He began to build a reputation as a tough—but fair—boss. But being a police sergeant was not always a serious business.

Each week the plainclothesmen would march a parade of Chinese gamblers into the station house. It was a ridiculous ritual of building up arrest statistics. For the most part the gamblers, generally waiters from Chinatown restaurants, didn't speak English. The plainclothesmen would make up the arrest reports with inventive names and places of birth. Once in a while, my father would be assigned as desk sergeant, where he'd have the job of entering the arrest information into a ledger. Young Ho, Old Ho, and One Hung Lo would all have been born in Shanghai. The gamblers would be hustled off to night court, where they paid the allotted fine, and they'd be back at their crap game before the night was over.

My father was less than a year into his time as a patrol sergeant when Joe Harley called and invited him for lunch near police headquarters.

During Rothengast's tenure as chief of detectives, the last vestiges of the O'Dwyer regime and the Harry Gross scandal were swept out the door of police headquarters. Changes were made in the Detective Division with lightning speed. Rothengast's mandate was clear: There would be no scandals while he was in charge.

Joe Harley had formed a close relationship with his boss. Both native New Yorkers from big families, they related on an intimate level. For Harley, it was an exciting time, working for a dynamic chief whose honesty was impeccable. And Rothengast was a powerful ally. According to Harley, it was as simple as this with Rothengast: If you were on his good side, he'd do as much as he could for you; if you weren't, watch out—no matter who you were.

During his time as chief of detectives, and later as chief police inspector, the highest rank in the department, Rothengast pursued a secret vendetta against J. Edgar Hoover. Although the chilly relationship between the NYPD and the FBI was caused more by a power struggle than anything else (New York city police brutality cases were investigated by the FBI, and other federal statutes also gave FBI agents, most of whom were non–New Yorkers, jurisdiction over the NYPD), perhaps the discord between the two law enforcement agencies can be traced back to Rothengast's grudge. At the advent of World War II, Fiorello La Guardia set up a clandestine unit called Special Squad One, which was to serve as a liaison between the NYPD, federal law enforcement agencies, and military intelligence. At the time, Rothengast was a highly decorated captain and was regarded with respect by both La Guardia and his police commissioner, Lewis Valentine. Fiercely patriotic, Rothengast wanted to lead the squad, and La Guardia thought him the perfect choice. But when Rothengast's name was sent to the FBI for a routine clearance check it was rejected by Hoover himself, because of Rothengast's Bavarian ancestry. According to the story, Rothengast never forgot this, and his resentment festered over the years. What had made Hoover's decision all the more bitter was that Rothengast's brother, U.S. Army Staff Sergeant John S. Rothengast, was killed in action in Germany just before the end of the war.

When Rothengast was promoted to chief of detectives he assigned two of his men to follow Hoover whenever the director came to New York. From the racetrack with mobster Frank Costello, to the Stork Club with Walter Winchell, detectives Willie Mulligan and Paddy Hogan tailed Hoover wherever he went. Rothengast was so admired by detectives that his secret investigation of Hoover became a bureau-wide cause. Even retired detectives helped out. The doorman at the Stork Club was ex-detective Harold Magee; retired detectives ran the security for the New York Racing Association. Retired detectives and moonlighting cops functioned as bartenders and limousine drivers, and thus Rothengast was kept apprised of every move Hoover made in New York. Rothengast built a dossier on Hoover that the FBI director himself would have been proud of.

According to my father and other sources, on leaving the police department in December 1953, Rothengast destroyed the file by setting it afire in a metal wastepaper basket. It's doubtful he ever intended to use the file against Hoover; more likely it was an insurance policy. Although, by all accounts, Rothengast's character was unimpeachable, rumors swirled that a member of his immediate family had a gambling addiction. When it came to his position in the NYPD, a job he loved, Rothengast was not about to leave anything to chance. After being burned by something as inconsequential as a German-sounding name, he put nothing past Hoover's wanton vindictiveness.

Perhaps only coincidentally, a little over a year after Rothengast retired, Hoover named a native New Yorker, James J. Kelly, as special agent in charge of the New York area. The FBI director finally realized the folly of having non–New York agents interacting with the NYPD. As time went by, and city cops of Rothengast's era sent their children through college and on to law schools at Fordham and St. John's Universities, the rolls of the FBI became filled with the names of city cops' kids—and Rothengast's grudge, and the rift between the NYPD and the FBI, were all but forgotten.

On a late winter afternoon in 1951, my father met Joe Harley around the corner from police headquarters in a restaurant on Kenmare Street named Patrissy's. Considered one of the better Italian places in the neighborhood, Patrissy's was frequented by the brass of headquarters. The restaurant had one big dining room, paneled in rich, dark wood and filled with tables covered with red-and-white-checked tablecloths. Joe Harley sat alone at a corner table and waved my father over. At first the two friends engaged in small talk, chitchat: Harley bringing his old buddy up-to-date on happenings in the DEA, my father regaling Harley with stories of Chinese gamblers. My father kidded Harley when, untempted by the various Italian delicacies on the menu, Joe ordered his usual lunch of a Western egg sandwich and a cup of coffee. My father ordered veal scaloppini, and, because it was his day off, a Dewar's scotch, served with a small bottle of club soda on the side. By the time the lunch was served my father had noticed a gleam in Harley's eyes. He had known Harley long enough to know when his friend was bursting with some juicy news.

"Do you have something you want to tell me?" Frank asked, eyeing Harley with good-natured suspicion.

"Nothing much," Harley answered, coyly dabbing his mouth with a napkin, "just that Rothengast wants you in his office on Wednesday."

Traditionally, in the police department, official word comes only after sufficient time for unofficial word to be given. Though Harley wouldn't come right out and say what the chief of detectives wanted to see my father about, even after intense prodding, my father knew from his friend's expression that it had to be good news. Still, a voice in the back of his mind, a voice born in Depression-era Archbald, was tapping out a distress signal. What if it wasn't such good news? Or what if things changed in two days?

The day of the meeting with Rothengast, my father sat in a luncheonette down the block from police headquarters trying to drink a cup of coffee and looking at his watch every minute or so. He had arrived a full hour early. He wore his best suit, one that he bought from a tailor in the Bronx, and one that he thought Hughie Sheridan would have been proud of. He was too nervous to eat, and just a sip of the coffee made his stomach sound like someone was shaking a sheet of aluminum in it. His watch finally read ten of nine, and he put a dime under the saucer and walked down the street toward police headquarters.

The front of the old building at 240 Centre Street still evinced some of its original elegance. The centerpiece of the limestone facade was a four-story clock tower topped with a dome that had once been gilded, but now was chipped and faded. The stairs leading to the entrance were flanked by stone lions and Corinthian columns. Inside the cavernous foyer, awash with bronze and iron grillwork, the marble staircase lay before him. Rothengast's office was on the second floor, and Frank walked slowly up the stairs looking at the brass plaques that lined the walls, dedicated to officers killed in the line of duty. Each time he walked up these stairs he looked for the name of Francis McKeon, whom he had known at the Academy. McKeon was shot and killed with his own gun on November 17, 1945, after a struggle with someone whom *The New York Times* described as a "crazed Negro janitor." It had been McKeon's first day back on duty after serving four years in the Navy during the war.

My father could hear his heart beating, and was sure the lapel on the new suit was bouncing up and down to the thumping muscle in his chest. He got to the stair where he knew McKeon's plaque hung, and stopped to look. The memory of the fresh young face, with a smile as quick as a cigarette lighter, came flooding back to him, and he imagined McKeon saying "Go ahead, Frank," urging him up the stairs.

Joe Harley sat at his desk in the anteroom of the chief's office as my father walked in. Harley greeted him with a wink of the eye and a strong handshake, then disappeared behind the smoked-glass door of the chief's office. A moment later, he returned and held open the door for my father to enter.

Rothengast sat behind a desk large enough to set for dinner. He was in his shirtsleeves and his tie was loose around his collar. His trademark double-breasted suit jacket hung on a clothes tree behind the desk. The chief motioned my father to sit, and, as was his wont, came right to the point.

"Frank, I'm going to give you the Four-One squad," said the chief.

My father's smile must have been infectious, because for a moment—and only a moment—Rothengast smiled back. In that moment, as my father digested the chief's words, the nagging voice that told him that something might go wrong evaporated like the smoke from one of his cigars. He thought of the cramped apartment at 2300. Then he thought of the tiny ramshackle house in which he grew up, and of his first days in New York, when he slept on the couch at Aunt Mary's. He thought of the first pay envelope, from his days at the credit union, which he kept in with his personal papers, and of the $12 he'd made that week. He thought of the squad commanders, the ones in the felt collars, whom he'd watched in awe while he worked for Hughie Sheridan. He knew that it was undoubtedly Harley's whispers in Rothengast's ear that had cemented the contract, the biggest of his police career, one that meant a significant raise in pay, one that signaled his star in the department was rising, one that would make his dream of a home for his family—which now included

131

Tommy, the fourth child—a reality. As these thoughts tumbled in his mind he realized that the chief was still speaking, and he forced himself to listen.

"I have full confidence in you, Frank," Rothengast said. "But there are a few things you should know."

He explained that the Four-One was a fairly busy detective squad, and one that seemed to get busier every day. Most of the thirty or so detectives who would work for my father had been at the Four-One quite a while, some of them sent there for disciplinary reasons: men with drinking and gambling problems, men caught in compromising positions with prostitutes, and some who had beaten confessions out of suspects. This squad, the chief cautioned, had for years been the carpet under which the department's fallen angels were swept. My father was to be the "new broom" that would sweep the place clean. It was important that the squad commander be someone not beholden to Bronx brass, not inculcated in the inbred ways of the Bronx Detective Division. What Rothengast didn't say then, but what my father found out later, was the Four-One detective squad, fifteen years prior, had been Rothengast's. In the chief's eyes, it was a special assignment.

Rothengast stood and shook my father's hand. "Remember, Frank," the chief said deliberately, "no scandals." At the door Rothengast told him that if any problems arose, he should call the chief directly. Then he asked my father if he had any questions. Frank had just one—one he wouldn't ask the chief. He needed directions to the 41st Precinct. He didn't know how to get there.

At the beginning of her stay at Willowbrook, the entries in Mary Clare's chart are almost daily. By late 1951, they are separated by months. Some refer to my mother's visits. There are no references to my father. The picture they paint of Mary Clare's short life is heart-wrenching and gruesome. Her temperature sometimes climbs to 105, and she seems to be suffering from viral infections all the time. She spits up any food she eats; the word "vomiting" is in nearly every entry. Her hands are encased in mittens, to keep her from putting her fingers in her mouth, which induces the vomiting. In one entry, she has been put in isolation—for fifteen days. She had developed ringworm and mumps. She convulsed often.

On the last page of the chart, in July 1952, my mother appears again, requesting that Dramamine, the motion-sickness drug, be administered to Mary Clare. On August 6, treatment with Dramamine is instituted, but the chart says that vomiting has continued.

The last entry, on August 8, 1952, is headed with the word "EXPIRED"—just as I have written it, in capital letters and underlined. The entry reads:

At 11:15 P.M. last night child was found by the attendant without pulse or respiration. Artificial respiration was instituted and the doctor on call was notified. At 11:30 P.M. Aug. 7th, child was pronounced dead by Dr. Fleischer. A telegram was sent to the parents. The body was examined and found to be without bruises or recent injuries. On order of Dr. Fleischer, body was removed to the morgue.

The cause of death was listed as bilateral pulmonary atelectasis. Mary Clare died choking on her own vomit.

There was no one home at 2300 to receive the telegram. My family had gone to New Hampshire to visit my mother's sister Mazzie at her farm. From a window in the old farmhouse, my father saw a New Hampshire state trooper's car pull in to the long gravel driveway. When the telegram went unanswered, Willowbrook contacted the NYPD, which sent word to the troopers to contact my father. Frankie, Eugene, and Tommy stayed with my aunt, and my father and mother drove in silence back to New York.

The day of my sister's funeral mass, thirty detectives stood on the steps of St. Nicholas of Tolentine, on Fordham Road, as the little coffin was carried to the hearse. It was a tradition in the police department of those days—when almost all cops lived in the city—to show support when family members died. How strange it must have been to see them there. A funeral mass for a four-year-old girl, guarded as if she'd been the mayor of New York. For my mother, truly, a part of her died that day, and sadness took up residence in a corner of her soul.

Every year, on the Sunday before Christmas, the whole family would go to visit Mary Clare at the Gate of Heaven Cemetery in Westchester County. Of my many childhood memories of this day, the clearest came when I was five. We drove through the wrought-iron front gate and past the wooden guardhouse to the parking lot, crowded with cars—the Sunday before Christmas is a big day for visiting the dead. My father had to park far from the cement paths through the cemetery's grounds. Dark gray clouds, like sagging stained mattresses, hung from the sky. My hands stung from the cold because my mittens were stuffed in my pockets. I was too old for mittens, I'd told my mother that morning.

We walked a great distance on the winding paths, my mother and father up ahead, leading the way; Eugene walked with his girlfriend, Diane, whom I liked because she played badminton and often had a catch with me in the backyard. Tommy walked by himself, reading the names off the headstones. I walked next to Frankie. We came upon our marker, a huge tree, barren and forlorn in its winter slumber. The rest of the way was on crusty snow, past headstones and monuments.

"Don't step on the graves," Frankie warned me. "You'll disturb the dead."

I tiptoed my way, careful to not bother the dead. My father stopped and looked around like an ostrich peering over the herd.

"Are you sure this is the right way, El?" he asked my mother. She paused, too, doubting her instinct, which would have found the grave in the middle of the night. Eugene reassured my parents that we were on the right path. Eugene's memory is like a Polaroid camera, and we continued silently on, the only sound the icy snow crackling beneath our feet. We looked for the name Duran on a headstone, as Mary Clare did not have a headstone and Duran was buried right beside her. I wondered if Mary Clare and Duran spoke to each other under the ground. When we finally reached the plot, my mother laid the Christmas ivy and poinsettias she carried on the undisturbed snow.

We stood in a circle and prayed. I didn't know what to say in my prayers, as I never knew my sister. So I said, I'm sorry I never knew you, and then my prayer was finished. My father looked down at his feet, which he stamped back and forth, a habit he'd acquired from standing fixed posts on winter nights in his early days as a patrolman. My brothers and Diane also bowed their heads. After a short while, my father lifted his eyes and gave us a quick tilt of his head, the signal to give my mother time alone. We waited in a bunch, twenty steps or so from her, our breath coming out in white puffs of smoke, our hands rummaging for warmth in the pockets of dress overcoats. I looked at my mother as she stood with her shoulders hunched, her back heaved in short, rapid sobs. She stood there for a long time, and I was most anxious to leave because I knew we were going to Patricia Murphy's restaurant for dinner afterward and Patricia Murphy's had a Christmas princess who wore a glimmering white gown and sat in an old-fashioned sled in the lobby and gave out candy canes to all the children. I pulled at my father's coat and asked when we were going to go.

"When your mother's ready," he said, as he stood there at attention. Finally my mother turned to us, dabbing the corners of her eyes with a handkerchief, her tears having left streaks from her mascara that looked like finger marks on dirty windowpane.

At the restaurant, Eugene and Frankie made a trip to the bathroom, then came back to the table bursting with laughter. Frankie told us that they'd met an elderly man whose hat had fallen into the toilet. He repeated what the man had said: "First my wife leaves me, then I lose my job, and now this!" I imagined the man's hat bobbing in the porcelain sea. My mother laughed hardest of all of us. But her laughter stopped suddenly, and I saw her fighting back tears. I went to her, and she clutched me, so tight I almost couldn't breathe. It was as though she was afraid that something would come to snatch me away from her, and this time, she would not let her child go. I saw that my father's expression was uncomfortable, nearly guilty. For what? I now wonder. For letting Mary Clare die? As if, as a cop, he had failed at his charge to keep his child safe from harm? Even if that harm was a disease? No. He shouldered the fault, because my mother needed to blame someone. For years it was her undying belief that the sulfa drug caused Mary Clare's condition, even after the doctors told her it was the viral infection. And even if it had been the sulfa drug, my mother needed some*one* to blame, not some*thing*. I knew, as only a child knows these things, that Mary Clare's death formed a chasm between my parents, and in that moment, in my mother's grasp, I knew too that that fissure also separated me from my father. He would give me up, to ease some of my mother's pain.

5

At the Bronx Historical Society, a real estate atlas from 1911 shows 1086 Simpson Street, then under construction, occupying lots 17 through 20, square in the middle of the block between 167th Street and Westchester Avenue. According to the atlas, the street front of the station house measured one hundred feet. On the south side of the building is a ten-foot-wide alley.

The station house took over two years to build and opened in 1914. The facade that faced Simpson Street was three stories high and made of limestone, which on the ground floor was rusticated in grand arches around the large and low windows and the doorway. The roof was terra-cotta, an elaborate assemblage of a forest-green tile that, at a certain time of the morning, glimmered in the sunshine. It was built by the reputable architectural firm of Hazzard, Erskine & Blagden. The design was called beaux-arts, or renaissance revival, and was to evoke, with its cornice and broad-hipped roof, the early-sixteenth-century palaces of Florence and Rome.

On the left side of the doorway, etched into one of the large foundational blocks, was the inscription "Police Department, City of New York, R. Waldo, Police Commissioner, MCMXIII."

Under Mayor William J. Gaynor, who had survived an assassination attempt in 1910, Rhinelander Waldo's term as commissioner—from 1911 to 1913—was considered quite an innovative time. It was then that the rank of "roundsman" was abolished and the modern "sergeant" took its place. Waldo oversaw the use of the first automobile in the police department, ordered new uniforms with heavy coats and large pockets to keep his men warm in the winter months, and instituted the three-shift platoon system. And he was a visionary when it came to municipal buildings.

While fire commissioner, a post he held before he was police commissioner, he devised an elaborate plan to build twenty-five additional firehouses in outlying areas of the city to quicken response time. As police commissioner, he initiated a similar, though scaled-down, proposal for police stations in the Bronx, to accommodate what Waldo foresaw—the coming population explosion of the borough. The Simpson Street building was to be the prototype for all those built in the Bronx after it. By 1911, plans were in the works for three new station houses and the rebuilding of two more.

But, except for the Simpson Street station house, Waldo's vision would not come to fruition. Perhaps, too involved in the grand scheme of things, the commissioner had lost touch with the everyday workings of his department. A scandal, which involved a small-time gambler named Rosenthal (who blew the whistle on the police department's involvement in gambling enterprises) and a dashing, crooked lieutenant named Charles Becker (who ordered Rosenthal's murder), brought about the commissioner's ultimate downfall. The Curran Committee, formed to investigate the scandal, found Waldo unfit and incompetent. The Simpson Street station house was the only one of its distinctive style built.

On the real estate atlas, the rest of Simpson Street is designated as residential, with building shapes colored in deep red to signify brick apartment houses, most with the code "5B" indicating a five-story building with a basement. On the far northwest corner of the block, several lots are taken up by Public School No. 20. An elevated subway station is marked at the intersection of Simpson Street and Westchester Avenue. The atlas shows the raised elbow of track where the train turns to run above Southern Boulevard directly behind the station house.

What the atlas didn't show is that in those five-story tenement buildings lived Irish, Germans, Italians, and the beginnings of the Jewish population that, with the completion of that elevated subway in 1905, grew by the tens of thousands each year. It didn't show that for the Jews and the Irish who lived in the squalor of the Lower East Side of Manhattan, the South Bronx was the real America, the place they had dreamt about on their voyage over, where harmony and opportunity lay.

When the station house opened, the entire population of its precinct was a suburblike 48,000. Over the next two decades, coinciding with the largest period of immigration of Jews from Eastern Europe, and the subsequent overcrowding of the tenement neighborhoods of the Lower East Side, the Jewish population of the Bronx would grow to 600,000, with the majority settling in the southern portions of the borough.

Even with the bulging population, the crime rate stayed remarkably low. Police blotters of the early 1920s from what would become the 41st Precinct (it was first designated the 62nd Precinct), read like those from an ideal midwestern town. Owners of unlicensed dogs, drivers speeding at a thirty-two-mile-an-hour clip along Southern Boulevard, and teenage boys roughhousing in the streets were the lawbreakers of the day. Yes, it was Prohibition, and raids on speakeasies were cited, and every once in a while there was a record of a cop discharging his weapon. Usually a rabid dog or a lame horse was the recipient of the bullet.

Thirty years after that atlas was made, during World War II, further waves of immigration to the South Bronx would occur. Blacks from the southern states and Caribbean people, mostly from Puerto Rico, flocked to the area to find wartime jobs in the factories of Hunts Point. (Northern blacks had lived in the Bronx since the 1600s, when they were brought as slaves to work the farms in the Morrisania area.) The war also brought with it rent control, first federally orchestrated, then run by the state.* Though once viewed as the height of egalitarianism, rent control and other influences would polarize the South Bronx and ultimately lead to its devastation.

But the Bronx was still a thriving place when, on a bright spring morning, my father drove his maroon '49 Nash Rambler down Southern Boulevard, under the elevated subway tracks, on the first day of his new assignment: April 2, 1951. Following the directions he'd been given at Bronx Detective Bureau headquarters, he passed Jennings and then Freeman Streets, where stout Eastern European women sold fruits and vegetables from wooden carts. Farther down, he passed the kosher chicken stores that lined the boulevard, and still more sidewalk vendors. He turned on Westchester Avenue, where the scent of Jewish delicatessens filled the air. The streets were teeming with people, Yiddish mixed with Spanish, forming a continuous hum.

He parked the Nash in the alleyway next to the station house and walked through the front entrance. He didn't notice that the archway around the door was rusticated; he didn't see the inscrip-

---

*In the 1960s, charge of rent control was taken over by the city.

tion on the cornerstone. My father *had* noticed the roof, and thought it a bit much for a police station.

Inside, he walked through the foyer and up to the desk sergeant and asked where he could find the squad room. He was directed up a flight of stairs to his right. The walls in the stairway were cracked and chipped. A waist-high wooden gate separated the squad room from the landing. Behind the gate, a bald man with a gin-ruddy face was seated at a desk typing a report with a deliberate two-finger style. At first, the detective didn't notice my father standing in front of him. After an awkward moment or two, he finally looked up at the tall young man dressed in a fine suit, and with only the slightest of interest asked:

"Can I help you?"

"I hope so," my father answered. "I'm your new boss."

The squad room was lined with a half-dozen or so wooden desks, on each a typewriter. The plaster on the walls, like that in the stairway, was chipped and the color of a nicotine stain. Inside the room, the first thing that caught my father's eye was a picture of George Washington hung rather oddly near the far top corner. The detective at the desk, noticing my father's questioning expression, shrugged and said "Bullet hole," and offered no further explanation.

In very little time, Frank realized that Rothengast's assessment of the detectives in the Four-One squad—that they were the fallen angels of the department—was, if anything, an understatement. One morning, early on in his new job, my father was standing at the top of the stairs by the gate to the squad room as a new uniform lieutenant was addressing the patrolmen mustered together on the main floor. Through the front door of the station house walked one of my father's detectives, Mike Hickey. The other detectives in the squad, my father knew, called Hickey the Inspector, because of his penchant for fashionable attire: natty hats and vests, always with the gold chain of his pocket watch fashionably displayed. Frank also knew that Hickey was considered the court jester of the squad.

In a moment, Hickey sized up the situation unfolding in front of him: the unseasoned lieutenant, the lines of patrolmen, most of whom were well aware of Hickey's reputation. Hickey winked to the desk sergeant, who immediately announced, in a commanding baritone, "Inspector in the station!" The lieutenant snapped to attention, greeting Hickey with a crisp salute. Hickey put his hands behind his back and walked slowly back and forth, inspecting the troops.

"Men," he said, deadly serious, "we have a situation. It seems a truck filled with Karo syrup has crashed into a chicken market on Westchester Avenue. There are syrup-covered chickens running wild in the street down there."

The patrolmen who knew Hickey tried to keep straight faces, but a few of them couldn't and spat out laughter. Those who didn't know him, including the lieutenant, stood agape, in astonished silence. Hickey didn't notice that my father was watching from the top of the stairs.

"I want you to approach the chickens with extreme caution," he continued. "They are extremely dangerous in this condition. So let's hop to it, the neighborhood depends on you."

Hickey dismissed the men, then spun on his heel and marched right past the befuddled lieutenant and up the stairs to the squad room. My father stepped into the doorway of his office and pretended to read a report, as the raucous laughter from below wafted up the stairs behind Hickey.

Though my father shrugged off Hickey's performance, there were other events that caused him to wonder what he had ventured into. One of the first murders that occurred during his time at the 41st was of a woman named Eugenia Fargus, who was killed in the basement of her apartment building. The police were notified by her husband, who said he'd found his wife dead around one o'clock in the morning. When Bill Carren, the detective assigned to the case, arrived at the scene, the victim was lying on the floor of the basement, naked, with a two-inch-wide knife wound in her forehead. Carren reported that the husband and wife had been drinking heavily that night. He also wrote that the husband's alibi was flimsy at best—he had told Carren that he left the apartment at eleven p.m. and returned two hours later. Carren told my father that the husband was his prime suspect. Carren had good reason for believing Fargus to be guilty: The husband had a prior arrest record, for robbery, and there were no witnesses who could corroborate his alibi. But the main reason Carren thought him the killer was the husband's occupation—he was a house painter.

Eugenia Fargus's body had been painted from head to toe with a dark-green enamel.

The husband was brought into the squad room numerous times and interrogated for hours, but didn't admit to the crime. Carren tried every trick he knew to elicit a confession. He threatened, he consoled, he even brought a Bible in one day and knelt and prayed with the husband. But still Fargus didn't break. Carren became so emotionally involved in the case, my father strongly suggested that he take his vacation—which he did, to a summer house in the Catskill Mountains. When he returned to the squad room a week later, he did so carrying a large cardboard box, which contained a three-foot-long blacksnake he had captured near his mountain cottage.

"I'm going to bring the husband in one more time," Carren told my father. "I'm going to lock him and this snake in the interrogation room until he confesses."

Carren never got the chance. My father remanded the snake to the New York City sewer system. The murder of Eugenia Fargus was never solved.

*   *   *

One of a squad commander's primary functions is the charge of scheduling and the assignment of cases. On the wall of the squad room, between the crisscross wire door of the holding cell and a sign above the fingerprint desk that read, "All officers must remove their revolvers before fingerprinting prisoners and must be accompanied by a backup officer, NO EXCEPTIONS," hung a blackboard lined in chalk. The days of the week were printed across the top, the names of detectives in pairs down the side. For the detective partners, the work week was five days. Each day included two tours—eight a.m. to five p.m., "day duty"; five p.m. to eight a.m., "night duty." The group of the detectives working a tour was called a team. Each tour was divided into individual time slots, with partners assigned to each slot. If a crime occurred during your time slot, you were assigned to it. This was known as "catching." If you caught a homicide or other major crime, you could be taken off the schedule, at the squad commander's discretion, to work the case to its conclusion. The squad commander had absolute and final say on anything concerning the chart.

Throughout his first month running the Four-One squad, my father was an enigma to his men. He arrived each morning before day duty started, and left each evening well after night duty began. But he seldom engaged the detectives in conversation and mostly stayed behind his desk (carved with the initials of past occupants, like an oak tree at a lovers' lookout), the office door halfway closed, readying the chart for the week, reviewing the crime cases being worked, and reading back records of others that were closed. His cool and distant demeanor was no doubt a cover for his uncertainty. He had gone from patrolman to detective squad commander in four years, a huge jump in rank and responsibility. He was only thirty-three, the youngest squad commander in the city. The natural trepidation he felt expressed itself, as it did most times with my father, inwardly.

Also, he took Rothengast's warning, "No scandals," very seriously. And he now knew that the sordid reputation of the men in the squad was deserved. Some of the reports he reviewed were shoddily written, others incomplete. The squad's arrest performance was mediocre at best. He thought that, individually, some of his men were savvy, street-hardened detectives. But an overall malaise, a lax attitude, seemed to permeate the squad as a whole.

The worst thing he could do, he thought, was give his men the impression that he was concerned with his popularity.

As a boss, my father was a natural. He had, for lack of a better word, balls. Maybe this boldness came from his instant rank in the navy or his time in the Detective District office. Or maybe it was born out of defiance, from years of seeing his father's servitude to the foremen in the mines. Wherever it came from, he had it. And he was about to show his squad that he did.

A month into his command, Frank reassigned his detectives to new partners. When the schedule went up, there was a great commotion, with loud, heated conversation and low grumbles. Some of the detectives had worked with their partners for years; in the police department, there is no more sacred a union. A detective named O'Brien stormed into my father's office and demanded to know what was going on.

"Things are going to change around here" was all my father said.

A few of the detectives complained directly to the bureau chief, who demanded an explanation. Chief Edward Byrnes had already made it clear that he was not in my father's corner. That first day of his assignment, just before driving to the 41st Precinct, Frank had stopped at the chief's office. "Don't make any mistakes," Byrnes had said coldly.

On a tribal level, the New York City police department has always run on an elaborate system of contracts—not the kind printed on paper and signed on dotted lines, but verbal ones sealed with a handshake or the clink of a glass of scotch. This can be dated back to the days of Boss Tweed and the beginnings of the corrupt Tammany regime, when promotion and desirable assignments were first offered for a price. Throughout most of the history of the police department, nepotism and ethnicity (for the most part Irish "taking care of their own") were the criteria by which sought-after assignments were granted. Chief Byrnes, diminutive in stature, with a halting, blunt delivery, was Bronx born and raised, and had spent his whole police career there. He wanted the Four-One squad for one of his own protégés. The thought of an outsider—a hayseed, for Christ's sake!—was a personal insult to him. But with Rothengast on my father's side, there was nothing Byrnes could do. When my father explained that he'd made the partner changes because he was unhappy with production, Byrnes, regardless of how he felt, couldn't countermand him. But, over the coming weeks, the 41st Precinct squad room was a very unhappy place, and my father a very unpopular boss.

6

Though in the civil service records, Frank McDonald was still officially a sergeant, his appointment as squad commander of the 41st Precinct brought with it the title of acting lieutenant, a rank created in 1925 by Commissioner Enright in order to bestow the appropriate authority and respect on detective squad commanders. My father had already begun work on losing the "acting" portion of his title, by readying for the lieutenant's exam.

He had discovered the fast track in the police department: pass the tests and have friends in high places. He had both the smarts and the access. He had placed in the top 10 percent in his first two civil service tests; the patrolman's and sergeant's exam. He had every reason to believe he would do as well on the lieutenant's test. But his vision of his future did not stop there. After lieutenant, the last level of civil service is captain. Higher ranks are bestowed by appointment. Just two more tests, he thought, and with the backing of people like Conrad Rothengast, who was about to be appointed chief police inspector, Frank McDonald's future in the police department was limitless. But my father's ambition only further exacerbated the division between him and his detectives.

As the president of the police board, from 1895 to 1897, Teddy Roosevelt oversaw a campaign to put an end to advancement by favoritism and graft. The first civil service exam for patrolmen was given in 1895. Roosevelt championed written tests and background checks for promotions. When he moved on to bigger things, and the corrupt machinery of the department began to grind once more, most of his reforms remained in place. But the model he created rewarded book smarts, not street smarts. There has long been a breach, in the police department, between commanders and their subordinates. Like battle-seasoned veterans receiving instructions on how to fight from army officers who had never been to the front lines, street-smart cops looked upon their book-smart bosses with sarcastic contempt. My father's early success and quick climb up the ranks included one little glitch: When he arrived at the 41st Precinct, he had absolutely no real experience as a street detective. His time in the Detective Division had been spent wholly in clerical, administrative, and political positions. He also lacked the intimate local knowledge possessed by the men who now worked for him, most of whom had grown up in neighborhoods of the Bronx. But this would change. It had to.

In preparing for the lieutenant's test, my father joined a study group that met in one of the midtown hotels, like the Astor, and took cram courses together at Delahanty's, the civil service exam school. In 1953, he took the test and aced it. He was thirty-five, and his career was proceeding as planned. The captain's test was next, and so were what Frank called the halcyon days.

The stories of the Rat Pack, the name sarcastically hung on the study group by one member's wife because of their late-night carousing, lived on for years in my home. After a few hours of study, they would go for dinner, and then continue late into the night at one of the hot spots of the day. They walked into restaurants and nightclubs like the Copacabana and Toots Shor's, and the sea parted. At Toots Shor's, Jackie Gleason would send them a round of drinks, or Phil Silvers would pull up a chair and sit with them, testing out his latest routine. When the check came at the end of the night—if it came at all—it would represent a fraction of what they had actually spent.

I have a photograph of the Rat Pack, taken in May 1956 in a place called Joe King's Rathskeller on Third Avenue in Manhattan. Seven men, all in finely tailored suits, are sitting on a banquette around a table draped in a checkered cloth. On the table sits a bottle of J&B scotch, and before each man is a small, straight glass. My father's arms are stretched along the banquette, around Jack Kelly and Frank Weldon, both squad commanders.

They were an impressive group. Two of them, Walter Fenn and Andy Leddy, had been B-17 pilots during World War II. Gus Harms, towering, with thick, blond hair, had been a member of the 1939 U.S. Olympic water polo team, and had won the Latin prize at Fordham University despite the fact that he was not Catholic. He also had his law degree before he took the entrance exam to the police department. Other members' reputations were formed during their police careers. Jack Kelly grew up in the Chelsea section of Manhattan, where his father owned a pet store and sold pigeons to West Side mobsters, some of whom took a shine to the friendly young man behind the counter. Before the advent of the Organized Crime Control Bureau, Kelly was considered one of the department's foremost experts on crime families. Mario Biaggi was well on his way to becoming the most decorated policeman in the history of the NYPD. And finally there was Frank Weldon, perhaps the closest of the group to my father. Soft-spoken, suave, with matinee-idol looks, Weldon might have been the best detective of the bunch. As heroin became the number one cause of crime in New York City, Weldon's investigations into the drug trade were legendary. He was also credited with solving the Wiley-Hoffert murders. Two women in their early twenties—one the daughter of a prominent surgeon, the other of a well-known writer—were butchered in their Upper East Side apartment. Before Weldon took over the investigation, the wrong man was indicted in the murders. As a result of Weldon's arduous detective work, the man responsible for the killings was caught and the wrongly accused man exonerated. The pilot for the *Kojak* television series was based on the case, with Telly Savalas playing Frank Weldon. (Quite possibly, this was the only time in television history when the real cop was better looking than the actor playing him.)

In the photograph, my father's face is full, nearly fat. His broad smile says there's no place in the world he'd rather be. Filled with confidence, he and his detective cronies were the young lions of the department. And though several of them worked in the Bronx, Manhattan, it seemed, was their private club.

One night, early in his time at the 41st Precinct, my father and several of the Rat Pack sat ringside to watch his old basketball pal Billy Graham fight Kid Gavilan for the welterweight title in Madison Square Garden—a fight Graham lost in a controversial decision. In a Greenwich Village bistro called the Bon Soir, the Rat Pack sat and watched as a young songstress from Brooklyn named Barbra Streisand made her professional debut. On another night, they went to the midnight show at the Copacabana, where Sammy Davis, Jr., was performing. Ushered down front by the maitre d', they were seated at a table next to Yankee stars Mickey Mantle, Hank Bauer, Whitey Ford, and Billy Martin. Just as the show started, Martin began to argue with a man at the table on the other side. Frank Weldon recognized some of the men Martin was screaming at as wiseguys from the Bronx. The shouting escalated into a wrestling match and few weak punches were thrown. Mantle and Bauer rushed to Martin's aid. Right in front of my father, one of the tuxedo-clad bouncers grabbed Martin from behind and in a low but authoritative voice explained to him that if he ever wanted to play baseball again he'd better leave right that moment. The next day, the fight was a front-page story in all the New York papers, the news accounts calling the table Martin had argued with "a Bronx bowling team." Frank Weldon called my father at his office the next day and said, "They're the kind of bowling team that drills holes in the balls with .38 caliber revolvers."

For Frank McDonald, these were the days and nights of being absolutely bulletproof. Nothing, it seemed, could slow down the juggernaut of his career. Very early one morning, after a night out on the town, he and five of the Rat Pack were riding home along the Bronx River Parkway. Frank Weldon was at the wheel, driving extremely fast, and didn't notice the garbage truck lumbering in the lane in front of him until he was almost upon it. Weldon slammed on the brakes and cut the wheel, but clipped the back end of the truck. Their car caromed out of control, flipping over, and ending upside-down in a ditch along the drive. Perhaps it was providence, or maybe it was the fact that there were six wide bodies filling every space in the car, but the most serious injury was to Frank Weldon, who broke a toe. My father didn't get a scratch. Not even a tear in his suit. He walked to a nearby gas station and called two of his detectives to come pick them up. The detectives chauffeured the lieutenants home. Life in the police department was that easy for my father; with a snap of his fingers, problems would vanish. The week after the crash, the study group met at Toots Shor's, and named the gathering "the wake," which it was called from then on. At the table they observed a moment of silence for Frank Weldon's toe, then lifted their glasses of good scotch for a toast.

Even my father's nascent investigative skills seemed predestined to greater things. On August 22, 1953, he was notified of the apparent suicide of a fairly well known doctor and his wife, who lived in a Parkchester housing development. Although Parkchester lay in the 43rd Precinct, one weekend a month, on a revolving basis, squad commanders in the Bronx would cover two precincts. Because running a detective squad was a twenty-four-hour, seven-day-a-week job (often my father would be awakened in the middle of the night at home by a phone call telling him he was needed at the office) the system was instituted to assure the commander at least one weekend a month of peace and quiet.

At the scene, my father saw that the doctor's wife was slumped on the couch in the apartment; the doctor lay on the floor near the doorway to the kitchen. Both bodies had foam around their mouths. On a coffee table sat two champagne glasses. The couple's twenty-one-year-old son and a male friend were also at the scene. It was they who had called the police. When the Bronx medical examiner, Charles Hochman, arrived, he determined that the couple had died from cyanide poisoning and that it was indeed a suicide pact. Hochman knew the couple—the doctor, William Fraden, worked for the city health department.

Hochman was well respected by detectives in the Bronx. Every year, the Bronx squad commanders would throw a birthday party in his honor. As the borough M.E., Hochman inspired many a story. He was known to perform autopsies holding a scalpel in one hand and a half-eaten Danish in the other. At one autopsy, of a prostitute who was murdered in Hunts Point, his dictation to the stenographer read: "A female, Negress, approximately twenty-five, five foot two inches, one hundred and twelve pounds, narcotics tracks on both arms, and well-traveled fore and aft."

In the Parkchester apartment that day, my father asked Hochman why, if it was a suicide pact, hadn't the couple both died on the couch? Why was the doctor's body on the floor near the kitchen? Hochman explained that cyanide poisoning causes inordinate thirst, and the doctor had most likely tried to crawl to the kitchen for water. Still, my father had his suspicions, not the least of which fell upon the couple's son and his friend. He thought their attitude too cavalier in the face of what had happened. In spite of his respect for Hochman, my father decided to open a murder investigation.

Nine months later, Harlow Fraden, the couple's son, confessed to killing his parents. The friend, Dennis Wepman, had been his accomplice. The two men were believed to have been in a homosexual relationship. The night of the murders, Wepman had stood at the doorway to the apartment, taking notes to be used in a novel he was writing.

Though the stars then seemed aligned in my father's favor, the future of the South Bronx didn't look as promising. In the decade after the war, when landlords became fed up with the rent ceilings imposed by state law, their frustration began to show in the upkeep of their buildings, which fell into disrepair. Throughout the 1950s, older residents of the Bronx were reluctant to leave their rent-controlled apartments; young ones, with the automobile and highway explosion in America, moved their new families to the North Bronx, Westchester, and, by the mid 1950s, Rockland County.

Meanwhile, inside the 41st a truce of sorts had been called. About a month after my father had reassigned the detectives to new partners, he reunited them. This about-face did not indicate that he succumbed to pressure from either his detectives or the Bronx brass. Younger than any of the men who worked for him, my father had made the move purely to send the message that he was the boss. The message was received. Although none of his men were about to ask him over to their houses for dinner, respect for my father began to grow in the squad room, and a transformation occurred in the detectives' attitude toward their jobs. Though a large percentage of the men did have sordid pasts, Frank's original assessment that most were good detectives was correct. For years before my father arrived, the inmates ran the asylum of the Four-One squad. Now they had a boss who asserted structure and chain of command, and the inmates became detectives again, and their inherent talents began to show.

In my father's first few years in the 41st Precinct, most of the homicides there were crimes of passion: drunken escalations of neighborhood grudges and outstanding debts; domestic quarrels, like the Eugenia Fargus case, that ended tragically. But, by the mid-1950s, with the infusion of heroin and the growth of teenage gangs, murders in the precinct not only came with alarming frequency, they were horribly arbitrary. One day, my father sat at his desk looking at crime scene photographs, the face of Mary Rozincoff staring lifelessly back at him. In one photo, she lay on her bed, her nightgown pushed up to her waist, her head positioned in the grotesque angle of death. He passed that face almost every morning on Jennings Street as he drove to work. In the winter months, she'd wrap her legs in burlap against the cold. Like the other street vendors, selling fruit and vegetables, she stood close to a trash can ablaze with a wood fire to keep warm. From the crime report on his desk, my father knew she had a son, a doctor who lived on Long Island. He imagined her saving each dime she made to send the son through medical school.

The crime report was an all too familiar story now: The intruder, a heroin addict, had popped the window of her ground-floor apartment on Southern Boulevard and, as she slept, smothered Mary Rozincoff with her own pillow.

During the investigation, Mrs. Rozincoff's son came to the squad room to speak to my father. As Frank began to express his sympathies, the son stopped him in mid-sentence:

"Where's the money?" he demanded. He had come not out of concern about the progress of the investigation into his mother's murder, but because he was convinced that police officers, and not the murderer, had taken her money. The two detectives working the case were standing at the door to my father's office and overheard the entire conversation. Frank looked at the detectives and then stared coldly at the doctor.

"Get the fuck out of my office," my father said, "or I'll have you arrested for interfering with a criminal investigation."

Whether or not he was within his rights to arrest the doctor didn't matter. What did was that the doctor believed him—he scurried past the now beaming detectives, and down the stairs. The detectives didn't say anything to my father, but they didn't have to. Their expressions told the whole story. My father was no longer the cold, distant squad commander. By 1954, three years into his tenure at the 41st Precinct, Frank McDonald was a boss for whom you wanted to work, and that loyalty showed in the performance of his squad. The "fallen angels" of whom Rothengast had warned had begun to build a different kind of reputation.

Mike Hickey once told my father that, years before, he had quit drinking for good when he found himself one midnight, dressed in full uniform, directing traffic in Teaneck, New Jersey. Hickey was also an inveterate gambler. This he didn't give up. He spent most days off at Aqueduct or at the New Jersey shore, at Monmouth Racetrack. One summer, my father and mother took a vacation in Spring Lake, New Jersey, and stayed at the Breakers Hotel, where Hickey always stayed. A perennial bachelor, Hickey spent each morning perfecting his golden tan on the beach. In the afternoon, it was on to the track. At night, Hickey would play poker with a group of guys on the porch of the hotel. One of Hickey's card-playing buddies was a knock-about actor named James Gregory. Years later, Gregory played the part of "Inspector Luger" on a TV sitcom called *Barney Miller*, about a New York detective squad. My father saw Hickey's mannerisms in Gregory's portrayal.

But when it came to work, Hickey was the consummate professional. Despite the Hollywood glamorization, detective work is for the most part painstaking and systematic. The investigation of a crime can mean hundreds of interviews, knocking on doors, talking to everyone and anyone, who might have a shred of valuable information. The detective then assembles this information—along, of course, with any evidence—and formulates a list of suspects. The part that comes next is what you mostly see on television—when the suspect is interrogated in the squad room. But before that ever happens, hours upon hours of detective work have been done.

Hickey had his own system of canvassing for information. His favorite saying was "Always look for the yenta," the neighborhood busybody who would sit in the window of her apartment and watch and see everything that happened on the block. Hickey's yentas helped solve a good portion of his investigations.

Mike Hickey and the other detectives who worked for him gave my father a detective squad ultimately regarded as one of the best in the Bronx (from 1958 to 1962, their arrest-to-crime ratio was at or near the top in the borough). But they also brought humor to their work without which the job would have been impossible to perform.

My father often told stories about Hickey. There was the time he assigned Hickey to investigate a series of robberies at Howard's, a clothing store. He said Hickey was the right detective for the job, given his fondness for fashion. The thieves were lowering themselves through the skylight of the store with a rope. Hickey decided to lie in wait for them, and sure enough, the first night he spent in the store, a rope dropped from the skylight.

The next day Hickey brought the suspects into court for arraignment. The magistrate, whom Hickey knew from Greenwich Village, where they had both grown up, was hard of hearing. On the stand, the D.A. asked Hickey to relay what he had witnessed the night of the robbery. Hickey began to answer in a normal tone of voice, but, every other sentence or so, he would just move his lips. The judge began to tap his hearing aid, becoming ever more frustrated as Hickey's testimony continued. An irascible character, he yelled at Hickey to speak up, at which Hickey again just pretended to talk. Finally, the magistrate came out from behind the bench and demanded that Hickey show him what had happened. From the evidence table, Hickey took the rope the thief had used and began to wrap it around the judge's legs, then around his arms, as he elaborated the thief's method. The whole courtroom was in stitches. Even the defendant was laughing so hard, tears were streaming down his face.

By the early 1960s, white flight from the Bronx was extremely fast. From 1960 to 1966, 205,000 whites moved out. In their wake, blacks and Puerto Ricans moved en masse from less desirable housing in Harlem and other areas, looking, as the Irish and Jews had decades before, for a better place to live. But for blacks and Puerto Ricans, the South Bronx was no longer the oasis it had been for the early immigrants. Throughout the 1950s wartime industry abandoned the Hunts Point factories. By the early 1960s, other industries were packing up the truck. From 1960 to 1966, 216 companies, manufacturing everything from apparel to machinery, left the South Bronx.

As their constituencies disappeared, Bronx politicians turned their backs on the community, and services vanished. As the 1960s approached, federally financed bulldozers razed block after block of tenement housing in the neighborhoods surrounding the 41st Precinct, and city-run housing projects were built. "Come one, come all" was the advertising catch-phrase of the day. But for those who came, there was little work. At the same time, an amazingly complex welfare system was instituted. Heroin addiction grew to epidemic proportions, and teenage gangs fueled the spiraling crime rate. From 1950 to 1960 murder-homicide arrests in the Bronx grew by 66.7 percent. By 1965, that number had more than tripled.

One by one, the delicatessens on Westchester Avenue, the kosher

markets on Southern Boulevard, began to close, their owners flee-
ing a neighborhood that was deteriorating before their eyes. Clothing stores, like Howard's and Crawford's, were first gated; then
they left and the premises became check-cashing stores, or they
were simply torched, their charred remains used as shooting gal-
leries. The stately apartment houses on Fox and Kelly Streets first
became run-down and eventually were abandoned. Police wore
air-raid hard hats, and later, riot helmets as protection from cop-
ings and bricks thrown at them from rooftops. Hunts Point, once
a bustling industrial area, became a wasteland; packs of wild dogs
roamed the lots of deserted factories. Drug pushers and prostitutes lined Southern Boulevard and Westchester Avenue where
pushcart vendors once hawked their wares. The murders piled up,
becoming, to my father, anonymous faces in crime scene photographs and numbers to be added to statistics. Some of them, like
Mary Rozincoff, stood out as exclamation points in the volumes
of murders. By the early 1960s, the 41st Precinct led the city in
virtually every major crime statistic.

At the beginning of his tenure at the Four-One, my father acted
as the administrative boss, assigning his detectives to cases. But as
the 1960s began and the sheer number of crimes began to over-
whelm his squad, more and more he found himself at crime scenes,
in abandoned buildings, in ramshackle apartments, and, in February
1962, in the dank, dark basement of 1171 Bryant Avenue.

On that cold winter day, as my father walked from a deli-
catessen around the corner from the station house, he was approached by a building superintendent from Bryant Avenue. The
super knew my father, as most of the neighborhood did by then.
The station house and the squad room had become a refuge from
the onslaught of crime and predators. The super was nervous, agitated. He said that there were four or five men in the basement of
his building with guns and that he had heard them plotting a robbery and murder. Nothing was implausible then in the 41st
Precinct. And just the week before, there had been a major gun

bust in the basement of another building in the precinct. My father went back to the squad room and rounded up two detectives to go with him to investigate.

My father, followed by the two detectives, all three men with guns drawn, eased open the door to the blackness of the basement. The only sound was the clanking of the boiler. Then something rustled in the darkness, and then there was the sound of metal dropping to the floor. My father crouched into shooter position, the technique he had learned twenty years before in the police academy. He held the Police Special with two hands, just as the instructors had taught. Up to this point in his career, he had never discharged his weapon on duty, and right then he said a little prayer to keep that streak alive. He heard the sound of a door creak before he saw the movement from the corner of his eye. Silently, he signaled to the two detectives. There was just enough light for Frank to make out the figure standing just a few feet away, holding a revolver pointed directly at him.

For a split second there was only deadly silence. Then, from the dark recess behind the man, he heard his name: "Frank, holy shit. Frank! Don't shoot, Eddy, don't shoot. . . ."

The seven men in that basement that day were all cops. The man who recognized my father was Vinnie Hawks, a lieutenant in the narcotics squad. He and my father had been in the academy together. The man holding a gun on my father was a detective named Eddy Egan. Frank knew Egan and had no use for him. One day, my father had walked into the squad room to find a prisoner hung by his wrists with handcuffs in the lockup cage. The prisoner had been put in that position by Egan, who had arrested him for narcotics possession and was trying to coerce him to inform on his supplier. My father had the prisoner taken down and ordered Egan out of the squad room, telling him that he never wanted to see him in the precinct again.

In the basement, my father was furious with Hawks. "Why wasn't I notified?" he screamed. Hawks tried to explain, but my father wasn't about to listen. He knew the thoughts that had surged through his own mind. One quick movement, by anyone, and he certainly would have fired. Had that happened, in all likelihood an all-out gun battle would have ensued. My father stormed from the basement, with Hawks apologetically following after.

Back in the squad room, my father called his boss, Red Walsh, then the detective district commander. Walsh told him that Hawks and Egan were working on a narcotics smuggling case and had asked for, and been granted, absolute anonymity. "It wouldn't have been so anonymous had seven cops killed each other in that basement," my father shouted as he slammed the receiver.

The stakeout in the basement of 1171 Bryant Avenue was part of an international heroin smuggling investigation. A mobster by the name of Tony Fuca lived in the building, and in the carriage room of the basement New York City narcotics detectives and federal agents had found nearly forty kilos of heroin, which had been smuggled into New York from France. Fuca had been arrested, but was released on bail. The narcotics cops and agents were lying in wait for Fuca's connections to come pick up the package.

The total amount of heroin was some 118 pounds, then the largest quantity ever seized in the United States; the case spurred a best-selling book and an Academy Award–winning movie. The French Connection case, however, came within a hair of being the biggest massacre of policemen in the history of New York City.

In the early 1960s, the burning in my father's stomach was constant. By then he fully realized that his once bright career had dimmed like a gray Bronx dusk. Often, in the middle of a shift, he would leave his office and walk to a luncheonette on Southern Boulevard to drink a milk shake, the lactose doing more harm than good. Sometimes, he would just walk around the neighborhood— down Simpson Street and across Fox Street. He remembers the overpowering odor of urine coming from the foyers of each of the buildings. He remembers the hollow deadness in the eyes of the junkie prostitutes and the frightened expressions of those who were chained to this neighborhood by poverty. There was also the look of anger in the eyes of some he passed. He had known poverty, of course, but what he now saw was far different from the whiskey-soaked version of his youth, the one wailed in barroom songs. In 1963, there was a murder in the precinct where a man stabbed his brother in the jugular vein with a fork. The argument was over a piece of chicken. Though it would take a decade for the South Bronx to die—the corpse set ablaze in a funeral pyre—by 1963 the bleeding within had begun. By then there was no longer any hope in the 41st Precinct. There was no longer any sense.

Later that year, my father went to the medical office in police headquarters. There an X ray showed that he had developed stomach ulcers. He too had begun to bleed. And for him, there was no longer any sense to being a cop.

In 1964, Mike Hickey died of a heart attack at Aqueduct racetrack with, as my father always remembered to note, two winners in his pocket. In some ways, Frank's last ounce of enjoyment in the police department went to the grave with Hickey. By then, he had taken the captain's test three times and failed. On the first test he had missed passing by a single point.

I never fully understood why my father failed the captain's tests. His preparations for the first of his attempts, in 1956, came before my recollection, but I do remember how, before his last try, he rarely read the thick exam textbooks, the ones that lay next to his gun on the top shelf in the hallway closet. Undoubtedly, the disappointment of so narrowly failing shook his confidence—it was the first scholastic exam of any kind he had failed in his life. But perhaps the reason for his subsequent failures lay deeper. If my father had become a captain, his police career would have been extended by five, even ten years. His time in the 41st Precinct had exacted a price, both emotionally and physically. Perhaps he just didn't want to be a cop any longer.

By the middle of 1964, the blustery days of the Rat Pack had faded to anecdote, told with a nostalgic air. Like someone left behind at a train station, my father watched as his study group, without him, climbed to the very top echelons of the police department: Jack Kelly would run the Bronx homicide squad; Gus Harms rose to the rank of deputy chief inspector and was, at one point, seriously being considered as a candidate for police commissioner; Mario Biaggi had begun laying the foundation for a second career as a congressman from the Bronx. The rest—except for Frank Weldon, who died in 1966 from a combination of ailments (he had his first stroke at a Rat Pack "wake" at our home in Pearl River)—reached at least the rank of captain and some rose as high as full inspector.

Several times during his last years on Simpson Street, my father requested a transfer. Each time his request was turned down. His tenure as squad commander of the 41st Precinct lasted for fourteen years, the longest anyone had held that position. Years after my father retired, Chief of Detectives Fred Lussen told him that the brass didn't want to move him, that the volatility of the precinct was such they were afraid a new squad commander would either fold under the pressure or stoke the flames that were then consuming the South Bronx. Fourteen years. Almost a death sentence.

In late 1964, though, my father finally received a transfer, to the Property Recovery Squad in downtown Manhattan, a desk job a universe away from Simpson Street. The man who took over the Four-One squad held that position for less than a year. Over the next half-dozen years there were at least four different squad commanders in the 41st Precinct.

My father retired from the police department on January 1, 1965. Some of his old gang threw him a racket, actually more a quiet dinner, at Tony Amandola's restaurant in the Bronx, the event about as festive as returning a library book. He was home early that night, poured himself a glass of buttermilk, sat in his chair in the living room, and read. "Damn guinea food," he mumbled.

A week later, he started his second career, as a security manager for Eastern Airlines; his office was at Kennedy Airport. If he talked about missing the police department, I didn't hear him. Rarely, in his cocktail hour or dinner table conversations with my mother, did I hear the names of his old Rat Pack comrades, or the other detectives who had worked for him. Instead, there was a new set of names mentioned: Howard Brunn, an ex–FBI agent who worked alongside him for the airline, and, later, Frank Borman, the one-time astronaut who became president of Eastern.

His new job took him to the skies often: to Boston, Chicago, Miami, and San Juan. On his return flights, when the pilot would settle the jet into a landing approach over New York City, and the South Bronx, my father didn't even look out the window.

Save the glory years of the Rat Pack, his time in the airline business was the happiest of my father's working life. As the years went by, he and my mother took full advantage of employee flying privileges, and saw most of the world. In 1968, Eastern Airlines was given the contract to transport the Vince Lombardi Super Bowl trophy from New York (where it was made) to wherever the game was being played. From 1968 to 1979, my father and mother attended ten Super Bowls, and all the festivities that surrounded the event.

Our first family vacation after my father took the job with Eastern was to Acapulco. In a pink Jeep with a striped surrey top, I rode with my brother Tommy, then sixteen and having just received his license, for miles along the Pacific coast, watching as a brilliant crimson sun slowly dropped into the turquoise water—a sight that is as clear now in my thoughts as it was thirty-some years ago. In some ways, the jet we boarded for that flight to Mexico was a kind of rocket ship that flew Tommy and me out of the cop universe, out from under that canopy of stars over the Police Camp. But for my mother—born into it, married to it, and, when Frankie joined the force, mothering it—the police department would always remain in the deepest level of her being. For my father, neither distance nor silence could separate him from the department. It was too much a part of him, it had taken too much from him, to forget that easily.

7

Just before Christmas a few years ago, I received a package in the mail. It wasn't a surprise. My father had called me several days before to tell me it was on the way. "I'm writing your book for you," he said.

In his familiar, strong, looping script—handwriting that was almost identical to his father's, and that I had once, as a kid, tried to forge for a note to my teacher, failing miserably—was fifty pages of his life; not just events and episodes, but feelings that made me weep several times at his tenderness. He wrote about my mother and their early life together, about the Rat Pack, all but a few now gone, "too soon," as he wrote. With fondness and respect, he wrote about Hickey and the other men who worked for him. In my mind's eye, I saw him sitting at the kitchen table, his glasses on, the only light on in the entire house the one hanging from the ceiling above him, the bargain-brand bulb bathing him in dull white, his pen flashing across the legal pad as the memories flashed across his mind. There was a scotch in front of him on the table. This I knew. I could tell when the scotch began to blur his still-fertile brain—the writing became just a bit larger and slightly sloppy. Still, he knew when to stop—writing, at least—as he would then sign off with a crooked "Keep the Faith, Dad."

The package also contained a large manila envelope of pictures. As I dumped them out on my bed, they spilled like pieces of a broken mirror onto the covers—fractured reflections of my family's history: my father with Eugene and Frankie, then just kids, on the roof of 2300; my parents at their wedding reception, a table with ten or so friends in the crowded Mayer's Parkway Inn; my mother, young and lovely, at Rockaway beach; my father in his police uniform at a St. Patrick's Day parade. As I looked at my father's young face I realized that the picture showed a man I never knew—startling black hair, almost handsome features, eyes that gleamed.

My thoughts went back to the one and only time I went with him to his job. The trip was to buy an Easter suit for me on Orchard Street, but he had to stop at the 41st Precinct on the way. Partly as joke and partly to keep me from wandering away, he put me in the lockup cage. Through the crisscross of wires I could see men in short-sleeve shirts, their ties loose around their necks. They smoked cigarettes and cigars. They called each other Hickey and Hoy, Squires and Martin. They sat at desks with old-style Underwood typewriters and rotary phones. They all wore guns on their belts.

One of the detectives, a man with a nose spread across his face as if he had been hit with a frying pan, asked me what I was in for. I blushed and said nothing. Through the half-open door, I could see my father standing in his office. I could hear his deep voice—a baritone sax, confident, in charge, rising above the chatter in the room. Several times he looked at me, but he didn't smile. I wasn't scared. Many times I'd overheard mention of the cage in his stories.

I stood quietly at attention, like a little soldier. My hair, freshly cut that morning at Enio's Barber Shop, was Vitalis-slicked to my scalp, my hands were at my sides, holding the bottoms of my short pants, my shirt was buttoned to the collar, my eyes were wide-open, inquisitive sponges, soaking in everything around me. There was something familiar about being locked in, watching my father through the cage.

I was his youngest child. My earliest memories of him are from the end of his police career, a time when most of his dreams were already dead. I wonder now how different things might have been had he never become a cop.

About the same time I received the package from my father, I was given permission to search back case files in the basement of the 41st Precinct station house. The precinct is no longer housed in the once grand structure on Simpson Street; the new vermilion-brick and dark-tinted glass building on Southern Boulevard looks more like an HMO than a police station. I was led down a staircase to a cinder-block hallway with thick metal doors painted red. My sergeant guide unlocked one of the doors. Inside, the walls were lined with metal shelves. Every inch of the shelves was taken up with thick cardboard boxes the size of large microwave ovens, squeezed one on top of the other. Each was marked with dates and type of crime. My eyes greedily searched for the era when my father ran the detective squad. At first, I saw nothing earlier than the late 1960s, a time when the 41st Precinct was burned to the ground. Most were marked with dates from the mid 1980s to the early 1990s, the crack cocaine era of devastation—box upon box with "Murder," "Rape," "Robbery" emblazoned on it in red Magic Marker. There were hundreds of boxes; thousands and thousands of individual records of still open cases.

They don't keep records that far back, my sergeant guide told me. I begged for one more look. On the top shelf of the far recess of the room, I saw the corner of a box I hadn't yet checked. I stood on a stepladder and pulled away the boxes that hid it. "Murders 1950s" was written on its side. My hand shook as I opened it. Inside were a dozen legal file folders—murders that had gone unsolved. My father's signature was on each DD 5, detective case report. The names that lived in his stories—Mike Hickey, Larry Squires, Bill Hoy—appear over and over again. The files also contained personal items from the victims and other articles of evidence: a small leather-bound address book, keys to a home, a crime tip written on toilet paper that crumbled in my hand. There were also crime scene photographs, each a graphic glimpse into my father's job:

In 1954, Samuel Tannenbaum, seventy-seven, the owner of a toy store on Freeman Street, stabbed forty times during a robbery.

In 1958, twenty-six-year-old Rosa Hernandez and her two-year-old daughter, murdered in their apartment at 660 Dawson Street. Both were beaten with the steel end of a mop handle, then drowned in a bathtub filled with scalding water.

In 1959, Nicholas Serico, sixty-nine, pistol-whipped to death as he pleaded for his life in the vestibule of his apartment house. The murderer made off with the $7 in his wallet.

The box also contained Eugenia Fargus and Mary Roznicoff's folders. The face in the Mary Roznicoff crime scene photo stared back at me just as it had to my father those many years earlier. Intently I read each file, and tried to imagine my father in this world of murder, one so different from anything I had ever known. My thoughts went back to a time when I was growing up in Pearl River. A boy a few years older than I had drowned in Nanuet Lake; his body lay near the diving board. My friends and I went to take a closer look as Mr. Eckart, the city cop and part-time life-guard, covered the boy with a coarse green blanket. As I watched the scene, transfixed—it was the first time I had ever seen a dead body—I felt a hand on my back. My father had followed me, and he put his arm around me and led me away. I had no way of knowing it then, but this was the reason my father had moved his family as far as he could from the world in which he worked: to keep his children from seeing what he saw all the time—cold bodies covered by coarse blankets.

Less than one year after my father retired from the police department, I stood in the garishly lit hallway of Columbia Presbyterian Hospital as nurses wheeled him by on a gurney. He had been rushed there for an emergency operation that removed three quarters of his ulcerated stomach and part of his ruptured esophagus. Nora, my mother's friend, held my hand as Eleanor walked alongside the gurney, her eyes moist and worried. Later, doctors told Frank that he had come perilously close to dying on the operating table.

When he returned home, he was gaunt and looked very old. He was forty-seven. For months afterward, he ate nothing but farina and oatmeal. He sucked on lollipops instead of cigars. Once in a while my mother would broil a steak for him, but my father could only chew it like bubble gum, then remove the pieces from his mouth and place them on the corner of his plate, which he hid, embarrassed, with a cupped hand.

That fall, after his operation, I played Mighty Midget football in Orangeburg. Most of the kids who played with me were the sons of New York City policemen. Both my coaches were city cops: Larry Kasperac, a traffic cop on Delancey Street, and Burton Armus, who had once worked for Frank Weldon and was then a detective in Manhattan. (Later he was the technical adviser to the *Kojak* television show.)

Still pale and frail, my father came to a couple of my games, and from the field I could see him standing off by himself, away from the rest of the city cops who came to watch their sons play. After the games, as he walked me to the car, some of the other cop fathers would approach to say hello. In their words, in their demeanor, there was respect. Even in his emaciated condition, even though he was now nearly a year retired from the department, in the other cops' eyes he was still a squad commander. But more than that, their respect came from the knowledge of where my father had worked, how he had done his job, and the price he had paid in doing it.

In his police career, Frank McDonald took the Roosevelt reforms and turned them upside down. He went from book cop to a street cop, and, as most of these cop fathers knew well, no one spends fourteen years as a street cop in the South Bronx and comes out whole.

DETECTIVE BROTHER

Frankie McDonald

There is no saint without a past—no sinner without a future. —Ancient Persian mass

1

At the departmental hearing, I sat waiting for my turn to testify. My hands were sweating; my tie and collar felt tight around my neck. I had never been on a witness stand before. The attorney representing Frankie had coached me on what questions to expect. I had told him the same words that I so often had told myself: "All my brother saw was a cop in trouble." The attorney's efforts only made me all the more uncomfortable, because they brought the night vividly back to my thoughts.

In the early winter of 1972, Frankie had stopped into Chuck's, the tavern where I worked at the time. Sitting at the bar, my brother seemed out of sorts, sullen and preoccupied. Perhaps he had had a fight with Pam, his wife, but he didn't say. Maybe it was the job, the recent cop assassinations at the hands of the Black Liberation Army, the ultra-militant splinter group of the Black Panther Party. Or perhaps it was money. The house, the kids, the bills were strangling him, and he just couldn't seem to get ahead

I wasn't working that night; I had stopped in to Chuck's, as I often did on my night off. I liked the attention my friends and customers gave me on my "busman's holiday." It was a weekend night, and the bar was filled with woozy coeds and long-haired college guys, usually fodder for Frankie's cynical humor. But he sat quietly.

Our plan was to find a place to hold a bachelor party for our brother Tommy, who was to be married the following month. I had suggested Gulliver's, a loud nightspot in Pearl River where I knew some of the employees. We only had one drink there, because the place was too crowded and besides, the bartender, a friend of mine, said that they didn't hold bachelor parties. But while there, Frankie met a city cop named Larkin whom he knew casually. The three of us left the club together.

Outside, Larkin, who lived a few towns away in Spring Valley, suggested we go to his house to play cards. At the time, I thought of myself as something of a cardsharp. I played in a weekly game where you could easily win or lose several hundred dollars. The truth was, I lost far more times than I won, but on several prior occasions I had bragged to Frankie about my cardplaying prowess. We agreed to pool our money, with me playing the cards. We left Gulliver's in two cars, Larkin driving ahead, and Frankie and me following. It was unusually warm, and the night was shrouded with a thin fog. As we followed Larkin along the back roads toward Spring Valley, I saw, in the darkness ahead, flashing lights that left streaks on the fog like the tails of Fourth of July fireworks.

The Spring Valley police car was stopped at an odd angle to the side of the road. In front of it was a large white sedan, an Oldsmobile or a big Buick, perhaps a Continental. As we slowly passed, Frankie's eyes were riveted to the scene: a lone cop was surrounded by six men, the occupants of the sedan. The six men were black.

I stayed in the car and watched the events unfold through the window: Frankie jumping out and running across the street to where the men stood in a circle around the Spring Valley police officer. At first he didn't know that the cop was an underclassmate of his from high school, until he was almost face to face with him. I watched as Frankie said something to the cop, and as one of the men grabbed his arm. There were shouts, heated words exchanged, but they were muffled by the distance, the fog, or my reluctance to hear them. Then I saw Frankie take out his gold shield, and hang it around his neck, as if to say, "That's who the fuck I am. . . ."

The flashing lights, the scene of the men surrounding the policeman, the still-bleeding memory of cop assassinations—all this, and too many beers—swirled like a vortex. It was as though, for Frankie, this was happening on the streets of Times Square or in Bedford-Stuyvesant, Brooklyn, the areas he worked as an undercover detective, and not in suburban Spring Valley. His two worlds had dangerously melded into one. Chin to chin with one of the men, Frankie screamed like a baseball manager fighting with an umpire over a bad call at the plate. For a moment, I sat frozen in dread, praying that he would just walk away. Finally, he did walk away, but not without parting words. I didn't hear him say *the* word; the lightning rod of a word that, in the early 1970s, when racial tension in New York City was stretched as tight as the skin of a snare drum, would blow everything out of proportion; the same word that I had heard come from the lips of every white cop I had ever known. But I made it a point not to listen.

Later, as we drove to Larkin's house, my brother sat in remorseful silence. I could tell he knew he had screwed up. We played cards most of the night in Larkin's finished basement, the walls hung with an extensive gun collection. But the laughter and conversation were forced, and for most of the night Frankie sat looking at the same can of beer in his hand.

That night, the Spring Valley officer wrote a report and left it on his captain's desk. The next day, the captain read the report and wrote a letter to the New York City police commissioner's office.

The commissioner's office filed interdepartmental charges and scheduled a hearing—an event that would change Frankie's life.

2

It seemed, while he was growing up, that Frankie would become anything but a cop. It wasn't the job itself that seemed so remote; rather, what was unfathomable was the thought that Frankie would follow his father's path. During his teenage years, the late 1950s and early 1960s, Frankie's relationship with our father ranged from antagonistic to outright hostile. Most of this discord revolved around Frankie's loathing of school and his rebellious nature. My father often lamented his lack of a college education. A natural student, he would've relished being in the company of those as devoted to books and learning as he was. The last thing Frankie relished was school. Eight years after he just barely graduated from St. Margaret's, the grammar school he was enrolled in when we moved from the Bronx, I was approached there by a nun named Sister Blasius, a square stump of a woman, who asked me if I had a brother named Francis. When I told her I did, her lips turned as white as a dying pope's:

"I guess I can expect you to be the same sort of bold article," she hissed.

What made the rift between my father and Frankie even more pronounced was the comparison my father made between his two oldest sons. The difference between my two oldest brothers is remarkable. It's hard to imagine that they came from the same family. By the time they were in their teens, Eugene—fair-haired, with clear azure eyes—was towering. Frankie wasn't short by any standard, except when he stood next to his older brother. Eugene had classic handsome features. Frankie's face was slightly pock-marked; his hair was reddish-brown, the color of the mud you see around the construction of a brick house, his complexion ruddy.

But greater even than their physical contrast was the difference in their personalities. Like my father, Eugene was inward-looking, contemplative, and analytical, while Frankie's emotions were mercurial. Eugene's feelings weren't easy to read; Frankie's were as obvious as neon signs. They both had tempers, a trait they (all of us) inherited from our mother, but Eugene's anger smoldered, while Frankie's was volcanic in its eruption.

When we moved from the Bronx, both Eugene and Frankie were enrolled in St. Margaret's. Some of the nuns there, a Dominican order, had come from the St. Nicholas of Tolentine school in Fordham. Just like the cops, they had made the escape from the Bronx to the suburbs. For Eugene, two years older than Frankie, and at that awkward age of twelve, when new friendships are hard to make, the nuns offered a familiar environment, and one in which he excelled. In Eugene, my father saw the scholastic opportunity he himself had longed for.

Frankie, on the other hand, spent much of his time devising ways to infuriate the nuns. Even before we moved to Pearl River, Frankie had begun to build a churlish reputation with them. One nun at St. Nicholas of Tolentine regularly hit him on the knuckles with a heavy wooden ruler. When he came home from school he'd keep his hands in his pockets so my mother wouldn't see the bruises. One day, the nun, who knew our father was a policeman, told him: "I wish I had your father's nightstick to hit you with."

By the time he was at St. Margaret's, Frankie had perfected the fine art of flatulent noises, using the one-hand-under-a-flapping-arm technique. He became so proficient with spit balls, he could hit the back of a nun's head from the last row of the classroom, where he always managed to sit. One time, he and a school pal, Willie Salvador, booby-trapped a nun's closets with piles of book bags. When she opened the door she was pummeled by the ensuing avalanche. But at St. Margaret's too, he paid a dear price for his antics; often Sister Therese Bernard would kiss her knuckle before administering a noogie to the back of his head.

When it came time for Eugene to choose a high school, my mother, of course, wanted him to go to a Catholic school. My father agreed, but there were certain hurdles that stood in the way. One was distance. The closest Catholic high schools, Bergen Catholic and Don Bosco, in Bergen County, New Jersey, were a twenty-minute car ride away. In addition, there was no school bus service from Rockland. But what presented the biggest hurdle was money. With four children and my parents' mortgage on the new home, there wasn't a whole lot left over. Though Eugene took the entrance exams for Don Bosco and Bergen Catholic, both of which he passed easily, my parents were resigned to the fact that they just couldn't afford the tuition ($25 a month) for a private school. In the fall of 1955, they enrolled Eugene in Pearl River High School.

When the pastor of St. Margaret's, Monsignor Toner, found out about my parents' plans, he paid a visit to our home. Toner had a commanding presence, despite his stooped posture, slight build, and generally wizened appearance, which made him seem older than his sixty years. His words that evening, though spoken with confessional softness, came right to the point:

"Eugene has too much ability to be wasted in public high school," he said as he sat in the living room drinking coffee from the good tea service.

My father tried to explain the family's financial situation. Toner, looking over his glasses at him, said: "There is always a way." My mother needed little convincing. They would find a way, she promised the monsignor. Two weeks later, Eugene was in Bergen Catholic.

To meet the cost of Eugene's tuition, my father took a second job, selling check-writing machines. Like the move to Pearl River, moonlighting was against police department regulations. But, for my father, Eugene's education outweighed any risk. Frank McCabe, the cousin my father lived with when he first came to New

York, sold the machines in his spare time, and did rather well. My father, however, was just not cut out to be a salesman. Accustomed to being the boss, he couldn't master the hat-in-hand posture. He ended up selling only about five or six of the machines: one to a liquor store in Rockland County, and the rest to businesses in his precinct. One of the machines sat in the attic of our house for years after. Still, my parents were able to cut enough corners to pay the tuition. My father brown-bagged his lunch instead of buying his usual corned-beef sandwich from one of the Jewish delicatessens on Westchester Avenue; my mother clipped coupons and invented new ways to turn canned tuna fish into family dinners.

Their financial sacrifice didn't go unappreciated. Eugene was awake before dawn each morning, studying his thick algebra, history, and Latin textbooks, the light over his desk cutting a triangle in the darkness of his room. In the winter months, before the sun rose, he would walk the mile across town to Bonamolo's, a candy store near St. Margaret's, where he would meet his friend Jimmy Moriarity and his car pool to school. He thrived in the strict atmosphere maintained by the Christian Brothers who taught at Bergen Catholic. Rarely was he the target of their discipline (except for the time he misplaced his tuba when the school band marched in the St. Patrick's Day Parade). And, as he had in St. Margaret's, Eugene finished his first year in high school at the top of the class. My father basked in his academic success.

There was no intercession by the monsignor when Frankie graduated from St. Margaret's. Undoubtedly, Toner was relieved to see him go. Still, my mother insisted Frankie have the same opportunity as his older brother. My parents chose Albertus Magnus for Frankie, a newly built school in Bardonia, New York, just a few towns from Pearl River in Rockland County. Despite his strenuous objections, Frankie was enrolled in the first class of the new school.

But although he showed up at Albertus each day, he rarely did any homework or even went to classes. Instead, he hung around the grounds, smoking Luckies. Maybe he'd sneak into the gym and shoot baskets. My father was furious when he found out, and several huge screaming matches in the living room ensued. Frankie didn't care how much his father yelled. Even then, no one, not even his father, could make him do what he didn't want to do. The school, however, settled the arguments—the administration asked Frankie to leave halfway through the first semester of his freshman year.

In October 1958, Eugene's junior year at Bergen Catholic, an event occurred that signified a rare collision of father and son's worlds.

Jimmy Moriarity, the designated driver of Eugene's car pool, was a notoriously late riser, and often the trip to school was a road rally so they'd arrive on time. Moriarity would barrel through the northern Bergen County towns of Montvale, Park Ridge, and Woodcliff Lake, alternately glancing at the road in front of him and at his wristwatch. One misty, gray morning that year, going at breakneck speed, Moriarity turned onto Broadway in Park Ridge, a sleepy road covered with a canopy of maple trees that ran alongside a reservoir. As he did, a white Lincoln Continental raced past in the oncoming lane, almost forcing him off the road. Moriarity got a quick look at the occupants of the Lincoln, two men in leather jackets. Eugene and the other students let go a torrent of choice words as Moriarity gunned the gas in pursuit. They lost sight of the Continental as it rounded a curve on Broadway; then they heard what sounded like an explosion.

On the other side of the bend, a blue Ford sedan was on its roof, its tires still spinning, smoke rising from the hood. Moriarity stopped the car and Eugene and his classmates piled out to see if the driver was all right. He wasn't. As Eugene approached the

Ford he could see the man hanging upside down in the car, blood dripping from his face, his neck at a forty-five-degree angle against the car's roof. At first, Eugene and his classmates thought that the Continental had cut off the Ford too. But then my brother noticed a three-inch round hole in the driver's side window. Moriarity ran to a nearby house and called the police.

That night, home from school, Eugene received a call from the Bergen County prosecutor, a man named Gil Gilissi. What Eugene and his classmates came upon that morning was not a traffic accident at all, but a mob rubout of man named Johnny "Baseball Bat" Scanlon. Scanlon was a convicted enforcer for a union goon squad on the West Side docks of New York. He had earned his nickname by beating two men nearly to death with a bat in a West Side bar. The prosecutor asked Eugene to come down to his office to look through mug shots of known mobsters in the hope of identifying the men in the Lincoln. My mother called my father at work.

"He's not going anywhere," my father said on the phone. "I'll be right home."

During his police career, my father had known his share of mobsters. With his Bronx squad commander pals, he often went to Joe Cago's Lido restaurant in the Castle Hill section. Better known as Joe Valachi (*The Valachi Papers* by Peter Maas), Cago's testimony in front of a Senate subcommittee documented the existence of the Mafia for the first time. From his days of walking a beat in Harlem, my father knew Tony Bender, Valachi's boss in the Luciano-Genovese crime family. Often, he and his Rat Pack were seated at tables next to mobsters at the Latin Quarter or the Copa. In the code of organized crime, at least in those days of "honorable" mobsters, being a cop's son brought with it a certain amount of immunity from reprisal. Though honorable on its surface, this professional courtesy was at root strictly business. In the late 1950s, when most crime families still shunned the lucrative distribution of heroin and other drugs, organized crime's main

sources of income were illegal gambling and vice. These operations depended on the cooperation of the police. This cooperation, generally given by crooked plainclothesmen, was paid for.
But, because of the sheer proliferation of daily numbers outlets
and houses of prostitution, and because they were busy enough
with more serious crimes, even honest cops, for the most part,
looked the other way. That is, however, until investigations into
murders and other major crimes necessitated information that
only those involved in organized crime possessed. On these occasions, it was not at all unusual for detectives to exert pressure on
the mob by closing down the vice operations, and even though
they would quickly reopen in other locations, such crackdowns
would cost the mob days of revenue. The threat of crackdowns
placed policemen, and their families, in an untouchable position.
Still, my father was not about to let Eugene be mixed up in any
prosecution of a mob hit.

"Over my dead body will he look at any pictures," my father
told Gilissi when he called that evening.

"I can subpoena him," Gilissi said.

"Go ahead and try," my father warned, "and I'll do everything I
can to keep him out of this."

Because of my father's strenuous objections, and perhaps because of his position as a detective-lieutenant in the NYPD, Gilissi
didn't press the matter and Eugene never looked at any pictures.
Jimmy Moriarity, who had gotten the best look at the men in the
Lincoln, was brought into the Bergen County D.A.'s office. But as
a witness, Moriarity proved to be of little help. For some reason
his recollection of the event became clouded. Perhaps only coincidentally, on graduating from Bergen Catholic, Moriarity, who
according to Eugene was only a fair student, received a full scholarship to the University of Bogotá in Colombia, South America.

The following year, 1959, the main topic of discussion at the dinner table was which college Eugene would attend. His top three

choices were Fordham University, Yale, and the Naval Academy. He was accepted by both Fordham and Yale, but not Annapolis. This probably had more to do with our family's lack of political pull than with any deficiency in Eugene's academic ability. At one point Fordham was his top choice. In his high school yearbook, under "Future Plans," he had written, "Fordham, to study law." But by the time he sent in an application and took the entrance exam, he had cooled to the idea of becoming a lawyer. Though Yale would have made both my father and Eugene happy, it was far too expensive, and too far above his station, to even consider. Although Eugene undoubtedly had the smarts to fit in at Yale, socially he would have felt out of place—he had a kind of civil service inferiority complex that permeated my family. My father started championing the State University of New York Maritime College at Fort Schuyler. For Eugene, it was an easy sell. In high school, his strongest subjects were math and sciences, and, from the time he was eight or nine, he was interested in ships. For a few years, our grandfather Pete was a caretaker at the Webb Institute on Sedgwick Avenue, one of the leading schools of naval architecture in the country. Pete often took Eugene on guided tours of the school and grounds. The thought of being a naval engineer felt natural to Eugene, and thrilled my father. In 1960, he was off to Fort Schuyler.

Meanwhile, Frankie literally labored through Pearl River High School. From his freshman year on, he worked two jobs. After school and during the summer, he'd work for a landscaper or a construction company, and each morning he awoke before light and went to work on the "honey wagon," the garbage truck. He took hour-long showers before he went off to school. He might not have even bothered (to go to school, not take the shower), if he hadn't noticed the attention the pretty girls were paying to the guys wearing the Pearl River Pirates football jackets.

In the classic underdog manner, a pose my brother Frankie

brought to an art form, he tried out for the football team at the beginning of his sophomore year, at the last possible minute. In the Bronx he had played his share of sidewalk games: stickball, Johnny-ride-the-pony, even a little basketball on the sidewalk with a half-deflated ball and the bottom rung of a fire escape ladder as the hoop; and though he had played football a few times, once in a semi-organized game on a hill in Valhalla (the team headed downhill was given the advantage), football wasn't really a city game. But in Pearl River then, it was big stuff. In 1959, the high school team won the county championship (the last time it did).

Frankie arrived at the first practice looking like a kid dressed up as a football player for Halloween. The only equipment left for him was a pair of pants at least two sizes too big, tiny leather shoulder pads, and a leather helmet, the kind you see in pictures of Red Grange. He wore high-top sneakers, because Mel's Army and Navy was already sold out of football spikes.

The captain of the team looked like a poster boy for high school athletics: six foot two, an Adonis build, ruggedly handsome, with reddish-blond hair. The coach, Max Talaska, a balding drill sergeant of a man, thought he would make an example of the latecomer in the baggy pants. He rounded the team into a circle and matched Frankie one-on-one against the captain.

As Talaska's whistle blew, the captain exploded out of his stance, knocking Frankie, who had to hold his pants up with one hand, on his ass. The whole team laughed, a sadistic grin cut Talaska's face, and the captain stood over Frankie like Cassius Clay later would over Sonny Liston. His face crimson, Frankie thought to himself: That will never happen again.

The second time, they met in a resounding crunch. Neither moved an inch, and the team responded with oohs and ahhs. The captain glared at Frankie. Frankie glared back.

The third time Frankie hit the captain so hard he stumbled

backward into Talaska, both of them winding up in a tangle on the ground. Humiliated, the captain ran from the practice field into the locker room, changed to his street clothing, and never returned to the team. Frankie started that year at offensive and defensive tackle, and the next year was the captain of the team.

In 1962, Frankie's senior year at Pearl River High School, I went with my brother Tommy to watch him play against the team from Tappan Zee, a neighboring town. The week before, in a game against Nyack, Frankie had dislocated his shoulder. Pearl River lost soundly to Nyack, 34–0, but Frankie made fifteen tackles on defense—half of them with only one arm. For the Tappan Zee game, my father taped a foam rubber pad to his shoulder and bound his arm flat against his side. Pearl River fell behind in the game, 20–0, but with one hand—literally—tied behind his back, Frankie made a dozen tackles. Early in the second half, he made a ferocious hit on a Tappan Zee halfback that caused a fumble and started an incredible comeback. Pearl River tied the score in the last seconds of the game, and when the gun sounded, the fans streamed from the bleachers to the field as though the Pirates had won the national championship, even going so far as to tear down the goalposts and hold a parade up Central Avenue after the game. A U.S. senator from New York, Kenneth B. Keating, happened to be in Pearl River that day for the opening of a local Republican club. He attended the second half of the game and afterward asked to be photographed with Frankie. In the photo—which ran in the next day's paper—the senator's arm is around my brother's shoulder and his eyes are on the young player in an adoring gaze. Frankie's expression seems to say he's not impressed by the attention: He's looking off to the side, at neither the senator nor the photographer. Later that year, he was voted All-County.

By then, Frankie had joined up with a quasi gang that called itself the Brothers. Nine or ten strong, all, like Frankie, were displaced city kids. Although they spent most of their energies on souped-up cars and shaping their pompadours, and although they paled in comparison to the Bronx gangs—the ones my father was so concerned with—the Brothers did have their share of rumbles, late-night carousing, and altercations with the law.

In 1963, the summer after they graduated from high school, the Brothers decided to take a trip together to the Jersey shore. They met on a Friday night in the Commodore Bar and Grill, a tavern in the middle of the town. The plan was to have a few beers and then drive down the Garden State Parkway in several cars. By the time they actually left, the time allotted for a "few beers" had grown by several hours. It was almost eleven p.m. when they began the caravan. Needless to say, when they arrived in the beach town of Wildwood, finding a motel that would rent a room to the ten of them—in their condition—presented a problem. To increase their chances, they decided to split up. Frankie rode with his friend Bobby Dunn and another teen named Louie, who was the driver of the car. As they cruised down the main drag in Wildwood, they saw two girls hitchhiking. They stopped the car and asked the girls if they knew of a motel with vacancies. Ten minutes later, they pulled into the motel's parking lot, with the hitchhiking girls in the backseat. In front of the motel were half a dozen guys drinking cans of beer. Just as soon as the girls stepped from the car, Frankie knew that picking them up had been a mistake. As he climbed from the car in the hope of mitigating any overreaction on the part of the girls' boyfriends, he was charged by one of them and the rumble began. Though outnumbered, Frankie and Dunn held their own (Louie, who never left the car, screeched out of the parking lot, leaving his two friends behind). Frankie threw a punch that landed square on the nose of the kid who'd charged him. The fight finally stopped when two Wildwood police cars showed up—all of them were arrested and placed in the town jail house overnight.

The next morning, the local magistrate looked at the lineup in front of him. The shirt of the kid Frankie had punched was covered in his own blood. Eyeing him, the judge said:

"Now that I know who lost the fight, someone tell me what happened."

Everyone began talking at once. The judge ordered silence, and picked Frankie as the spokesman for his side. Frankie relayed the story of the hitchhiking girls and their boyfriends' ire.

"We didn't want any trouble," Frankie pleaded to the judge. "I'm going to be a policeman."

The judge leveled a glare at Frankie and said: "Son, I'd be willing to bet you will never become a cop."

Frankie's declaration to the judge in Wildwood was perhaps the first time he told anybody his dream of becoming a cop. He certainly hadn't discussed it with his father. Their relationship, unlike the one my father had with Eugene, remained tenuous at best. And when Frankie joined the navy, right out of high school, my father seemed happy to see him go. It might straighten him out, he said. Frankie's car accidents, his brushes with the law, and his volcanic temper caused, for my father, too much disharmony, and—his ultimate accusation—too much unhappiness for our mother. My father always deflected his own feelings onto his wife: "You're breaking your mother's heart," or "I won't have you hurting your mother this way," he would often say when Frankie came home late or in trouble. Utter falsehoods. My mother's heart could never be broken by Frankie: he was so much more *her* son than my father's. That anger, that independence—these were all things Frankie inherited from her, along with her sense of humor. My mother didn't condone Frankie's wildness, but she accepted it. But for my father, Frankie was the black sheep of the family. And as Eugene fulfilled all of my father's expectations, the distance between Frankie and our father lengthened.

I have two photographs from that time. In one, Eugene wears

the dress whites of the Maritime Academy, a pristine poster boy with sleek lines, razor edges, and a cream-colored complexion. In the other, Frankie, ruddy-faced, wears his navy uniform: a boxed, stiff sailor hat, bellbottom pants with buttons, clumsy mirror-black shoes. Eugene is the officer, Frankie the swabbie.

The navy did not straighten Frankie out. At least not right away. While on shore leave, a month after he was assigned to Jacksonville, he got into a fight over a girl in a sailor bar. The Shore Patrol was called and he ended up spending Christmas in the brig. Soon after, an official-looking letter from the navy arrived at the house. In it, Frankie's captain explained that he was writing because he knew my father had been in the navy and was a lieutenant in the New York City police department, and that he therefore would appreciate the severity of Frankie's insubordination. My father read the letter at the kitchen table and shook his head in disgust, then carefully put it back in the envelope and placed it where he would see it every day: in his closet, up behind his gun.

Frankie sent me postcards from places like Madrid, Rome, and Hamburg. I pinned them to the wall next to my bed. At night, I would listen to Marv Albert's "Scoop" and "Yes!"—his radio play-by-play of the Knicks games—and pretend I was Cazzie Russell hitting a jumper from the corner, keeping sharp for when Frankie came home and we would play sock basketball again.

Frankie also wrote to our father. It was in one of these letters that he first told him that he wanted to become a policeman. When my father read the letter, he shook his head, folded it back into the envelope, and stuck it deep on the top shelf of his closet, right next to the captain's letter.

Though my father maintained his suspicions of his second son, Frankie had begun to change. He wrote to a high school English teacher named Miss Warren, whose class he had rarely attended, and asked if she could suggest books for him to read. Lying on his bunk, rocking to 45-degree angles in a "tin can" destroyer called the U.S.S. *Bigelow*, Frankie, for the first time, discovered treasures like *Crime and Punishment*, *Our Town*, and *A Connecticut Yankee in King Arthur's Court*.

His newfound serious attitude kept him out of further trouble, but fun was still on the agenda. While in port in Germany, he and two of his mates took shore leave and found themselves in a nearly empty beer garden with a handful of other sailors and locals listening to an oompah band. When the band took a break, one of Frankie's mates asked the members if they would mind if he and his friends played a few songs. Frankie climbed onstage and sat behind the drum set, and the two other sailors, after hurrying back to the ship to retrieve their electric guitars, quickly set up next to him. They began the set with "Wooly Bully" and followed with "I Want to Hold Your Hand" and several other Beatles tunes, then the new rage in rock and roll. On hearing the familiar music, sailors wandering past the beer garden began to pile in, and by the end of the first set the place was packed with navy men dancing with the local girls. They played late into the night, and even a few members of the Shore Patrol came in to listen.

In March 1966, Frankie was honorably discharged from the navy and began classes at the Delahanty Institute. Twenty-five years earlier, my father had sat in the same classrooms in the Delahanty building on Thirteenth Street and Fourth Avenue—the same corner where for seven years my grandfather had worked as a traffic cop.

The night he graduated from Delahanty's, Frankie went to his old haunt, the Commodore, to celebrate, but none of the Brothers were around. A few had gone on to college, but most hadn't, working in construction or in gas stations. By 1966, at least six of

the original ten Brothers were in the marines and the army, seeing heavy action in Southeast Asia.

The Commodore was just not the same without his friends, so
Frankie headed to a bar called the Deer Head in West Nyack, a
few towns away. There he sat alone, looking out the window as it
began to rain, when he noticed a girl step from a car. She wore a
tan raincoat and had her hair up. She was pretty, with round eyes
that twinkled and a small, sweet smile set in a jaw that perhaps
was a touch too pronounced but gave her face an overall happy
expression. Frankie's eyes were fixed on the front door as he
waited for the girl to enter. When she did, he realized he knew
her. That's Pam, he said to himself. She had dated a guy he played
football with in high school. He remembered that Pam and a
group of her friends had been at every one of his games. He
caught her eye and gave her a little wave. Pam waved back, and
Frankie turned back to the bar, feeling the blood rush to his face.
While he sipped his beer and gathered his courage to approach
her, Pam walked over to him.

After they talked for a while, he asked if she would like a lift
back to Pearl River. "Sure," Pam said, with a smile.

Gallantly, he opened the door to the Impala for her, hopped in
himself, and gunned the gas, leaving a testosterone spray of gravel
behind. A half-mile or so from the bar, with one hand on the
steering wheel and the other stretched out on the back of the
bucket seat where Pam sat, he took a turn too quickly and the car
hydroplaned off the road and into a ditch. A tree limb cracked the
windshield, and smoke poured from the engine block.

Pam, unhurt and totally calm, said: "I guess you're not the best
driver in the world. You've given me a ride twice, and both times
you got into an accident."

Frankie looked out over the hood of the Impala at the rising
steam, and then quizzically back at Pam.

"The night of your graduation?" Pam said, trying to engage his
memory.

"Jesus," Frankie muttered, holding his face in his hands, remembering then that Pam was his friend Willie Ahlmyer's date, and that both of them were in the backseat of my mother's car when he crashed it.

Like Frankie, Pam was a transplanted city kid; she had lived in Brooklyn until she was ten. She even had cops in her family. Her grandfather, on her mother's side, had once been the chief of police of Savannah, Georgia, but, she confided to Frankie, his primary source of income was a very lucrative bootlegging business. Her paternal grandfather, Joseph Lawler, owned a famous restaurant in the Singer building in downtown Manhattan. His customers were Wall Street financiers, Tammany politicians, and Broadway actors. Two of the bartenders who worked for him went on to fame as legendary New York saloonkeepers: Sherman Billingsley, who ran the Stork Club, and Toots Shor. Pam's grandmother was a Broadway actress who went by the stage name Lucy Lord and performed in musicals and light operas.

But when Pam's grandfather retired from the restaurant and handed the reins over to Pam's father, Michael, and his three brothers, the business began to decline. Pam told Frankie that her father and uncles ran the place into the ground. One time, at the restaurant, Pam's father stuck a fork in a small-time bookmaker to whom he owed several thousand dollars. A lieutenant from the 1st Precinct by the name of Hiller, a customer and a man who knew the price of a drink—and the money he was saving by not paying for it—was more than happy to make the incident magically disappear from the police files. After Michael paid him off, the bookmaker was happy to keep his mouth shut.

Soon after the restaurant closed, Pam's mother filed for divorce and moved to Montvale, New Jersey, with Pam and her brother, Clem. There she worked as a waitress in a restaurant called the Steak Out, popular with the New York City cops living right across the state line in Pearl River.

The young romance burned bright and hot, and even though Pam's mother looked at Frankie suspiciously when he came to pick her up—no doubt convinced that he was some sort of demolition derby driver, bent on steering her only daughter into a twisted-metal wreck—she eventually became resigned to, if not happy about, the fact that Pam and Frankie were a steady item.

The following May, Frankie took the police entrance exam at George Washington High School in upper Manhattan. He had crammed every night for weeks, sitting at the same desk his brother Eugene, doing his high school studies, had used. At night and early in the morning, before he left for his construction job, the same triangle of light cut through the darkness over it. Frankie's face was tight with worry when he returned to the house the day of the exam. He had little faith in himself as a student, and no experience that hard study paid dividends.

A couple of months later, while he waited for the results of the police exam, Frankie married Pam in a ceremony at St. Margaret's, followed by a small reception in the back room of a modest restaurant called the Old Hook Inn. They spent their honeymoon moving into a tiny one-bedroom apartment behind an Esso station in Pearl River. Pam had a calming effect on Frankie. They held hands and giggled together. He bought a Volkswagen Beetle—which, compared to the muscle cars of his past, made me laugh.

About a month later, Frankie drove the Volkswagen to the George Washington Bridge bus terminal to pick up a copy of *The Chief*, a civil service newspaper where the answers to the exam were published. His hands trembled as he sat in a coffee shop there and compared his answers with those in *The Chief*. By his count, he scored 92. When he received the official result, he found his actual score was 94. With the 5-point bonus given to veterans, his final mark was 99.

3

Although my father still bathed in the glow of his oldest son's success (Eugene had graduated Fort Schuyler with a degree in nuclear fission; then he married his head-turningly beautiful high school sweetheart, Diane Schurerer, and took a job in Newport News, Virginia, where he worked as an engineer on a crew that was replacing the reactor core in the nuclear-powered aircraft carrier U.S.S. *Enterprise*), the subtlest of changes occurred within my father while Frankie was in the Academy. Perhaps he became caught up in his son's enthusiasm; maybe the sight of Frankie in the gray Academy uniform stoked memories of his own youthful optimism as a rookie cop. Frankie, too, seemed to warm in their relationship. He would often stop at the house on Blauvelt Road on the way home from the Academy. I would see his Volkswagen pull in the driveway from the window of my bedroom, and run to the front door. On hearing Frankie's car, our father would put down the book or paper he was reading and wait expectantly for the door to open. They would sit across from each other in the living room: Frankie drinking a beer, my father sucking on hard candy in lieu of the cigars he could no longer stomach. As Frankie would relay the day's events, my father would intently measure each of his words, and judiciously produce statements like "Make sure you keep your nose clean."

Though Frankie would bristle a little at such comments, he seemed happy to have someone with whom he could talk about "the Job." It was on this common ground that Frankie and my father forged a new connection.

My mother would bristle too and, as she always had, come to Frankie's defense. "You don't have to tell him that," she would say to my father. "Frankie knows what to do."

There had always been a deep connection between Frankie and

189

my mother. Her love for him—for all of us, her boys—was obvious and fierce. Yet I never truly knew how she felt about Frankie becoming a cop. She was proud, of course, but would have been proud no matter what his career choice. Still, I remember something melancholy about my mother then. Sometimes, as she listened to her son's cop talk, she would put down her crossword and close her eyes like someone listening to a sad aria on a radio. I realize now that that song had played for the whole of my mother's life, and, for her, it was both painful and impossible not to listen to.

Frankie's first friend in the police department was a fellow recruit named Jimmy McDermott. They actually met while they were both walking from Grand Central Station on the day they were to be sworn in, the first day in the Academy. Like most of the close friends Frankie would make in the department, McDermott was something of a character. Tall and slim, with a wide, freckled face that would be right at home in County Cork, McDermott thought of himself, in Frankie's words, as an instant "hairbag," police parlance for a cop who has been in uniform for a long time. As the two young recruits walked into the elevator in the Academy building on Nineteenth Street, Frankie pressed the button for the second floor, where he knew the swearing-in was being held. "Where do you think you're going?" McDermott asked as he pushed the button for the eighth floor. "The ceremony is all the way upstairs." As Frankie began to disagree, McDermott stopped him in mid sentence. "Listen, I was already on the Job, it's on the eighth floor," he said, filled with bluster. McDermott's confident demeanor made Frankie doubt his own information. When they got off the elevator on the eighth floor there was nothing but a large, empty room. By the time they got back to the second floor, the recruits had already been seated in alphabetical order. All 600 of them had to stand to make room for the latecomers, who, because of the closeness of their last names, sat right next to each other. As they did, the first deputy in charge of personnel shook his head and sarcastically announced: "You two are really starting your career off on the right foot."

As it turned out, Jimmy McDermott hadn't actually been a member of the NYPD; rather, he had worked as a policeman on the New York Central Railroad. When Frankie learned this, he called Jimmy "Choo-choo," a name that caught on with the rest of the Academy cops.

Often, Frankie would meet McDermott at a soda fountain near his home in the Bronx, comparing notes on their nascent police careers and drinking egg creams. The setting was appropriate. For they were kiddy cops, both with innocent visions of what lay ahead for them in the Job: saving the city and the like. And, though Frankie was already well indoctrinated into the world of saloons, he was content passing the time in soda fountains with Jimmy, who didn't drink. Besides, Jimmy was as funny as anybody he had ever met in a bar. Funnier.

One day, Jimmy invited Frankie and another friend up to meet his wife and children. On the train uptown, he warned Frankie not to stare at his wife. "She has this nervous twitch," he said, vaguely explaining that she had been in some kind of accident before they were married. "When people stare at her, it kind of kicks up," Jimmy said. "What the hell are you talking about?" Frankie asked. But Jimmy was adamant. "Please, for my sake, don't stare." Frankie shrugged and promised he wouldn't stare.

On the sidewalk outside his apartment, Jimmy's wife, a pretty girl with dark hair and a round Irish face, stood holding on to a baby stroller with one hand, and the hand of a small child with the other. As Jimmy introduced them, Frankie smiled thinly, then quickly averted his eyes. For a moment she looked at him quizzically, then knowingly at her husband, and then back to Frankie. "He gave you the twitch story, didn't he?" she said with resignation. "I don't have a twitch, he tells everybody the same thing."

* * *

Though, in Frankie's era, the Academy term was only supposed to last six months—910 hours of intensive classroom, physical, and firearms training—he wouldn't actually graduate until May 15, 1968, one year to the day from his swearing-in. Several times during that period, his class was assigned to bolster the manpower in precincts and other units. Less than a month into the Academy, Frankie was assigned to the 47th Precinct in the northeast Bronx. Fearing a reprise of the 1964 and 1965 Harlem race riots, the police brass had decided more cops were needed at the precinct level throughout the city. During his four months at the 47th, Frankie saw little action. The 47th Precinct then was a relatively peaceful command, a residential Italian-American enclave. Plus, the police department's paranoia about riots proved just that, paranoia. Mostly, Frankie was assigned either to be the third man in a patrol car—sort of a watch-and-learn position—or to stand a post on a quiet block. Even though the recruits were allowed to wear blue uniforms—summer-weight shirts and pants—and the lapel pin of the precinct, rather than the traditional Academy grays, Frankie couldn't help but feel like an uninvited outsider. For the most part, he kept his mouth shut and did as he was told.

At the end of that summer, Frankie and Choo-choo McDermott were assigned on a barrier detail for the West Indian Day parade in Brooklyn. When the parade was over, the two Academy rookies began to load the blue wooden sawhorses back onto a truck. They were dressed in civilian clothes—T-shirts and jeans—but both wore their service revolvers on their belts. As they were finishing up, a clearly shaken man approached and told them that someone had been shot just a block or so away. McDermott leaped from the back of the truck, and both he and Frankie ran, following the man to the scene. There a victim lay on the sidewalk, alive, but with a gunshot wound to the chest. The people gathered around on the sidewalk explained that the person responsible for the shooting was in the building in front of which the man lay. Frankie and McDermott unholstered their guns and ran up the stairs. As they reached the third-floor landing, an apartment door opened and a rifle appeared—not pointed at the rookie cops, but barrel first. Frankie grabbed the rifle, and Choo-choo cuffed the man holding it. Just as they began to march their prisoner down the stairs, a group of people arrived, whom Frankie and McDermott believed to be precinct detectives. Later, Frankie found out that in fact they were plainclothes policemen in a detective training unit and still patrolmen in rank. But at that moment, the rookies had every reason to believe that these were detectives, and when the plainclothesmen told Frankie and McDermott to escort the victim to the hospital, while they brought the suspect into the station house, the recruits followed orders.

In the Academy, off-duty guns and a statue called the Mayor's Trophy are awarded to recruits who prove the best in academics and physical condition, and (this category was the most prestigious) make the best arrest. Though they didn't say it at that moment, both Frankie and McDermott believed that they had made the arrest that would secure them the ultimate Academy prize.

In the back of the ambulance, on the way to the hospital, the victim told the two fledgling cops what had happened. He was sitting on the stoop when a man who lived in the building told him to move. When he refused, the man went up to his apartment, returned with the rifle, and shot him point blank. As the man told the story, obviously in shock from his wound, his eyes began to roll up in his head. Frankie held the man's hand as he was wheeled into the emergency room, reassuring him that everything would be all right. But though the doctors valiantly tried to save him, they couldn't. The man died right there on the operating table, with my brother still holding his hand.

A couple of hours later, Frankie and McDermott returned to the station house. As they reported to the desk, a sergeant handed

McDermott an envelope that contained his handcuffs. McDermott asked the sergeant what had happened to the man he and Frankie had arrested. The sergeant told him that the man had already been processed into the system and was at that moment being arraigned in court. McDermott was beside himself. How could the guy be in court without the arresting officers? he asked. The sergeant shook his head. "You didn't arrest him, son," he said. "Those plainclothes guys did."

"We arrested him!" McDermott screamed. "It's a murder case and we arrested him!"

That night, Frankie stopped by the house to tell my father the story. Coincidentally, my father happened to know the squad commander of that particular precinct, and the next morning he gave him a call. "What's going on?" my father asked. "The kids got gypped out of a collar, a nice collar. The least you could do is write up a 49." (A UF 49 is a letterlike interoffice memo form; to give you an indication of the bureaucracy of the police department, if you fill out only half the page, it's called a 49A.) My father asked the squad commander to send a UF 49 to the police commissioner's office, or at least to the precinct commander. The squad commander did neither, and the "gun," the award for best arrest, went to a recruit who foiled an armed robbery while he was off duty. A good arrest, but not a murder.

When the summer of 1967 folded into a chilly New York fall, Frankie thought he would finally be sent back to the Academy to finish his training. He wasn't. As the Christmas holidays neared, he was assigned to Traffic Safety Unit B (the descendant of Tom Skelly's traffic squad). Housed in the old 18th Precinct, by then called Midtown North, Safety Unit B was responsible for the traffic detail in the heart of Manhattan. With just a few months of police experience and no experience as a traffic cop, Frankie found himself in the middle of Herald Square, in front of R. H.

Macy's department store—at Christmastime—besieged by relentless traffic, hordes of package-laden pedestrians, and tourists asking directions to the Statue of Liberty. Though at first he wasn't that familiar with Manhattan, Frankie quickly learned the locations of subway entrances, bus routes, and landmarks. He bought and carried with him the *Red Book*, an information guide to New York. Within just a few days, he had all the material on Midtown memorized.

Just like any other unit of the police department, Traffic had its share of Runyonesque characters. One afternoon, a few days before Christmas, Frankie took his lunch break in the basement of the Horn and Hardart Automat on Thirty-fourth Street and Eighth Avenue. In police parlance, the basement was known as a "coop," a place to have lunch or sneak a cigarette break. That afternoon, while Frankie was eating a sandwich, a traffic cop named Kirby came in and sat at a nearby table. About the size of a city mailbox, but somewhat wider, with a flat, whiskey-burned face, Kirby had worked the corner of Thirty-fourth Street and Eighth Avenue for over twenty years. He knew just about everybody who worked near that busy intersection, and Christmastime was very lucrative for him. Frankie watched as he unbuttoned his choker—the old-time police blouse with a double row of buttons—and removed a handful of envelopes. Each of the envelopes contained a card or note wishing Kirby a happy holiday, and a five- or ten-dollar bill. Though a fair distance away, and pretending not to watch, Frankie could barely contain his laughter as the veteran traffic cop commenced a running commentary on each gift. For his part, Kirby didn't care who was watching, and became more animated with each envelope, until he finally opened one that had two one-dollar bills in it.

"Can you believe this?" he said incredulously, holding the bills between two stubby fingers like he was holding the tail of a dead mouse.

"A fuckin' deuce! The cheap bastard! Merry Christmas my ass, I ought to give it back, da prick."

Years later, when Frankie was working City-Wide Street Crime, he read that Kirby had retired after thirty years. The local businesspeople erected a plaque for him that still hangs on his corner of Eighth Avenue.

It was while working the Christmas traffic detail that Frankie made his first arrest. And with it, some of the veneer peeled off his new career.

The day following the arrest, looking haggard, he sat in the living room and told my father the story. He said it was the toughest fight he had ever been in. With a knowing smile, my father told Frankie that he had better get used to it: New York was filled with tough guys. Frankie took a sip of his beer, nodded, and said, "And some of those guys are women."

The arrest occurred two days before Christmas, while Frankie was assigned to Thirty-third Street and Seventh Avenue. About four o'clock that afternoon, the cars on the side block were stopped dead and backed up all the way to Sixth Avenue. When Frankie walked down Thirty-third Street to investigate, he saw a very large woman spread-eagled on the hood of a cab. At first he thought it was an accident. But as he drew closer, he realized that the woman was drunk. As he went to grab her hand and help her off the cab, she wheeled and whacked him across the side of the head with a nearly empty bottle of Four Roses whiskey, knocking his hat halfway across the street. Frankie was more stunned than hurt, but as he tried to pull the woman out of the street, she removed one of her shoes and with it began beating him on the head. Meanwhile, a crowd gathered around to watch the show.

Frankie said that it got to the point where he was going to have to do something. From his utility belt, he removed the little rubber club called a day stick, but it proved useless, he said, like trying to fight a grizzly bear with a hot dog.

As the woman continued to pummel him with her shoe and the fist of her free hand, the crowd swelled to Times-Square-on-New-Year's-Eve proportions. Blood streamed from Frankie's nose, and his face was red from the mortifying predicament. As the woman backed up, readying for another charge, he had had enough. My brother balled his left hand into a fist, and when she was nearly on him, he hauled off and punched her as hard as he could flush in the face. Wheeling backward, she slammed into a pillar of a building, the force of the collision knocking off her wig, exposing a completely bald head. Stunned by the sight of the hairless woman, Frankie tried to collect himself. But he had little time, in a moment she was up and coming at him again. Finally, a cop from a nearby post arrived and called in a 10-13, "Cop needs assistance." Ultimately it took a half-dozen cops to get the woman in cuffs and in the backseat of a patrol car.

Her name was Bernice Williams, he found out. As he filled out the arrest card in the back room of the station house, Bernice sat cuffed to a metal chair, a broomstick wedged underneath the arms of the chair, immobilizing her like the safety bar in a roller-coaster car. The veins in her bald head throbbed as she fought against her restraints. She let out wild, whooping screams and spat at anyone who passed. Across the room, a thin cop wearing glasses was filling out "alarms," forms on stolen cars. For a long while, the cop sat quietly going about his work as if oblivious to Bernice and her antics. Then, without warning, after one particularly eardrum-piercing scream, he stood, walked over to her, and put his hands on the back of her chair. With frightening speed, he drove her across the tile floor, ramming her headfirst into the cinder-block wall. The force of the impact, Frankie said, was so hard that Bernice's stockings exploded. Without saying a word, the cop went back to his desk, sat down, and continued his task, as Bernice slumped, semiconscious, in the chair.

The next day, at court, Bernice was sober and, incredibly, none the worse for wear. She pleaded guilty to the assault charge and, having a record of attacking policemen, was immediately remanded to jail for six months. On the way out of the courtroom she winked at Frankie.

The incident taught Frankie a lesson. Though he wasn't completely a wide-eyed innocent when he went into the police department, his intentions in becoming a cop were perhaps the purest of any of my relatives who joined the force—he really thought he would be helping people. For all Frankie's atomic anger, underneath he was something of a Boy Scout: He coached Mighty Midget football even though he didn't have a son playing for the team; in a family crisis he could be counted on as the first there and the last to leave. For him, the uniform of the police department was a perfect fit, the teams clearly defined—the good guys wore the blue shirts. But he quickly found out that the job had a way of crushing virtuous traits under the heel of a shined brogan. In the New York City police department, the lines between good and bad became blurred very quickly. Bernice Williams was his introduction to the ambiguity that would cloud many of his experiences as a cop.

For me, the wonder of Frankie's story was enhanced by the difference in the two worlds—the one in which he worked and the one that my father had moved us to. The sign on Veterans Parkway, the exit road off the Palisades toward town, read: "Welcome to Pearl River, the town of friendly people." But among the townfolk, our little hamlet was better known as "lily-white" Pearl River. The only thing I knew about black people was the stories I heard from my father, and with Bernice Williams, the stories contributed by my brother.

While I was growing up in Pearl River, I did know one black kid—not even a whole family; he was an exchange student of sorts who came from Georgia and lived with a family named Graf. I never knew the particulars of why Lionel Macon moved to Pearl River. He was a very dark-skinned child with a big, fast smile and close-cropped hair. We would play basketball in the driveway of the McKeons' house, and when one of the kids called him nigger or spade, Lionel would go into his "happy darkie" routine: His smile grew to his ears and he shuffled his feet.

It was surprising to me, of course, that he wasn't very good at basketball. I mean, he was okay, but just okay—he never did live up to his color on the court. When we all went to high school, with those racist preconceptions in place, the coaches made a spot for him on the junior varsity team. Once, I sat near Macon in the stands watching our varsity squad play against Mount Vernon, a predominantly black team from lower Westchester. During the warm-up, I watched Macon as he intently watched the Mount Vernon team: their lithe black bodies glistening, gracefully cutting through the air to the basket. No one dunked the basketball in those days, at least no one among the puny white players of Pearl River or the other white towns of Rockland County. Yet at least three of the Mount Vernon squad slammed the ball through the hoop, bringing waves of murmurs from the crowd. Mount Vernon won that day, by at least 50 points. With every basket they scored, Macon clapped and whistled. I was angry that he was rooting for the other team. Now, I realize that Pearl River was not, could never be, his team.

Even before Macon's arrival, there were signs that Pearl River was less than welcoming to black people. One of these signs was the controversy caused by a statue of St. Martin de Porres.

When I was about eleven or twelve, my best friend on the block was a boy with a wide, freckled face and bushy brown hair named Henry Reynolds. The two of us would ride our bikes and play softball with the other kids on the block in the parking lot of the Jewish camp at the end of McKinley Street. I always wanted to be on Henry's team. He could hit a softball farther than any of the other kids. He was the oldest of a family that numbered six or seven then, and seemed to add a new member every year. His house was filled with runny-nosed babies in drooping cloth diapers.

Henry's father was in the merchant marine, and not at home much (enough, I guess, to keep his wife always pregnant). Mrs. Reynolds was a gentle, temperate woman, with a soft Irish brogue and a baby permanently clasped to her breast. She was also very religious. Every morning she would load the passel of kids into a dark-green Pontiac station wagon and drive to Mass at St. Aedan's, the new parish church built just a few blocks from McKinley Street.

One late summer night, after dinner, I went down to visit Henry to see if he wanted to take a ride on our bikes. He was sitting on the front stoop of his house, his hands under his chin, his eyes cast down to the ground between his sneakers. He couldn't leave the house, he said, because his mother was at the hospital and he had to watch his brothers and sisters. I didn't ask what was wrong. Henry was not much of a talker.

For an hour or so we sat together in silence. Then Mrs. Reynolds pulled into the driveway. I could see her face was streaked with tears as she rushed by us and into the house without saying a word.

As Henry and I walked our bikes up Champ Avenue, nearing the top of the long, steep hill, he began to explain: His brother John was very sick, and had been rushed to Good Samaritan Hospital that afternoon. I can't recall exactly what the illness was, but I do remember clearly that John's condition was very severe. At first, doctors weren't sure whether he would live. There was talk of brain damage if he did.

I kept vigil with Henry those few days. His father, I think, was away at sea, and his mother spent the time at John's bedside or in St. Aedan's praying to Martin de Porres, patron saint of sick children.

For those not versed in Butler's *Lives of the Saints*, Martin de Porres was black. Though he was born in Peru, of a Peruvian father, his mother was a colored freedwoman from Panama, and Martin inherited his mother's complexion. He founded orphanages and foundling hospitals in Peru, where he lived all of his life. Unlike St. Anthony, my mother's favorite saint, whose statue I would find in every church I visited, and whose illustrated image I'd see in the pages of my religion books, St. Martin wasn't well known—I had no idea who he was or what he looked like. But Mrs. Reynolds knew of the saint. And if a miracle was needed to save her son, it was Martin de Porres who could perform it.

Within a few days, John's condition improved dramatically. And a week or so later, he was home, pale and thin, but heading towards full recovery. When John came home, Mrs. Reynolds was as happy as I can remember seeing her. Her eyes flickered like altar candles, her normally rigid countenance was replaced with the serene glow of an elderly nun on Easter Sunday. Her prayers had been answered.

About a month later, she pulled into her driveway with a box the size of a refrigerator in the back of the station wagon. It contained a four-foot-high statue of St. Martin, which she and Henry promptly positioned on the front lawn of her home. This was her way of showing her gratitude for the saintly intercession. But for the neighbors on McKinley Street, who reacted to it with absolute outrage, it was a threat to the very harmony of the block. No sooner was the statue of St. Martin on the lawn than neighborhood phone lines buzzed with the news.

The family that lived next to the Reynoldses was especially infuriated. One neighbor suggested that they glue a lantern to it so people would think it was a lawn jockey. A city cop who lived up the block said the only thing the statue was missing was handcuffs. One night someone, I never knew who, spray-painted part of the statue's face white.

Mrs. Reynolds answered the neighbors' desecration and snipes by having a brick grotto built around St. Martin and placing a spotlight on the lawn, shining it on the statue day and night. The Reynoldses also acquired an ill-tempered German shepherd who was given just enough leash to reach almost to the street. A stroll past their house would prompt Rommel, the dog, to fly from his lair under the bushes, his chain unraveling with the speed of an anchor chain on an ocean liner, until it snapped taut, yanking Rommel into midair while he bared a mouth filled with frightening teeth. The kids on the block were terrified of Rommel. Even Skipper, my dog, judiciously took the backyard route behind the houses across the street from the Reynolds home on his way to visit one of his paramours in the developments near St. Aedan's.

For a while, McKinley Street became sort of a tourist attraction. Our stickball and touch football games on the normally quiet street were constantly interrupted by curious townsfolk who would drive slowly past to gawk at the statue on their way to mass at St. Aedan's. As the months, then years, went by, the grumbling subsided somewhat. But, for as long as I lived on McKinley Street, St. Martin was never welcome there.

By April, Frankie was back in the Academy building. But again, his stay wouldn't last long. At 3:15 in the morning of April 5, 1968, Police Commissioner Howard R. Leary issued an emergency order that mobilized his entire 28,788-man police force into a thirteen-hour-a-day, six-day-a-week work schedule. The day before, on April 4, Martin Luther King, Jr., had been assassinated in Memphis. Frankie's class was once again assigned to the streets.

Though major rioting erupted in cities across the country—Washington, D.C., Chicago, Baltimore, and Pittsburgh—in New York there were only scattered episodes of violence and looting. The night after Dr. King was shot, a band of black teenagers swarmed through Times Square and Columbus Circle, breaking windows and engaging in fights, and looting occurred in Harlem and Bedford-Stuyvesant. The fear of violence, however, was much worse than the violence itself. Rumors of bombing and mass assaults flooded Manhattan. The paranoia reached such a pitch that on the Friday after Dr. King was assassinated, major corporations like Time, Inc., General Electric, and RCA closed early because of rumors that swarming black mobs were headed downtown.

Though racial tensions would remain extremely high throughout that summer, and indeed, for several years after, within a week after Dr. King's assassination New York was, relatively, back to normal.

During those weeks, the only swarming Frankie saw was of prostitutes around their prospective customers' cars. He was assigned to a post on Thirty-first Street and Eighth Avenue, a few blocks south of the General Post Office building. That strip of Eighth Avenue was favored by hookers known as "tunnel hostesses," who serviced the Jersey trade that came through the Lincoln Tunnel. One night, one of the prostitutes became especially infuriated about Frankie's presence, which had seriously affected her business. Brazenly, she went to the police call box and made a citizen's complaint, saying in an obviously slurred voice that Frankie was harassing her. Frankie took the phone from her hand and spoke to the lieutenant on the line. He explained that the woman was a prostitute and intoxicated. Instead of sending a patrol car to check the validity of the complaint, the lieutenant told him to put her back on the phone and completed the complaint form. Frankie learned another early career lesson that night: Doing your job does not necessarily mean you're not going to get in trouble. Indeed, he would find out, sometimes the harder you did your job, the greater the opportunity for it.

In May, Frankie finally graduated from the Academy. The ceremony was held at the Armory, on Sixty-seventh Street and Lexington Avenue. This time, Frankie, and Jimmy McDermott, would be on time.

The day before the ceremony, my father waited anxiously for him to stop by the house. That week Frankie had filled out what was called a wish list, his top three choices of precincts. My father called Gus Harms, his old Rat Pack cohort, now a full inspector.

"He wants something close to home," my father said. "If there's anything you can do, I'd appreciate it."

With Harms' rank, it would only be a matter of a phone call. But just in case he didn't come through, my father also called the clerical sergeant at the Academy, who had once worked for him as a detective in the Four-One squad.

More and more, Frankie stopped by the house to speak to our father. I would watch how our father straightened in his chair and leaned toward his son when Frankie told a war story or asked a question. They had a way of talking to each other that seemed to exclude everyone else in the room. Frankie had finally found a way of scaling the wall around my father. And in some ways, this newfound closeness was even greater than the usual feeling between father and son. They both now belonged to an insular brotherhood. They were cops.

When Frankie arrived late that afternoon, my father handed him a yellow receipt—the credit slip for his service revolver, which he had turned in on his retirement. Frankie would take the slip to a gun store on Broome Street, near police headquarters. There he traded in the slip for his off-duty gun, a Colt Cobra. Though the event was about as ceremonious as a third beer, the torch was effectively passed that day.

With my father's help, in the middle of May Frankie was assigned to the 34th precinct. He'd been in his new command only a couple of days when he was sent with a detail to Columbia University. He and a dozen other rookie cops were secreted away in a university-owned building in Morningside Heights, one of many such squads housed in Columbia-owned buildings.

A few weeks before, while Frankie was still walking the Eighth Avenue beat, students at Columbia University had commandeered several buildings on campus and held three university officials hostage, including the acting dean, who was barricaded in his office for twenty-four hours. The siege began as a dual protest, against the construction of a university gymnasium on Morningside Park, which the protesters believed was a racist endeavor, meant to serve university students and not the poor residents of the neighborhood; and the university's association with the Institute for Defense Analysis, which the protesters believed aided the war in Vietnam and studied methods of controlling antiwar protests. The uprising was led by Mark Rudd, the campus president of Students for a Democratic Society (SDS) and was joined by members of the Congress of Racial Equality (CORE) and other black organizations. The seizure completely shut down the university. Classes and other school activities were canceled. It also focused the eyes of the entire nation on Columbia.

For several days, university officials wavered between requesting police action and resolving the dispute themselves. Even the faculty was divided on the issue, with an ad hoc group of professors siding with the demonstrators. But as the days drew on, and an outside mediator's efforts proved fruitless, the prospect of the conflict ending without police involvement became increasingly remote.

By 1968, anticop sentiment had reached perhaps the highest level in modern history, especially among two groups: college students protesting the war in Vietnam, who viewed police as representatives of the establishment; and parts of the black community, who saw cops as racist. For public relations–conscious police department officials, the Columbia riots were a potential nightmare. The last thing the police department needed then was to be drawn into a student protest rife with racial overtones. Still, on April 30, at 2:30 a.m (a time, as one police official quoted in *The New York Times* put it, "when Harlem was asleep"), at the university's request, a force of 1,000 New York City cops wearing riot gear swept onto the campus, removing and arresting the protesters. Although the police tactics that night were widely criticized, and there were several reported injuries to students (and policemen), the raid effectively brought an end to the occupation. But it did little to ease the tension.

Throughout that spring, the campus remained a tinder box. Rallies and protests were common. There were rumors of further occupations, and agitators with bullhorns stirred the already strained emotions. Columbia asked the police department to maintain a presence in case tensions erupted again. The school officials wanted the cops on the premises, but they also wanted them out of plain sight.

As the days went by, and the likelihood of another student takeover lessened, cops assigned to Columbia became lulled into a boring routine. Frankie and the others in his squad spent their time playing cards and eating hero sandwiches from a local deli. But one day, there were rumors that a planned protest had the possibility of turning violent. A speaker at a rally promoting the protest had announced: "We are taking the campus back."

The lieutenant in charge of Frankie's detail was a man named Dan Brady, who lived in Pearl River. When the phone rang in the cops' basement apartment, Brady picked it up. On the line was a deputy chief checking on manpower. Brady, in a field general's tone, told the boss that he had "a hundred men with hats and bats at the ready." Overhearing this, the dozen or so cops in the room, including Frankie, looked at each other, perplexed. A half-hour later, the deputy chief arrived. On seeing just Brady with the twelve officers—plus the decks of cards and the remnants of the sandwiches—the chief became incensed.

"You told me you had a hundred men here!" he shouted.

Brady shrugged. "How was I supposed to know you weren't the enemy?"

The next day, Brady's secret squad was reassigned, the rumors of trouble proved unfounded, and Frankie was placed at a post at the main gate to the university, at 116th and Broadway. Though he was well aware of the antipolice sentiment on the campus (and practically everywhere else, for that matter), he hadn't realized how deep it ran. Like a Buckingham Palace guard, he stood stone-faced as students passed calling him "pig" and giving him the finger. His orders were explicit: Do not engage the students for any reason. One student, a girl no more than nineteen, spat in his face as she walked by. Later that same night, Frankie stopped by the Commodore for a beer and relayed the story to another city cop.

"Right now," the cop said philosophically, "it's us against everybody else. It's time to circle the wagons."

Frankie was the first to come to the aid of a friend in trouble, but with cops, sometimes the distress signals aren't so clear. Such was the case with Jimmy McDermott. Frankie's close relationship with his first friend on the force lasted only through the term of the Academy. It goes that way in the police department. As my brother often said, you make intense friendships with partners, even fellow precinct or unit members, and then transfers jettison those people from your life.

On graduating from the Academy, McDermott was sent to the precinct in Central Park This was the cause of a great deal of good-natured ribbing by Frankie and others of their Academy class. McDermott had thought of himself as something of a "super-cop," one who would right all the wrongs in the city. In Central Park, he ended up policing nuts and squirrels.

Periodically, throughout their careers, my brother and Jimmy ran into each other at police rackets and functions. They even talked on the phone once in a while. McDermott eventually worked his way out of Central Park and into the 32nd Precinct in Harlem, the precinct my father had worked in his short tenure as a patrol sergeant. There McDermott built a reputation as a very good cop, and ultimately he was assigned to the Emergency Service Unit. For the most part, Emergency Service is made up of the true elite of the department. Some cops do gain entrance into Emergency Service by being "hooked up," police parlance for having good connections, but by and large those cops are the exceptions. According to my brother and others, Jimmy McDermott earned his way into Emergency Service.

As the years went by, my brother all but lost touch with his old Academy pal. He had heard through the grapevine that Jimmy had become involved in politics: first in the Bronx, where he lived, and later with American sympathizers of the struggles in Northern Ireland. Then one day my brother learned that Jimmy had died—by his own hand. At Jimmy's funeral, Frankie was told by other cops that Jimmy had some kind of trouble with one of his kids. But what was obvious to Frankie, and the rest of the cops gathered in the church that day, was that Jimmy McDermott's emotional problems ran much deeper than those caused by even the worst of family disputes. The night of the incident, he had had an argument with his kid on the steps of his home. At some point during the argument, he went inside his house and got his gun. He then returned to the front stoop, and right in front of his son, he shot himself in the head.

According to a recent survey by Columbia University, policemen are four to five times more likely to kill themselves than are regular citizens. There are obvious reasons for this, not the least of which is that they have guns. But the tragic ending of Jimmy McDermott's life demonstrates circumstances that no statistics can capture. Sometimes, cops who are heroic, devoted, and, like Jimmy, have a sparkling sense of humor live with inner demons so ferocious that even in a job fraught with as much peril as theirs, the most dangerous person such a cop will ever face is himself.

4

The apartment in Pearl River where Frankie and Pam first lived was in a Victorian house on Henry Street, one of the houses built during the 1920s, when industrial growth brought prosperity to the town. The windows in their living room looked down on the Esso station. They had a threadbare couch, a secondhand dining room set with unmatched chairs (all gifts from Pam's mother) and one of those old-fashioned, round-edged refrigerators that hummed like a mosquito zapper in a Texas roadside diner. Frankie was twenty-four, Pam just twenty-two.

When Pam gave birth to Laura, their first child, she was in labor for nearly twenty-four hours. In the waiting room of Nyack Hospital sat Eugene and Diane, Pam's mother, Ann, and Pam's brother, Clem. One of the nurses told Pam she had better hurry—because, the nurse said, her family was waiting on her.

Pam assured the nurse she was trying her hardest.

With the arrival of Laurie, the first order of business for the new parents was to find a bigger apartment—no easy feat in Pearl River, a town almost wholly made up of private houses. Buying a house was then well beyond their reach. After a few weeks of searching, they finally found an apartment slightly bigger than the one they had, near the center of the small business district on Franklin Avenue. It was a convenient location for Pam, who, without a car, could walk to the laundry with the baskets filled with dirty diapers, and to markets for groceries, baby clothes, and formula. But it was nearly impossible for a young family to exist in suburbia on Frankie's starting yearly salary of $7,022. Though Frankie worked "around-the-clock" tours, his schedule changing every week (day tours for five days, "four-to-twelves" for five days, midnights for four days), he managed to pick up some extra money working part-time for a construction company he had worked for in high school. Though moonlighting was still against regulations, the police department looked the other way as long as cops didn't work as bartenders or strikebreakers, or take any job that necessitated the carrying of a firearm. One side job he had was at a rail shipping company on Thirty-third Street and Twelfth Avenue. One day a week he'd work an 8 p.m–to–8 a.m. shift on a loading dock, guarding the "crib car," a railroad car loaded with such desirables as cameras, stereos, and other items with a propensity for growing legs. In the wintertime, it seemed the coldest place on the planet—an open loading dock next to the Hudson River. Frankie'd stuff newspaper in his shirt, constantly walk back and forth, once in a while sneak a few hundred yards down Twelfth Avenue to grab a little warmth from a trash can blaze, something the longshoreman called a Harlem heater.

With Frankie working an extra job, and Pam home nursing Laurie, they didn't exactly have a bustling social calendar. When they did try to have some fun, it mostly consisted of inviting friends over for a few beers and a pizza, or, once in a while, a dinner out at an inexpensive restaurant called Steak & Brew, which served unlimited pitchers of beer during the meal. Frankie had continued his friendships with some of the Brothers, who had then returned from Vietnam. Several of them—Bobby Myers, Willie Ahlmyer, and Bobby Stevenson—had joined the Orangetown Police Department. Frankie and Pam also struck up friendships with other New York City cop families in Rockland. One of the cops, Phil McAleer, a sergeant on the West Side of Manhattan, told Frankie he was wasting his money paying rent and should buy a house instead. Frankie told Phil that he'd love nothing better, but didn't have the money for a down payment. By the late 1960s, homes in Pearl River had already begun to climb in price; long gone were the $500 down payments of our father's day.

"Ask your dad to help you out," McAleer urged.

For Frankie, going to his father for advice—even to use his influence for assignments in the police department—was one thing, but going to him to borrow money was quite another. McAleer's suggestion, however, had planted an idea that would begin to consume Frankie's thoughts: He would get the money for a down payment somehow, even if he had to work three jobs.

After he was pulled from the Columbia University detail, in late May 1968, Frankie was brought back to the 34th Precinct and assigned to a foot post. He was finally a cop with a precinct.

Though there are cops who are happy to walk a beat (Christy Smith, a cop Frankie worked with in the 34th Precinct, was a foot patrolman the whole of his thirty-year career and was known as the mayor of Dyckman Street), Frankie had greater aspirations. The first step up the ladder for a beat cop is a "sector car." In one of their living room chats, Frankie asked my father the best way to go about getting assigned to one. "Get noticed," my father said, advising him to "build a batting average" and "make a lot of arrests." Frankie took the advice to heart and quickly learned the street.

In those early days on the beat, he arrested a number of purse snatchers—who preyed on elderly women walking home from church on St. Nicholas Avenue—and shoplifters near the stores on Broadway and 181st Street. One of the first tricks he learned was to look for the glassine envelopes that junkies would leave behind on the sidewalks in front of buildings where they got high. Quite often, on the rooftops of those buildings, he would catch an addict in the act of shooting up. One day he found a shooting gallery on 165th Street and in it saw dozens of handbags with broken straps. That address became a gold mine of arrests for him, as he would wait for junkies to return with a just-snatched purse, or from copping their drugs. He once foiled a confidence team that had convinced a woman they were bank examiners trying to catch a crooked teller. The con men had talked the woman into helping them—by making a withdrawal from her account. Frankie didn't make the arrest, turning the case over to the detective squad, but he bolstered his standing in the precinct.

For Frankie, the job was fun. He liked the way he looked in the uniform. He liked the authority it gave him. But most of all, he liked that he was good at the work. It was as though the whole of his prior existence had led him to his job: being the son (and grandson) of a cop; his childhood on the streets of the Bronx; the tough-guy persona of his football days and with the Brothers. His life experience, his bloodlines, had endowed him with an inherent knowledge of police work. Even all the disappointments of his school years, the nuns who had told him he would amount to nothing more than a hooligan, mattered little now. Or so he thought.

One night he was taken off his regular beat and assigned a post at a dance at Mother Cabrini High School. The nun in charge of the festivities came to Frankie and, in a frightening replay of his days in St. Margaret's, ordered him to move from his post to another position.

"Excuse me," Frankie said resentfully. "I don't think I work for you."

The nun's face went white with anger, a look Frankie was all too familiar with.

"We'll see about that," she said, as she turned and stormed away.

Fifteen minutes later, a radio car pulled up, the window rolled down about four inches, and a gravelly voice came from within.

"Did you speak to the nun?" the sergeant asked curtly.

Frankie admitted he had.

"Well, when she tells you to do something, you do it! And don't give her any more shit." The window went up and the radio car pulled away.

Frankie stood there for a moment or two, his jaw scraping his shoes. Given his history with nuns, the irony of the event left him with only unprintable words to express his feelings.

At the end of the dance the same nun approached Frankie and Billy Rutter, the other cop assigned to the school, and handed them each an envelope. Inside was a crisp $5 bill. Frankie's first exposure to police corruption was perpetrated by a nun.

Along with Jimmy McDermott, Billy Rutter was one of Frankie's first friends in the police department. They had been in the Academy together, and were both assigned to the 34th Precinct. Rutter also lived in Rockland County, and often they car-pooled to work. Frankie would kid Rutter about his patchwork Corvair, which he was always putting junkyard parts into. Rutter was an affable fellow with an easygoing sense of humor. He needed one. Not only did he take a ribbing about his car, he wore a bad toupee, which, after several Budweisers, would invariably slip to the side of his head, making him look like an accident victim.

One night, when Frankie was reporting for a night tour, the captain of the precinct, John Charles Daly, a dinosaur of a cop, well into his sixties, was walking down the steps of the precinct house. "Jump behind the wheel of that radio car, son," Daly ordered. "We're taking a little ride."

Two days before, *The New York Times* had printed a front-page exposé on cops cooping on duty. The story had rankled the brass at headquarters, and had even drawn Mayor Lindsay's attention, so orders were issued to precinct commanders to put an end to cops catching catnaps instead of bad guys. The best-known coop in the 34th Precinct was under the 207th Street Bridge, which was the exact location where Daly directed Frankie to drive.

Frankie knew that there was a real good chance of someone getting caught. But as a rookie cop, who had spoken all of six words to his captain (*"Good morning, captain,"* twice), he wasn't exactly in a position to try and talk Daly out of his plans. Sure enough, they pulled under the bridge, and there sat a sector car. But the worst was yet to come: As they rolled closer, their headlight illuminated the scene of a cop, in full uniform, taking a tire

off an abandoned Ford Fairlane. On a closer look, my brother realized that the cop was Billy Rutter. Holy shit, Frankie muttered,
holding his forehead in his hand. The captain stepped from the
car. Rutter, still holding the tire under one arm, addressed Daly
with a crisp salute. Meanwhile, Rutter's partner was sound asleep
in the radio car.

For weeks, Rutter thought Frankie had set him up. But finally, after buying him a few Budweisers, Frankie convinced him it was
none of his doing. With the two new openings in sector cars
(Rutter and his partner were demoted to foot posts), Frankie was
assigned Sector G, or George, and his new partner was a cop
named Paul Gibbons.

Lanky, with a wild head of straw-colored hair, Gibbons had a
reputation as an arrest machine. A seasoned cop, he taught Frankie
the nuances of radio car patrol. "Keep turning corners" was his
catch-phrase. Though simple, the tactic was brilliant. With Gibbons at the wheel, the green-black-and-white Dodge radio car
took on the characteristics of a panther, prowling the darkness of
the Washington Heights side streets. Each corner they turned
gave them the element of surprise. That first year together, Gibbons and Frankie led the precinct in arrests—and each arrest paid
a dividend.

"Collars for dollars" was a favorite saying of cops in those days.
With each arrest, overtime in court put Frankie one step closer to
a down payment on a house. Though money, and the prospect
of one day owning his own home, were important to Frankie,
he wasn't a mercenary. There was enough crime in Washington
Heights then that he and Gibbons didn't have to rely on collaring
drug users who boosted radios from cars and steaks from super-
markets to survive. Instead, they tried to focus on those who sold
them the heroin. And, information on dealers was easy to develop. A junkie facing a bust—and however many days in jail, with

the horrors of withdrawal—would inform on dealers without so much as a second thought.

For Frankie, just as the collars brought him closer to the down payment, they also brought him closer to his ultimate career goal—the gold shield of the Detective Division.

In his last years at the 41st Precinct, my father had worked for the man who then ran the Bronx Borough Detective Division and since then had become the chief of detectives. About this time, he arranged for Frankie to have a meeting with the man. During the short meeting at the chief's office, Frankie was promised that he would "get a call."

Though Frankie'd only been a cop for a few years then, using my father's influence to open the door to the Detective Division wasn't that big a favor. There were plenty of detectives with less time on the job than Frankie had whose entry into the division was secured by their fathers, who worked as bartenders on Fordham Road or in cop bosses' haunts in Manhattan, the contract having been sealed with the picking up of a small bar tab and a wink of the eye. Many a contract to the Detective Division was made after mass in the parking lot of St. Margaret's Church. In fact, the Catholic church itself often wielded its formidable influence to secure promotions and assignments in the police department. One contemporary of my father's, a detective who lived in Pearl River, had once studied to be a priest. He kept up friendships with his fellow seminarians, and one of them rose to become the personal secretary to New York's then archbishop, Francis Cardinal Spellman. While still laboring as a patrolman, the ex-seminarian called his priest friend and asked for a favor. Soon after, the chief of detectives received a call from Spellman, and a promotion to the Detective Division was arranged.

But Frankie once told me there is an old adage in the police department: "When you're in, you're the best; when you're out, you're a pest." My father was out, and Frankie never received the call he was promised.

* * *

After a year together, Frankie and Gibbons were assigned to the "school car"—a promotion of sorts, patrolling one of the busiest sections of Washington Heights—George Washington High School and the immediate surrounding area. Because of increased violence in the schools, a result of severe overcrowding, extended school hours to make up time lost during teacher strikes, and the increase in juvenile illegal-drug use, a special unit was formed in December 1968 to patrol school grounds and the areas immediately around them. The overcrowding in George Washington High was so bad the school held three sessions a day. The crime problem around the school reached the point where shop owners would lock their doors—some even shutting down completely—during school recesses.

In June 1969, Frankie and Gibbons responded to a call about an unruly crowd assembled outside the high school. An agitator who billed himself as a Black Panther was preaching from the front steps. The principal demanded of Frankie and Gibbons that the man be removed. When Gibbons tried to grab the agitator's arm, the would-be Panther (it turned out he was not a member of the party) punched him in the jaw, knocking him sprawling down the steps. Frankie began to wrestle the man, trying to get his cuffs on him. Gibbons, dazed but back on his feet, went to Frankie's aid. Meanwhile, the crowd became hostile. They chanted for the man's release. Frankie called for backup as he and Gibbons dragged the agitator through the crowd, being pummeled and pulled. When they finally got into the radio car, Frankie sighed with relief. But the students surrounded the car and began rocking it. He was sure they were going to tip over—the car was at least up on two wheels. Just then he heard the sirens of the backup on the way. For Frankie and Gibbons, those sirens were like the bugle of the cavalry.

The backup teams were led by a tough veteran sergeant who had no qualms about using his nightstick, and the scene escalated into a riot. Finally, Frankie was able to move the radio car through the mass of students and cops. Safely away from the scene, the two partners looked at each other and shook their heads.

"That could have been really bad," Gibbons said, with typical understatement.

In the backseat, the agitator's attitude changed dramatically. He became polite and soft-spoken, no doubt sure that he was headed for a beating in the station house. He didn't receive one. Frankie and Gibbons were content to have escaped with their lives. Later, Gibbons complained about his jaw, which had taken the first blow. He had it checked at nearby Columbia Presbyterian Hospital and found it had been slightly fractured. From that day on, it clicked when he talked.

With each passing month of 1968, violence against police became more frequent and frightening. In August that year, two police officers responding to what turned out to be a false alarm walked into a trap and were shotgunned. Though they survived, both were badly wounded. In November, a bomb exploded outside a Harlem station house, close enough to shatter most of the windows. But cops weren't just victims: In September, off-duty police officers had attacked members of the Black Panther Party outside a Brooklyn courthouse where a Panther was on trial for assaulting a cop. Lines had been drawn. The sides were clearly delineated. Things, as Frankie would say, were heating up.

Frankie and Gibbons's next step up the precinct ladder was an assignment to the "narcotics car." What was ludicrous, the narcotics car was a regular patrol car, about as inconspicuous as an ice cream truck during a heat wave. By 1969, there was a nationwide explosion of drug abuse. In New York City, desperate narcotics addicts—and the business of supplying them drugs—became the number one cause of crime. Nowhere was this more in evidence than in the 34th Precinct.

Washington Heights was then a neighborhood in transition, with a high percentage of teenagers—the sons and daughters of a recent Hispanic infusion into the area. It was also easily accessible from New Jersey, just over the George Washington Bridge. This was the time when Washington Heights first became known as a drug bazaar, a marketplace for suburban as well as local users. The narcotics division of the NYPD then numbered only 800 full-time cops. By 1970, there were over 40,000 narcotics arrests, nearly 70 percent of those for heroin. Of the more than 100,000 felons arrested that year, nearly 20 percent admitted to being addicts. And it seems likely that the number who chose not to confess their addictions would boost that percentage significantly higher. These statistics also did not include dealers and suppliers of narcotics, a percentage of whom—at least the smart ones—were not addicts. Even at the most conservative estimates, the narcotics business was now responsible for fully half of felony crimes.

The brain trust at police headquarters worked full-time trying to stem the rising crime rates. Meanwhile, an inspector of the 5th Division decided to abolish the narcotics car and strip away the obvious indicators that marked cops in the street. In the precincts of the 5th Division, including the 34th, uniform cops assigned to the narcotics units would be put in plainclothes and unmarked cars. It was a radical move, but it worked. Soon after, Police Commissioner Patrick Murphy authorized the use of up to 5 percent of each precinct's uniform force for this innovative program. His edict was carried out despite two major roadblocks. One, department regulations forbade uniform cops to work in plainclothes (although a few special squads, such as gambling and vice, were exempt from this rule). Two, there were no funds available for unmarked cars. A waiver was obtained to override the plainclothes regulations, but finding the money for the cars was impossible, because New York City was entering a fiscal crisis that would last for a decade. In an unorthodox move, cops were authorized to use their personal cars as undercover vehicles. Some of the cops assigned to the narcotics units balked at the idea, but Frankie and Gibbons both decided to do it. Gibbons had little to lose, since he drove a green 1962 Volkswagen Beetle, but Frankie had just bought, with a few dollars down and a heavy monthly loan payment, a brand-new Plymouth Duster. The police department would pay for gas but not for repairs of any damage incurred in the line of duty.

For Frankie, if his new assignment meant a couple of dents in the Duster, so be it. The new unit was his chance to see real action—to "get noticed," as his father advised. Though undercover policing has its downside (in the heat of the chase it is hard to tell the good guys from the bad; undercover cops are regularly involved in scary near-misses with the uniform force. And, for drug dealers, the difference between an undercover bust and a stickup team looking to rip them off is nearly imperceptible), for Frankie, the rewards were well worth the risk. For him, Undercover was a field where gold shields grew like dandelions.

Though this makeshift approach to police work was irregular, to say the least, the unit was an immediate success. The arrest rate grew considerably, and with it, Frankie's reputation.

For the first time in his career, my brother did not wear a patrolman's uniform to work. Instead he donned jeans and a Jets football jersey, number 13 (belonging to Don Maynard, one of his favorite players). His hair was long, nearly shoulder-length, red near the ends, and it curled up in the back. To the seasoned observer he still looked like a cop, that was for sure. The Irish-ruddy complexion and his thin lips pressed in a tough-guy smirk remained even when the uniform came off. But he certainly didn't look like the other city cops, and he certainly fooled the bad guys often enough.

But being this new type of policeman brought with it a kind of split personality. In Pearl River, Frankie was struggling with all the typical problems of other young suburban marrieds: money and children, trying to plan and save for schools, doctors, Little League and soccer teams. In Washington Heights, he was a guerrilla fighting a battle on darkened city streets, in alleys and on rooftops. At home he was a father who put his whole heart into trying to build a home for his family. In the city, that heart was often covered with a bulletproof vest.

In 1970, Pam gave birth to their second daughter, Patrice. Now, with two babies in diapers, she had little time to worry about her husband, but she could not stave off the dread that accompanied each story Frankie told when he returned from work. She lived in a kind of suspended terror. Each time the phone rang late at night, a cold shiver ran through her. One night, the local TV news led with a story of an undercover cop killed in Washington Heights. The report did not give the name of the officer, pending notification of his family. Pam sat in front of the TV watching the on-the-scene report—the police cars with "34" emblazoned on their sides, the flashing lights, the dark street starkly illuminated by the TV lights—and felt her heart race.

As soon as he had the chance, Frankie called Pam to tell her he was all right, and that, because of the shooting, he would have to work late. Lying awake in their bed, she had answered the phone on the first ring, and, during the short conversation with her husband, pretended that she hadn't watched the news.

About the same time, there had been a rash of robberies and murders of taxi drivers in New York. Cabbies, concerned about their safety, refused to work the late-night shifts, causing a shortage of taxis on the streets. Those who did drive at night equated black people with crime and often refused to pick them up. They also sped away from fares with destinations in high-crime neighborhoods like Harlem and Bedford-Stuyvesant in Brooklyn. The city began discussions of allowing off-duty cops to work as cabbies on the night shifts, when most of the crimes occurred. It was not an original idea. In Philadelphia the program had been instituted some years earlier with great success. As in Philadelphia, the New York cops would carry their revolvers.

For Frankie, and other industrious cops, the program was a godsend. Once he obtained his taxi driver's license, he could just show up at night at any number of cab companies and be assured of work. And even though the moonlighting cops were mostly assigned cabs without a Plexiglas partition—this innovation came about in response to the wave of violent crimes—the money was good, even terrific. Cabbies in those days kept 49 percent of all they made, plus tips. On the average, Frankie was taking down $100 a night from his second job. With extra money like that coming in three, sometimes four nights a week, a down payment for a home was squarely in his sights.

Pam wasn't thrilled with the idea of spending so much time alone, not to mention that her husband was now working two of the most dangerous jobs in New York. But she, too, was excited by the prospect of a home of her own, and she tried not to worry.

Though it meant incredibly long workdays, sometimes stretching to seventeen or eighteen hours, Frankie enjoyed driving a cab. It gave him the opportunity to learn the city: the location of landmarks, of good restaurants and hotels. He learned the streets— knowledge that later on in his career would prove invaluable. He learned the fastest routes to the airports and knew his way around the maze of Greenwich Village. He even learned the outer boroughs, Brooklyn and Queens. Whether because of his desire to make as much money as he could, the swaggering confidence he had as a tough guy and a cop, or the revolver strapped in his ankle holster, he never refused a fare, no matter how dangerous the destination or what color the skin of the hand waving him down.

One night, after dropping a fare off in the theater district, he drove up Eighth Avenue, where a man flagged him down. He pulled over, and the man held the door open as two other men appeared from a doorway and jumped into the backseat. Something was wrong. He asked the destination and one of the men said only:

"Just drive uptown."

Frankie watched his three passengers in the rearview mirror. At one point his eyes met those of one of the men, and they held each other's gaze for some moments. Again, Frankie asked where they wanted to go, and again "Uptown," was the only answer. Frankie gently reached his hand down his leg and removed the revolver from his ankle holster, then slid it between his legs. Every fiber in his body, all the experience of his two years on the street, told him that this situation was not good. He kept watch in the rearview mirror as furtive glances were exchanged among his passengers. He decided he had to do something to put himself at the advantage. He casually removed the revolver from between his legs and held it against the steering wheel, then turned again to the backseat and in an overly friendly tone asked the destination once more.

"Right here," said the spokesman of the three. "You can leave us right here, man."

Between them, they barely had enough for the two-dollar fare, paid in nickels and dimes.

As often happens between partners, Gibbons and Frankie became good friends. On many occasions, Pam and Frankie went to the Gibbonses' home in Babylon, Long Island, to visit; a few times they stayed overnight. Gibbons later moved to Pearl River. But, as close as they became, sitting in a car with each other for at least eight hours a day, five days a week, going on three years, there were, as there are in the best of friendships, uncomfortable times. What bothered Frankie most about Gibbons was how much he liked to talk. He wasn't a braggart, which Frankie would not have put up with. What poured from Gibbons's mouth was just a constant babbling monologue about anything and everything. Over their years together, Frankie learned to tune his partner out, nodding and "mmmming" his way through the verbal barrage.

Gibbons thought himself a bit of a gourmand, and on dinner breaks, he would often stop at a local butcher shop and order a shell steak, then go to the Legion Diner and have the short-order cook broil it for him. Sometimes he would go to Yingie's Chinese restaurant and emerge with an amazing array of cartons of spare ribs, sweet-and-sour pork, fried dumplings, and other delicacies. Invariably, as Frankie and Gibbons sat eating behind the Isabella Nursing Home, their favorite meal-break coop, a call would come over the radio to which they would have to respond. Frankie would take his time and replace the covers on his food, but Gibbons would just toss it out of the window. If the call proved inconsequential, Gibbons would sit like a dog under a dinner table watching Frankie eat. "What? You're not going to give me none?" he'd ask.

Though at times Gibbons wore on his patience, Frankie's partner had an innocent quality that was quite endearing. One of his favorite hobbies was baking. The cop who for several years made the most arrests in the 34th Precinct also made holiday cookies and elaborately frosted cakes, which he would sometimes present to other cops in the precinct on their birthdays. Gibbons also had a reputation for the kind of frankness that made even the most jaded cop's jaw drop. Whether it was his vasectomy or any aspect of his sex life, no matter was too personal or sacrosanct for him to address, and rank was never an obstacle to disclosure. Often, Frankie would hold his head in his hand as his partner approached a commanding officer and began a discussion on the most intimate of subjects.

Another aspect of Gibbons's personality that wore on Frankie was his hypochondria. He was always complaining about his back, his kidneys, a twisted ankle, a cold he was sure was going to develop into pneumonia. He called in sick often, for the slightest of reasons. He did, however, have one malady that was not psychosomatic—asthma. Several times he collapsed during chases.

One day, when Frankie and Gibbons were still in the sector car, they had received a call to respond to the Dyckman Houses on Nagle Avenue. It was a medical emergency involving a baby, and an ambulance was also directed to the scene. But Gibbons and Frankie, just a block or two away, arrived first. In the lobby a table was set up and several tenants were collecting signatures for a petition to fix the elevators: They were out of order, and had been apparently for some time. The baby was on the twelfth floor. Both Frankie and Gibbons charged up the staircase. Frankie was nearly to the twelfth floor before he realized Gibbons was no longer behind him. There was no time, however, to locate his partner. The baby's mother stood in the open doorway of her apartment screaming hysterically.

Inside the dining room area, on a waist-high hutch, the baby lay in a plastic bathtub. She was so small, so completely motionless, that to Frankie the tiny girl looked like a doll. A blue doll, because the baby had ingested the bathwater and couldn't breathe. When Frankie was a child living in our Bronx apartment, a neighbor, Mrs. Farrell, banged on the door screaming that her baby was drowning in the bath. Frankie remembered my mother running into the Farrells' apartment, picking the baby up by his feet, and slapping him hard on the back. Emulating her, Frankie took the infant and gave her a whack. As though a thermos jug spigot had opened, a gush of water spilled from the baby's mouth, and she began to cry. Just then, the Emergency Service Unit and the ambulance workers came into the apartment. A sergeant arrived and asked what happened. When Frankie told him, he said: "Write this one up, it's a good one."

On the way down the stairs Frankie saw Gibbons sitting on a landing, an oxygen mask on his face.

"You okay, Paul?" he asked.

More embarrassed than anything else and in a voice muffled by the mask, Gibbons said: "Keep this to yourself."

After an examination at the hospital, the baby returned home that same night, and for months after, Frankie kidded his partner on his missed shot at being the hero. Although paradoxically long-winded and short on breath, Gibbons had one trait that Frankie completely admired: He was absolutely fearless.

On a hot early-fall day in 1970, Gibbons and Frankie sat in the Duster, stuck in traffic on 177th Street. Gibbons tugged uncomfortably at his red-raspberry summer shirt, regaling Frankie with several theories on how to solve New York City's traffic problem. In the middle of his rhetorical riff, a call came over the radio about a robbery in progress just two blocks away. Gibbons opened the door and jumped from the car. Frankie was about to follow, then realized he couldn't leave the Duster, with only a thousand or so miles on it, in the middle of the street. It took him maybe five minutes to snake his way through traffic to the building where the robbery was taking place. When he arrived, there was no sign of Gibbons. Then, as Frankie was about to enter the building, two shots rang out. A woman passing by began to scream, and pointed into an adjacent alley. There a body lay motionless. From where he stood, all Frankie could see was that the form was wearing a bright red shirt.

For a split second, he stood paralyzed in horror, believing his partner lay there dead. But just as quickly the fear evaporated: Gibbons's high-pitched shout for help came from the building. Frankie drew his service revolver and raced up the steps. A door to an apartment on the fifth floor was flung wide open. Inside, Gibbons and one of the robbers were on the floor, wrestling for Gibbons's gun, which lay just out of their reach. With a surge of adrenaline, Frankie flew into the apartment and in one graceful motion, as hard as he could, kicked Gibbons's opponent in the face. Reeling backward, the man slammed into the wall, then slumped unconscious back to the floor.

Gibbons thought he had shot the man who'd fallen to the alley. He hadn't intended to, he told Frankie in a quivering voice, but his gun discharged when the other robber jumped on him. But in fact Gibbons hadn't shot the guy. The man in the alley was trying to escape through the window, the same way the two suspects had entered the apartment. The technique was called a stepover: Burglars would go out a hallway window, then jump to an apartment window ledge to one side of the hall window. The man who lay in the alley had missed the hallway window ledge in his attempt to escape and fallen the five stories.

In several minutes, the apartment was filled with uniform cops who had responded to the second call of "shots fired." When the patrol sergeant arrived, having seen the one burglar lying in the alley, and the unconscious one in the apartment, he asked Frankie what had happened. Still confused by the rapid events, Frankie said he wasn't sure.

"Well, I'm taking a walk," the sergeant said. "When I come back have a story."

Whenever a cop shoots his gun, a detailed written report is filed, and the gun has to be tested by ballistics. Though Gibbons denied that he meant to fire his weapon, and even though he was undoubtedly within his right to shoot if he had intended to, the fact that his weapon had discharged meant a full investigation. And several aspects of the incident didn't fall in Gibbons's favor: Frankie had arrived on the scene after the fact, and there were no other corroborating witnesses; also, there was the physical condition of the two robbers—the man in the alley seriously hurt from the fall, and the man in the apartment with quite a dent in his head from Frankie's size 11 shoe.

Back at the station house, filling out the numerous reports (Gibbons, who had wrenched his back in the struggle, had been taken to the hospital for tests), Frankie was approached by a clerical sergeant. The sergeant, perhaps realizing that for him the case had all the characteristics of a nightmare of forms and reports, dropped an application for a newly formed unit in front of Frankie.

"Why don't you and your partner give it some thought," the sergeant said.

The application was for a unit called Anti-Crime, an experimental, undercover squad that would almost immediately become one of the most heralded crime-fighting tools in the history of the New York City police department.

5

On the night of May 21, 1971, as two New York city police officers lay clinging to life in New York Hospital, my brother Frankie and his fill-in partner, a cop named McQuaid (Gibbons had called in sick), were working Anti-Crime in the 34th Precinct. Two days before, Patrolmen Thomas Curry and Nicholas Binetti had been sitting in a patrol car stationed in front of Manhattan District Attorney Frank Hogan's home at 404 Riverside Drive, a quiet and fashionable street that winds along the Hudson River. Six days earlier, Hogan's prosecution of thirteen Black Panthers for conspiring to bomb police stations and kill police officers had resulted in a not-guilty verdict on all counts, a verdict that had left the police department vibrating from shock. During the trial, angry Panther demonstrations outside the courthouse erupted into near riots, and the home of the presiding judge, John M. Murtagh, had been firebombed. Racial tension in New York City was explosive.

Still, Curry and Binetti had every reason to believe that a long, boring night lay ahead of them. Why, given the verdict, would the black militant organization want revenge against Hogan now?

Just fifteen minutes into their night shift, which began at nine p.m., a dark maroon Buick slowly rolled by, going the wrong way down a one-way street. The cops wheeled their patrol car in pursuit, and, some six blocks south of Hogan's building, pulled up alongside the Buick. Just as they did, the residential street exploded with the crackle of a .45-caliber machine gun. Over twenty rounds were discharged. Curry and Binetti were shot in the face, body, and arms. Their patrol car slammed into a parked car. The Buick disappeared into the night.

On the twenty-first, *The New York Times* received the Buick's license plate, accompanied by a letter from an ultra-militant splinter group of the Black Panther Party. The last part of the letter read: "The domestic armed forces of racism and oppression will be confronted with the guns of the Black Liberation Army, who will mete out in the tradition of Malcolm and all true revolutionaries real justice. We are revolutionary justice. All power to the people."

That night, as Frankie and McQuaid cruised the streets of northern Manhattan in the Duster, the radio blared to life. The initial "10-13," "Cop needs assistance," was quickly followed by a "10-40," one of the most urgent of calls. With my brother at the wheel, the partners raced down the Harlem River Drive toward a housing project on 159th Street facing the Harlem River, where the Polo Grounds baseball stadium once stood. By the time they arrived, not more than a few minutes after the initial call, the small streets within the project were jammed with emergency vehicles, ambulances, and police cars with sirens blasting and lights flashing. It seemed every police officer in Manhattan, on duty or not, had responded to the call.

The information imparted over the radio during the first few minutes after the shootings was sketchy, even dead wrong. The first reports said that two housing patrolmen had been shot. In actuality, the victims were two regular patrol cops; their names,

Frankie would learn later, were Waverly Jones and Joseph Pia-gentini. The description of the shooters was vague at best: two young black males, wearing dark clothing. Piagentini and Jones had responded to a call for assistance, a woman who was superficially stabbed, but had refused help. The two cops were shot in the back as they walked from the Colonial Park Houses, the official name of the Polo Grounds projects: Jones three times, once in the back of the head, killing him instantly; Piagentini, thirteen times. There were bullet wounds in Piagentini's hands. He had lain dying on the ground and tried to cover his face as the last of the bullets—fired from his own service revolver, which had been taken from him—were pumped into him.

Frankie turned the Duster from the gridlock that lay before him and raced to a location known as the hole. On the northern edge of the projects, a steep block wall topped by a wire mesh fence ran alongside the access road to the Harlem River Drive. Beyond the access road lay Highbridge Park, a huge wooded tract that rolled and rambled from the Polo Grounds projects to the very northern border of the 34th Precinct. Anti-Crime cops from the 34th knew this fence well—especially the torn-away portion of it. Criminals who lived in the Polo Grounds projects and feasted on the residential and business areas of Washington Heights used the cover of Highbridge Park and the hole in the fence to make good their escape. Frankie pulled to the shoulder of the access road, and he and McQuaid leaped from the car. The park lay in front of them, a huge black ocean of woods. The only sound was the leaves rustling in the light night breeze, and the distant wail of police sirens. They knew a search of the woods would be senseless—like trying to find someone in Central Park. Instead, Frankie and McQuaid jumped back in the Duster and headed back to the Three-Four, holding on to the hope that the killers had the same idea.

Adrenaline, fueled by anger, pumped in Frankie's veins. Though his tour was supposed to end at midnight, he and McQuaid worked until the sun rose. They stopped and searched dozens of suspicious characters on the street. They tossed a bar on Amsterdam Avenue, one that McQuaid knew had a sordid clientele, searching every single patron, including the bartender, and came up with nothing—not so much as a nail file. Word of the dead cops had already reached the streets. It didn't matter to Frankie and McQuaid that they were performing illegal searches, and that nothing they would find would hold up in court. For them, and most every police officer in New York that night, there was only one objective: find the cop killers.

The consensus among investigators assigned to the case was that the shooters of Piagentini and Jones did escape the projects through the hole in the fence and most probably crossed the Harlem River into the Bronx by the High Bridge, a pedestrian span. But if in fact they had, they had done so in the minutes before Frankie and McQuaid arrived.

A few days later, the girlfriend of one of the shooters, who lived on Fox Street in my father's old precinct, told police she had overheard a conversation between her boyfriend and several other men, the very night of the shooting. She remembered one man saying that one of the cops was a "brother"—Waverly Jones, who was black. Another man in that apartment answered: "A pig is a pig."

Though most of the BLA members responsible for the cop killings were eventually brought to justice (one was killed in a shoot-out with cops in St. Louis, others apprehended as far away as San Francisco), the months and years of the BLA siege wrecked the city's nerves, further polarized the already strained relationship between the NYPD and the black community, and pushed cops into a wartime mentality.

In a twelve-month period during 1971 and 1972 alone, ten New York City police officers were killed in the line of duty; another dozen were maimed. I knew their names well. The city cops in Pearl River would repeat them like a mantra: Foster and Laurie, Piagentini and Jones, Curry and Binetti, Cardillo . . .

During that twelve-month period, Frankie went to at least half a dozen cop funerals. He stood among the sea of navy blue. He saluted with a sparkling-white-gloved hand while the single bagpiper hauntingly played "Amazing Grace" as the coffin was carried by sturdy blue shoulders into the church, and he would wipe the tears that had begun to form in the corners of his eyes while the piper played "Coming Home" and the coffin was carried to the hearse. Each time he would try not to look at the widow and family, but each time his eyes would be drawn to them. He knew—all cops knew—the routine the widow had been forced to endure. Soon after the cop had been shot, a phone call would have been made to the home of the dead officer. It would have been cryptic, the call, with not a lot of information imparted. Soon a police car would have arrived, to drive the worried wife to police headquarters, where a ranking officer would tell her that her children no longer had a father. . . . At each of these funerals, Frankie thought of Pam, watching late-night TV, waiting for him to come home from work. He thought of his two little girls, Laurie and Patrice, snuggled in their Little Red Riding Hood comforters in their bedroom. When he looked at a dead cop's widow, not even the white gloves could soak up the tears that would stream down his face.

The house Pam and Frankie had set their sights on was just off Forest Avenue in Pearl River, on a street covered in the spring and summer with a cooling canopy of trees, lined with modest split-level brick and wood homes with neatly kept lawns strewn with plastic toys and divided by tarred driveways on which were parked tricycles and Ford station wagons. On the top of Forest Avenue was a 7-Eleven, where preteen girls and boys would walk to buy Slurpies and grape-flavored bubble gum, and young teen-agers would buy cigarettes and smoke them clandestinely behind the store.

And a few blocks down from the 7-Eleven, on Middletown Road—the AOH's St. Patrick's Day parade, held here on the Sunday after March 17, had grown to be one of the biggest in the country—was a tavern called the Grasshopper. The walls of the "Hopper" were dark-stained panel, hung with New York Jets schedules and cheesy Budweiser's mirror signs. The tables had checkered cloths, and toward the back, there were red Naugahyde booths. The bar, on the left as you walked in, ran the length of the place. There, seated on bar stools, on any night of the week, would be patrolmen, detectives, retired detectives, the rank and file, most of whom worked, or had once worked, in the precincts of the Bronx and Manhattan. Cops weren't the only ones to patronize the Hopper; there were firemen (so many Jack Ryans in the fire department lived in Rockland County that they were numbered. Jack Ryan Number 7 moonlighted as a bartender at the Hopper), local businessmen, and, on weekends, all of their wives. But for all intents and purposes, the Hopper was a New York City cops' bar, "Bronx North," as it was sometimes called, the mirror image of any number of bars across the street from Bronx precinct houses. By then, the wave of cops who had emigrated to Pearl River during the mid-fifties was neatly tucked into suburbia. The sons of cops and firemen, who became cops and firemen themselves, bought homes and staked their claim to a town that was now their birthright.

Though Frankie continued driving the taxi to save money for the down payment, and though he was still racking up the collars, the bills seemed to eat up every dime. Although every fiber in his body told him not to go to his father for money, ultimately he did just that. My father took a bank loan for $5,000 and solemnly handed the payment book to my brother. When Frankie took the payment book home, he noticed that the loan officer had made a mistake: What was supposed to be a three-year repayment plan instead was a two-year plan. With the loan my father gave them, and a few thousand that Frankie had saved, he and Pam closed on the house near Forest Avenue. But now they had two large monthly payments, the mortgage and the loan, and the financial strain was immense.

Pam suggested that she take a job. The neighbor across the street could watch the children during the day, she reasoned. "I'll find a way to make more money," Frankie answered. Perhaps the prospect of not being able to provide for his family was too great a blow to his pride. Other cops in Pearl River could afford homes, why couldn't he? But other cops weren't the only ones with whom Frankie compared himself. Eugene was well on his way to a meteoric rise in business—criss-crossing the country, with a promotion and a bigger, more impressive house with each transfer. Although the competition between Eugene and Frankie for their father's attention had waned with time, Frankie always felt an underlying jealousy of his older brother's success.

"I'll just work more nights in the cab," he promised Pam.

As the months went by, even with the extra work, the monthly nut seemed harder and harder to make. Several times Frankie had Pam choose between paying the mortgage and paying my father's loan. Each time, he paid the latter, and pretended, in conversations with my father, that he was doing just fine.

One day, Pam saw in the "help wanted" section of the *Journal News* an ad for a waitress in a local restaurant. Though she had been around restaurants most of her life, she'd never actually worked in one. How hard could it be? she wondered. The restaurant, Hoppin' John's, was located in Tappan, just a few miles from Pearl River. She called the number and was told to come down right away for an interview, which she did. With the help of a small lie, saying that she had experience, she was hired on the spot. Though Pam was worried about his reaction, her nervousness disappeared when Frankie walked through the door.

"I got a job," she said straightforwardly. "And don't start yelling, because we need the money."

Surprisingly, Frankie's reaction was subdued. The reality was, they desperately needed the money.

Frankie and Pam's financial problems coincided with the Knapp Commission. Like its predecessors, the Lexow Committee in my grandfather's day, the 1914 Curran Commission, which unseated Police Commissioner Waldo, and the Harry Gross case of 1949, when my father was a young detective, the 1970 Knapp Commission investigated police corruption, mostly centering on the plainclothes division and a newly formed narcotics investigation unit. One of the star witnesses for the Commission was Frank Serpico, a name that in my house was uttered as a curse. According to my father and brother, and therefore, the law in our family, the world was divided in half. You were either a "stand-up guy," sort of a Jimmy Cagney character going silently to the chair, or you were a rat. And Serpico, in my home, was the quintessential rat. Both my father and brother were honest cops. If nothing else, the financial struggles that plagued their lives were ample evidence of their refusal to take anything but their salaries. For Frankie, the Knapp Commission was just more fuel for the anti-cop fire that burned so brightly in the early 1970s, but even that Frankie had gotten used to. Being called a pig didn't bother him much anymore. But corruption was all around him, and though the Knapp Commission would not directly affect his life, Frankie watched, ringside, as the commission shattered the lives of cops close to him. One such cop worked with Frankie in Anti-Crime.

Within Dan Diggins's circle of friends, it was common knowledge that Matty Sirica, Diggins's brother-in-law, was a thief. The joke was that Matty could steal a hot stove. He worked as a maintenance mechanic at Kennedy Airport. With easy access to freight hangars, Matty had a veritable shopping mall at his disposal. Still, except for an occasional power tool or stereo speaker that "fell off the truck"—or in this case, off the plane—Diggins rarely took advantage of his brother-in-law's expertise. But on a clear October morning of 1971, a brand-new $800 transponder for a Cessna 150 sat wrapped in brown paper like a T-bone steak on his kitchen table—compliments of Matty.

It was a Saturday, and Diggins had been doing some jobs around the house—spreading grass seed and fertilizer, preparing the lawn for winter. He enjoyed keeping up his half-acre in the suburban Rockland County town of New City. With all the overtime he was putting in at Anti-Crime, he wanted to take advantage of this rare day off. His job in the new unit placed him in the highest-crime neighborhoods and had instilled in him a newfound appreciation for his home: the dirt in his flower garden turned over for its winter slumber, the garage swept and tidied, the house newly painted. That Saturday, Diggins would have been happy to spend the rest of the afternoon doing chores, but he had a contract; and a contract with a fellow cop always took precedence, always drew him away.

The promise had been made two weeks earlier, in a bar called Maruffi's on the corner of Baxter and Bayard Streets across from the back entrance of 100 Centre Street, the Manhattan Criminal Court building. Perhaps it was made at one of the tiny tables with checkered cloths, where Phillie the waiter presided, serving hero sandwiches that arrived from the basement kitchen by dumbwaiter. Or maybe it was at the long oaken bar, where Hawkie, so named because of his enormous hooked nose and tiny squinting eyes, swooped down, landing ice-cold beers before cops who laughed raucously at last night's fruitless chase of a perp. These same cops also talked in hushed confessional tones, lips moving in expressionless faces, and eyes, like those of a nun standing in front of a testing class, scanning the room assessing everyone. In those days, just prior to the Knapp Commission, there was a lot of assessing. Rumors of cops wearing wires circulated in station-house locker rooms and in places like Maruffi's. Like other cop bars—the Jesse James across from the Five-Oh precinct, French Charlie's in the Five-Two, the Melody Lounge in Washington Heights near the 34th, the Pub on Queens Boulevard, across from the Queens County Court house—Maruffi's was a church where the cop brotherhood congregated. Here the confidences that bound this fraternity were passed, asylum was found, the legendary blue wall of silence was transubstantiated into fake stucco.

If cop bars are churches, then Maruffi's was the cathedral. Cops from all over Manhattan waited there for arraignments across the street. The seasoned ones, the cops who could predict the wait by the court calendar or the day of the week, would know whether their appointments with the D.A. were hours or days away. Diggins had gone through the ritual of lodging a prisoner at 100 Centre, submitting prints at the Bureau of Criminal Identification at police headquarters, and then heading back to the Criminal Court Building to put his name on the waiting list at the complaint room. He figured his wait to be three or four hours. He went to Maruffi's to pass the time in quiet contemplation.

Huey Collins was at the end of the bar—a fixture, wearing his black raincoat over his uniform, as he always did, even when it was ninety-eight degrees. Cops and court officers filled the tables, Phillie the waiter yelled to the sandwich maker in the basement, and Hawkie cursed about this or that. As Diggins sat at the bar sipping a cold one, a cop from the 19th Precinct named Bill Phillips appeared at the door. Phillips had thin dark hair, combed back, and muttonchop sideburns. His eyes twinkled with the look of either a sinister practical joker or a conscienceless killer. He sidled up next to Diggins at the bar. Although they didn't work together, Diggins knew Phillips fairly well. The Anti-Crime cop was a flying buff, and Phillips owned the NYPD Flying School at MacArthur Airport on Long Island. The school wasn't sanctioned by the department; Phillips just used the name. But a number of cops had learned to fly, and obtained their private pilot's licenses, at Phillips's school. Diggins had taken a couple of lessons there himself, but his job in Anti-Crime, and the responsibilities of his new home, kept him from seriously working toward his license. He made a promise, however, to both Phillips and himself, to pursue it when he had the time.

The NYPD Flying School owned a couple of single-engine Cessnas, a Cherokee, and a $14,000 twin-engine Cardinal. How a patrolman got the money to underwrite such an enterprise was something known only to Phillips. And Diggins, even in the sanctity of Maruffi's, would never ask.

Phillips was, in my father's vernacular, a "bright lights" guy. He had a reputation for dressing in immaculate suits, doing up the singles bars on the East Side of Manhattan, and hanging around KGs—known gamblers—and other sordid types. Diggins also knew that Phillips had been "flopped" from the detective division, losing his gold shield for accepting drinks "on the arm" (for free), at one of his East Side haunts. The incident, though, gave Phillips almost martyr status among some cops, who viewed the bust in rank as unusually cruel punishment for something many had done. After a few beers, Phillips casually asked about Diggins's brother-in-law, Matty. He dropped a few not-so-subtle hints about one of his planes needing a transponder, a transmitter that sends pulse signals to air traffic control radar. Though Diggins was wary of Phillips, this was a favor that could be exchanged for flying lessons sometime in the future. He promised to see what he could do.

The following week, Phillips called Diggins at his house and asked about the transponder. The call bothered Diggins for two reasons. First, in the covenant between cops, a single promise is usually binding. Second—and more important—conversations like this one were never held over a phone. Though Diggins was a smart cop, highly regarded by Frankie and his other partners, he foolishly shrugged off his suspicions.

Early the next week, Matty, as usual, delivered on the order.

The transponder, shipped from the Cessna plant in Wichita, Kansas, was taken from the Flying Tigers freight warehouse at Kennedy. A few days later, when Diggins next ran into Phillips, again at Maruffi's, he told him that the package had arrived. Phillips asked if he would be able to bring it to him at the flight school the following Saturday in exchange for a quick hop out to Montauk, and Diggins agreed. That Saturday, as Diggins grabbed the plain brown package and headed for the door, the phone rang.

After agents assigned to Whitman Knapp's investigation, armed with a warrant, had searched his home, Diggins thought about the voice on the phone earlier that afternoon. He hadn't recognized it. There were only two words spoken—"Don't go"—then the click of the receiver, and the dial tone. The Knapp agents didn't find the transponder, which lay at the bottom of the pond on Merrick Road. Still, they didn't give up on Diggins, interrogating him for months afterward. Every day, the threat of prosecution hung over him. He was reassigned from Anti-Crime to the seclusion of a desk. Just a week after agents searched Diggins's home, Whitman Knapp announced that William Phillips would testify before his commission. And, for three days, he did. Though Frank Serpico was perhaps the most high-profile witness to testify (thanks to Peter Maas's best-selling book and Al Pacino's portrayal of him in the movie) most people familiar with the proceedings agree that Phillips's testimony was the most damaging to the police department. In a villainous star turn that put his face on the front page of every New York paper and in the lead story on every televised newscast, Phillips was nothing short of brilliant. His testimony seemed as frank as it was riveting. He was well spoken, well dressed, and handsome, but the story he told in front of the bank of microphones belied all of that. He was perhaps the most corrupt and evil cop in the modern history of the New York City police department. He shook down drug dealers for hundreds of thousands of dollars. He extorted protection money from mobsters and pimps.

Phillips had been caught by a sometime private detective and eavesdropping expert by the name of Teddy Ratnoff, who was hired by the Knapp Commission to bug the East Side apartment of Xaviera Hollander. Hollander, perhaps better known as the Happy Hooker (the title she gave her autobiography), ran a high-class whorehouse out of her apartment. Ratnoff, who had a dubious past himself, struck up a friendship with Hollander, greed being his primary motive. Ratnoff's initial association with the Knapp Commission was as a supplier of highly technical bugging devices, but he quickly sensed the possibility of making more money from the commission by offering to set up situations where dirty cops would be taped. A madam and whorehouse, he thought, would be the perfect bait. The trap for Phillips was set in P. J. Clarke's, a well-known saloon on the East Side. The Knapp Commission used several retired federal agents, whom Phillips knew casually, to help reel him in. At a back table at Clarke's, the agents told Phillips of a madam looking to go "on the pad," jargon for paying protection. That very night, and in several subsequent meetings, Phillips was taped, compliments of Teddy Ratnoff's expertise, arranging protection for Hollander.

As tough and slick as Phillips thought himself to be, when he was caught he immediately "turned," agreeing to wear a wire for the Knapp Commission. As a result of his testimony, scores of cops lost their jobs and some were jailed. At least one committed suicide. Because of death threats to Phillips, the NYPD provided protection for him during and after the hearings. He was moved to another city, where he received full pay and wrote a book (with Leonard Schechter) called *On the Pad* about his experiences as a crooked cop. For a while it looked as though he had escaped his own criminal career unscathed. The New York State district attorney's office, however, was preparing its own case against him. Phillips was ultimately convicted of murder. While still a policeman, he had killed a pimp and a prostitute on the East Side of

Manhattan. During the trial he was represented by F. Lee Bailey, on appeal by Henry Rothblatt. He lost, and was sent to prison.

When the investigation of Diggins subsided, he put in for a medical retirement on account of a leg injury sustained on duty years earlier. The NYPD fought the request, but eventually gave in to an avalanche of doctors' reports. The day Diggins turned in his badge and gun to the paymaster at police headquarters, he walked over to Maruffi's for the last time. As he looked around the barroom, filled with cops in secretive conversations, he wondered which one was the angel on the phone . . . and which, if any, of them were wearing a wire.

Less than a month after the Knapp Commission hearings began, Police Commissioner Patrick V. Murphy unveiled the innovative "City Wide Anti-Crime Section." The undercover units on the precinct level had been so successful that the commissioner decided to expand the concept and form a unit that would focus on high-crime areas throughout the city. The charter members of this new unit would be taken from the precinct Anti-Crime units and the Tactical Patrol Unit (an elite mobile unit used to respond to riots or protests, and to augment precincts during flare-ups in the crime rate); the whole of the Taxi-Truck Surveillance Unit, a squad formed as a result of an increase in truck hijackings and taxi crime, would also join.

The head of the Taxi-Truck unit was Terry McKeon, who lived in Pearl River. It was in his driveway where I played basketball with Lionel Macon. McKeon's brother, Francis, was the cop whose memorial plaque hung on the wall of the staircase at the old police headquarters.

Though my father called McKeon to put in a contract for Frankie, chances are he would have been picked for the squad without my father's help. Frankie and Gibbons's record in precinct Anti-Crime spoke for itself.

In the coming months, the Knapp Commission would maintain its choke hold over the Department, and because of the nature of the unit (undercover, and in high-crime neighborhoods, an arena rife with the possibility of corruption) applicants were put through a stringent series of background investigations. Police brass was not about to take any chances. Frankie's personal index was cross-checked with the Internal Affairs Division, the Civilian Complaint Review Board, the Disciplinary Records Unit, the Public Morals Division, and the newly formed Organized Crime Control Bureau, among other interdepartmental agencies. Though Frankie's record was clean, even exemplary, the background checks were only half of the admission process. The other and possibly more weighty half was the personal interview.

Interviews for the unit were held in a small office in the Queens Safety Division headquarters in Flushing Meadows Park, the site of the 1964 World's Fair. Frankie sat in a metal folding chair in front of two wooden desks behind which sat a lieutenant named Joe Bainer and the then chief of detectives, Joe Borelli. Borelli did most of the talking. He asked about Frankie's past assignments, arrests he had made, and why he wanted to join the unit. After about twenty minutes of this, Bainer, a gravel-voiced, lantern-jawed man, finally spoke:

"You ever been in the Legion Diner in the Three-Four?" he growled.

Frankie answered that he had.

"Did you ever get a cup of coffee for nothing?" Bainer asked, glaring at Frankie.

No, Frankie answered.

"You're full of shit," said Bainer.

On that note, the interview was over. Frankie was sure Bainer didn't want him, and the disappointment must have shown: When the obligatory photograph was taken, the chief of detectives, seeing the downcast expression on Frankie's face in the picture, turned to Bainer and said: "Boy, this guy don't like you."

But, in November 1971, both Frankie and Gibbons were among the charter members of the new unit.

6

The summer of 1972 my brother had a cookout—one of the first parties held at his new home. The redwood deck off the back of the house had not yet been built. Nor had the dormers been added for the kids' bedroom, or the extension, the "new room," where Frankie later held his annual Christmas Eve party. There was a patio, a patchwork of square slabs of slate, with weeds sprouting between them. He had a portable, round charcoal grill on which sizzled hot dogs and hamburgers. There was a Styrofoam cooler filled with Bud. Paul Gibbons came with his wife, Pat, and so did some of the other cops from Anti-Crime. Some of the Brothers came, Bobby Myers and Ahlmyer among them. Billy Rutter showed up late, wearing a T-shirt with "P.I.G." printed on it. Under the letters, the shirt read, "Pride, Integrity and Guts." We all laughed and clenched our fists in a show of solidarity.

The summer before, between my junior and senior years in Pearl River High School, I smoked my first joint in a fort in the woods behind some kid's house. A half-dozen of us sat cross-legged on the plywood floor, passing it back and forth. "Don't bogart it," someone said to me. We drank Boone's Farm apple wine. Though it was sickly-sweet, I guzzled it down. My head began to spin like the label of the Sly and the Family Stone record on the stereo, and I began to loudly sing along.

"Keep it down, man," I was warned. "You'll attract the pigs."

I laughed in response, what with the buzz in my head and the absurdity of the statement.

I was torn between the cop universe I had been born to and this tepid social rebellion left over from the 1960s. Only now, looking back, do I see the dichotomy of that situation. Watered-down as it was, that social rebellion was still an expression of peace and love, words of which I had little understanding. By then, in high school, I had plenty of friends who had grown up outside the insular cop society I had known as a child. Their fathers, like mine, had worked hard and built homes and futures for their families. But in their homes there was communication and love that were as alien to me as Latin. I can remember being at a friend's house watching, astonished, as his father kissed him good-bye on the cheek. My father's most outward display of emotion was a pat on the head, and even that was more of a slap. No fault lay at his door. Nor is it my intention to elicit sympathy. I know now the myriad of reasons why my father could not express his love: his job, his impoverished youth, his own father's alcoholism. Still, as a young man I felt that in his relations with me he acted more like a squad commander than a father, and my communication with him resembled that of a subordinate to a boss. Often he'd search my room, barreling through the cherished teenage boundaries. Once he found a stack of pornographic magazines. He removed them, and never said a word, sexuality being far too intimate an issue to be discussed in my home. In the world of an Irish Catholic cop's family, sex was shoved in the back of a drawer, like the metal box in my mother's bureau where my father locked his off-duty gun. Instead, a Catholic priest named Joyce provided sex education. With a slight Irish brogue, Father Joyce would lecture the class on male and female vessels and the damnation that awaited those who aroused themselves or others before the consecration of the sacrament of marriage. With all his talk of vessels, I was never quite sure if I was being lectured on maritime history or sex. As Father Joyce was an ex-seaman, perhaps it was the former. Another time, my father found a small bag of marijuana in my sock drawer. He left it on top of the dresser for me to find when I came home that afternoon. A whole day went by, a family dinner, then breakfast the following morning, eaten in stony silence. The wait was excruciating. Finally, he told me to take a ride with him in his car, his favorite venue for lecturing. I sat expressionless on the seat next to him. He rattled off his stock phrases—"not under my roof," and such. He told me he hadn't told my mother, because "It would break her heart." He said that if I were arrested it would shame the whole family. He reminded me that he had been a policeman for twenty-three years (as if I could have forgotten), and that my brother was now a policeman. "I've arrested people for what I found in your room," he said. "So has your brother."

I said nothing in response. It seemed that the only time I talked to my father was during these lectures. But silently I seethed. I didn't care about the shame or his law enforcement background. And I didn't need his cop words.

On the other hand, there was Frankie, and my enduring hero-worship of him. In the summer of 1972, after I graduated from Pearl River High School, I took the job I mentioned earlier as a bartender in Chuck's Pub, a small, dark tavern, the last store in a mini-mall on Middletown Road in Pearl River. The clientele was mostly college-age kids who went to Rockland Community, or were home from out-of-state schools. Sometimes Frankie would stop in with his cop friends—Paul Gibbons, Billy Rutter, and others. Once in a while, on my nights off, I would go out with them.

The world in which my brother and his friends worked—with its abandoned buildings, drug addicts, murders—was so alien to the suburban world where they lived and raised families, it was impossible to go from one to the other without some time in a decompression chamber. Although it didn't happen often, I loved being with Frankie and his cop friends during these times. They were like cowboys in town after a month-long cattle drive, tinning their way into sporting events and clubs where civilians had to wait on line, and out of speeding tickets with local cops.

On one of these nights, I sat in the backseat of Paul Gibbons's family car, a station wagon, the kind with the wood paneling on the sides. We were traveling so fast the tires squealed with each bend in the road. There were six of us—myself and Frankie, and four of his crazy cop friends—jammed into the car with beers between our legs and empties rolling around the back cargo area. We flew down Route 340 in Sparkill, deserted at this early morning hour, and passed St. Thomas Aquinas College, a future stop in my staccato pursuit of higher education. I pointed the campus out to Gibbons and he slammed the brakes, pulling the car to a screeching halt. A small cement pool with a fountain in the middle decorated the lawn of the convent adjacent to the school. A cop named Seely bolted from the car, ripping off his clothing like a crazed lover—first his shirt, then, hopping on one leg, his pants, next his underwear, and finally his ankle holster. He stood on the brick ledge that surrounded the pool, bent over, and spread the cheeks of his ass in a salute to us left behind in the car. The cops and I laughed wildly as we watched Seely's performance. He held his arms straight out from his sides, bent his knees, and did a perfect belly flop into the pool. The water was only a foot and a half deep. Seely rose from the blackness and turned to us, glistening and scraped, raising his fists and howling like a mad dog.

"He's a little fucking nuts, isn't he, Frankie?" I asked.

"He's a good cop." Frankie shrugged, as if that, measured against Seely's insanity, constituted a wash.

Yeah, I thought, the citizens of the Bronx must sleep soundly knowing Officer Seely has the watch.

As Seely stood howling, the others dashed from the car. Clothes were strewn across the lawn of the nunnery. One by one, the naked cops dove into the pool. Lights went on in the convent. Frankie and I leaned against the car, the only wallflowers, laughing and sipping our beers.

Down the winding path from the convent came the lights of a compact sedan. The night watchman stepped from the car with St. Thomas emblazoned on its side, his eyes wide as he took in the scene: the four naked men, the piles of clothing, and the guns lying on the grass. Frankie, the only cop clothed and remotely sober, approached the guard, reached into his back pocket, and pulled out his badge, flipping open the leather case to give the guard just a flash of his shield. "Fish and Wildlife," he said with the utmost sincerity. "We think there are goldfish missing from this pool."

The cops stepped from the pond and in single file casually walked past the befuddled guard, picked up their clothing and guns, and piled into the station wagon.

It was while watching such playfulness and unbridled emotion that I began to formulate the idea that joining the force didn't have to mean being straitjacketed in my feelings the way I thought my father was. It was seeing my brother and his friends so uninhibited that made me think that perhaps I, too, could become a cop.

By the summer of 1972, the City Wide Anti-Crime Sections, later renamed the Street Crime Unit (SCU), had become the kind of police work true crime authors and TV producers live for. Originally consisting of some two hundred cops divided into twenty ten-person squads, the unit was first housed in the Queens Safety Division headquarters, but as it grew, it moved to the Harbor Precinct Building, a kind of Bat Cave on Randalls Island, under the Triborough Bridge. The cavernous room was divided into sections partitioned by rows of lockers. Each team's section resembled backstage at a Broadway play, or Central Casting. In lockers and on hooks hung on the walls were costumes decoys would wear. They ranged from "streetwalker" garb to the black suit and white collar of a Catholic priest. (An early publicity shot of the unit was taken and appeared in the newspaper. The police commissioner immediately received a call from the archdiocese and decoys were forbidden to wear the priest outfit.) The squads were broken down into three-person teams, each consisting of one decoy and two backup cops. The decoy, dressed as a streetwalker, a lost tourist, or, in parts of Brooklyn, as a Hasidic Jew (there were no complaints from the Jewish sector), would attract muggers, drug dealers, and confidence men. When a crime was committed—and only when the crime was committed—the back-up team, alerted by a prearranged sign, would rush in and make the arrest.

Frankie's squad was assigned to high-crime areas in Brooklyn and the Bronx, but mostly to Times Square—in the early 1970s, a veritable Sam's Club crime store. Prostitution, drug dealing, and cons of every conceivable kind happened twenty-four hours a day, seven days a week. Just the criminals in and around the Port Authority Bus Terminal would have kept Frankie's squad in court most of the time. The work became so routine that Frankie's team made a game of it—"Pick the Perp." As they drove the streets of Times Square in taxicabs, the undercover vehicle of choice, they would keep a scorecard among themselves, each team member getting a chance to guess which street character would commit the next crime.

Because of his size and his unmistakable cop looks—only the dumbest of crooks would have tried to take him off—Frankie always worked as a backup. Several cops rotated as the team's decoys. Paddy Quinn played such a realistic drunk, he was mugged by the same guy twice in one week. After the first arrest, the mugger was whirled through New York's revolving-door justice and back onto the street. The second time, Quinn even tried to lose the mugger, to no avail. Ironically, in real life, Quinn didn't drink. Another decoy, Freddy Shroeder, played a character the team called Fenwick Babbitt, an upstate businessman looking for kicks. He wore a short-brimmed hat and a loud sports coat. Shroeder was so believable in his role that once, only moments after he stepped from the undercover cab, he was inundated by a posse of prostitutes. There were so many of them swarming around him, fighting over him, pulling him by his arms, he couldn't get his hands free to lift his hat to signal for backup. Frankie also worked with Mary Glatzle, known as Muggable Mary. During her career as a decoy, Glatzle was "mugged" some 500 times.

The new unit seemed perfectly suited to Frankie's personality. Never the conformist, he felt stifled by structure and chain of command. Compared to the rest of the department, the Street Crime Unit was assembled along less "military" lines, with sergeants and lieutenants working alongside their men—and women—in tight-knit undercover teams. It was an environment in which Frankie's police skills thrived. But, sometimes, felons stumbled right into him.

While Frankie was working as a backup along Forty-second Street west of Eighth Avenue, a strip lined with pornographic movie houses, two men walked out of the fire door of one of the theaters and, right in front of him, rifled through a wallet. Frankie signaled the team, and the men were apprehended. When my brother walked into the theater he asked the manager to turn on the lights so he could find the wallet's owner. The expression on the manager's face was of utter disbelief: "In this theater?" he said. "The lights haven't been on in this theater for thirty years."

As an image of the most graphic of sexual acts flashed on the screen behind him—and with the sound of zippers quickly being closed all around—Frankie announced to the startled audience the name found in the wallet. Reluctantly, the owner identified himself. As he stood, he realized his pants had been cut by a razor and most of his backside was sticking out.

For Frankie, however, there was one important ingredient the unit lacked. Though he made close friendships with his partners in his immediate team—Shroeder and Quinn—and with his sergeant, Buddy Ayers, who lived across town from Frankie in Pearl River, as a whole the unit lacked the camaraderie that he had experienced at the precinct level. SCU cops were treated like an invading army in the neighborhoods, and in the station houses, where they worked. Animosity arose within the ranks of precinct cops who viewed the unit as headline and glory grabbers, while they, roving targets in uniforms, were given little credit. The SCU was also far more competitive than precinct-level units. It seemed to Frankie that everyone in the SCU was trying to forward their careers—even if it meant stepping over their comrades on the way. The administration of the unit didn't help matters any; they encouraged competition by instituting a point system for arrests—a score card. Robbery arrests garnered 3 points, as did gun arrests; grand larceny on the person (taking money without physical force, like a pickpocket or a confidence scammer) earned 2 points; a stolen car earned 1. The incentive was promotion. The top fifty point holders would be promoted to detective. The system wasn't altogether fair. Decoys, for example, who took the greatest risks, made fewer arrests than did the backup team. And luck, being in the right place at the right time, was far too big a component. Some cops who led in point totals didn't deserve promotion, while other cops, lower on the list, did.

Although Frankie saw the unfairness of the system, he quickly realized that it *was* the system. He made up his mind to work as hard as he could, make every arrest that he could, and hope that luck was with him. It was. When the list for promotion to detective was posted, his name was on it. He had his gold shield. He had been a cop less than four years.

Just a few months later, it would be taken away from him.

7

The hearing for the incident in Spring Valley was postponed several times, so for a few months Frankie lived in limbo, not knowing whether he was going to retain his rank and stay a part of SCU. He had pleaded not guilty to the charges (and years later, when the case was reviewed at his request, he was exonerated). But at the time, he didn't want to take a "five-day rip," a suspension. In the argot of the police department, getting such a strike on your record is known as "picking up a nail," and it marks you—forever—as damaged goods.

Strange as it seems, the only time he didn't think about that night was when he was working. He put every ounce of his energy into policing. It was what he was good at, and the only source of relief. He had obtained his detective's gold shield even quicker than his father had. When he was away from the job, he was the classic dark, Irish figure, guilt-ridden and self-deprecating. I hated that he gave that voice so much power. One episode, one night, one mistake was all it took. And that one mistake outweighed thousands of days of hard work, years of sacrifice and struggle.

As far as the police department was concerned, Frankie's fate had already been sealed. From outside the hearing room in the newly built headquarters at One Police Plaza, Frankie called the "wheel," the clerical officer at SCU, to find out his assignment the day he entered his plea. He was told he had been transferred to the 50th Precinct. At first Frankie thought he meant the 50th Detective Squad. Several gold shield Street Crime cops had made the jump from his unit to squads. But the assignment officer told him that this transfer was back to uniform.

"Tell the boss I'm coming right up," Frankie said on the phone.

No punishment could have been worse—a transfer, a demotion, a nail, and what's more, to the quiet precinct of Riverdale. His thoughts went to the house. How could he afford it now? He was struggling as it was, at detective pay. Things were caving in, and he couldn't let that happen. He would talk to his C.O., Captain Flynn, he thought. There must have been a mistake, and Flynn was the one who could rectify it.

When he arrived, he found Flynn's office empty. The captain had left only the message "Tell him I'm gone for the day."

Frankie had some time coming, so he put in for vacation. He needed space and distance to think. He needed time to decide whether to go back into uniform or leave the job entirely.

A year before, Eugene had moved into a new home in St. Louis. By that summer, Diane was pregnant with their third child. Eugene had invited Frankie and Pam out several times to see the new place. Each time, Frankie put him off. But the day he found out he was being demoted, he called Eugene and took him up on the offer.

Although Eugene was completely unaware of the circumstances, he knew as soon as Frankie got off the plane that something was wrong. There was none of the usual brotherly razzing from Frankie. No jokes. Just a handshake and a subdued greeting. That first night in St. Louis, Eugene and Diane proudly gave Frankie and Pam a tour of the house, a four-bedroom colonial, built to their specifications. After the children were put to bed, the two couples played board games in the family room, paneled in rich, dark mahogany, with a natural-finished plank floor and a brick fireplace. Though the girls, Pam and Diane, drank wine, and the brothers polished off the better part of a bottle of Johnnie Walker Red, the conversation was awkward.

The next afternoon Eugene suggested that Frankie take a walk with him to see the neighborhood. They made small talk as Eugene steered through a just-built subdivision with saplings and sodded lawns, and up a hill to a section of larger homes. He pointed out where the quarterback of the St. Louis Cardinals, Jim Hart, lived. Finally, after a mile or so, Frankie could no longer hold back his emotions.

"They're trying to screw me," he said, and he began to tell Eugene the story he had assembled: While he was on duty, someone had spat at his partner, and Frankie had overreacted by grabbing the man and throwing him to the sidewalk. Because of the altercation, he had been brought in front of the Civilian Complaint Review Board. As a result of the complaint, he said, the department was taking his gold shield. Frankie then said something that made Eugene stop and glare at his brother in disbelief: "I think I'm going to quit."

Eugene had no way of knowing that his brother had altered the events. Nor did it matter much. Lies, and secrets kept, had always been the language of our home—the language of a cop home.

They walked together for some time in silence. Then Frankie began to remark about how nice the area was where Eugene now lived. "What are you going to do if you walk out now?" Eugene asked. This was the perfect place to raise a family, Frankie said, stalling. "What else do you want to do?" Eugene said. I'm sick and tired of New York, Frankie answered. "Have you given it much thought?" Eugene asked. I gave them my soul, Frankie said, shaking his head.

As they turned onto the block where Eugene lived, Frankie stopped. His eyes were red and filled with tears. "I don't know what I'm going to do," he said.

When Frankie returned from St. Louis, he did report to the 50th Precinct. Inside the station house, he approached the desk lieutenant and said he was newly assigned. At first, the lieutenant thought he was a detective or an Anti-Crime cop. But when Frankie asked for permission to leave so he could turn in his gold badge at police headquarters, the lieutenant suspiciously eyed the sight before him: the long, unkempt hair, the sour, defeated expression.

"I'm starting to get the picture," the lieutenant said.

As Frankie turned to leave, the lieutenant yelled after him with contempt: "And get a haircut."

My brother sat in his car in the parking lot of police headquarters and stared at the gold badge in his hand. He remembered when he had shown it to his father for the first time. It had linked them even more than the uniform, like a Cracker Jacks ring for members of a secret society. Certainly, at times, he felt as though the badge contained magical powers. Sometimes he would reach to his wallet just to feel its outline. And each time he did, it assured him of who and what he was.

The keeper of the shield room in headquarters, a civilian employee, was straight out of Dickens. Old, wrinkled, with purple veins popping from his face, he reached over the desk with bony fingers, snatched the badge, and, with an indifferent flip, tossed it into a box—a cardboard coffin for dead careers.

For me, that fall of 1972 was a schizophrenic time. On the one hand, I enrolled at Rockland Community College, where I spent more time in the lounge with the suburban student body, holding onto the longhaired remnants of the 1960s—playing card games like hearts and casino, smoking pot in the parking lot—than I did in class. But on the other hand, I nurtured a halfhearted desire to become a cop. My schooling was being paid by a federal grant under LEEP, the Law Enforcement Education Program. RCC had instituted a police science curriculum to accommodate Rockland County's many New York City police officers' sons and daughters who were now of college age and were interested in law enforcement careers. I didn't have to pay tuition, nor was I beholden to my father. Nor, for that matter, did I have to attend class to get a passing grade. Most of the instructors either had worked with my father or had been my brother's bosses. But this familiarity, and the grant, only made me take the whole thing less seriously, even though the grant came with the stipulation that the student become a police officer within two years of graduation. Otherwise, it would be considered a loan, and would have to be repaid. So cavalier was I about my college career, I cashed one of my $75 book allowance checks at a topless bar called Mel's.

At night, I worked at Chuck's Pub, the first of several bars where I worked in my late teens and early twenties (the legal drinking age in New York State then was eighteen); my days off were spent at the racetrack. My father hated my lifestyle, especially working behind the bar. "You're spinning your wheels," he said more than once. It wasn't, however, as though he was pressuring me to become a cop. Only six years had passed since he retired, and the disappointment of his police career still burned in his stomach. Anyhow, I'm sure he thought I didn't have what it takes to become a cop. At the time, he was working as a security manager for Eastern Airlines, and he once tried to get me into the baggage handlers' union. He even set up an interview for a ticket agent position. But I was supposed to learn rudimentary typing. I didn't bother, and didn't get the job. He extolled the virtues of the Transit Authority and the Sanitation Department—the twenty-year pension and the city paycheck; no doubt his high opinion of these was born of the dire financial situation he grew up in. But I was interested in neither. I'd work until three a.m., then go to friends' houses to party or to an after-hours place to play cards. I'd drive home, my eyes squinting against the morning sunlight, and pass bus stops filled with people hurrying to work or school, even friends on the way to RCC. In my youthful arrogance, driving a souped-up Pontiac LeMans and always walking around with a couple of hundred in my pocket, I thought of them as suckers. On several occasions, I walked into the house while my father sat at the kitchen table eating his breakfast of cornflakes and prune juice. He didn't even look at me as I half staggered up the stairs to my room.

I moved out of the house several times during this period, only to have to slink back when I lost a job or owed too much to the bookmakers. My moving out was always a melodramatic ritual: My mother cried as she stood on the front steps watching me go, while my father sat in the living room, his face hidden behind the *Journal News*, undoubtedly whispering "Good riddance" under his breath.

In 1974, I took a job in a place called the King's Arms, a restaurant and dance club in Tappan, New York. The crowd was mostly older (at least to me then) married couples and cheaters. One night my father—now, in my vernacular, "the old man"—stopped into the restaurant for a drink. It was a rarity for me to serve him over the bar. I felt awkward, and, for some reason, a little bit ashamed. A few days later he said, "You're working in a mob joint." I told him that the place was owned by a couple of

Englishmen. "I don't care who you think owns it," he said. "There's mob money behind it."

He came to this conclusion because of Joe DiMassio, the bartender who worked with me. A Dean Martin look-alike, DiMassio was one of the funniest people I've ever known. His dyed hair was as black as shoe polish. He drove a Godzilla-sized candy-apple-red Cadillac convertible, and had a bevy of ex-wives and current girlfriends, whom he would juggle as expertly as a Wallenda. Before the King's Arms, Joe had worked in a place called Connie's Cloud Room, near La Guardia Airport in Queens. At Connie's, he worked with a waitress by the name of Alice Crimmins, who became one of New York City's most infamous murderers. She strangled her two children. The Cloud Room was also notorious because its owner, Conrad, was gunned down one night as he walked from the restaurant. Because there was no robbery motive, police thought Conrad, a known gambler, must have just dealt with the wrong people. Right after Conrad was shot, Joe moved out of Queens and up to Rockland County. My old man knew of Joe's exotic past. "The guineas always put one of their own close to the operation," he said more than once. Though my father had spent many nights in places like the Bronx restaurant owned by Joe Valachi and other known mob hangouts, I didn't believe his statement about the King's Arms. When I told him he was wrong, he squinted and shook his head. It was bad enough his son was working for mobsters, his expression said, but that he didn't even know it was an inexcusable offense. I would later, however, work in a club where I wasn't so naive. And in my rebellion against my father, relish the thought of how he'd have reacted to my toy-gangster friends. Back then, I thought of myself as much more suited for a life on the periphery of the law than one upholding it. I spent a lot of my time at Aqueduct and Roosevelt racetracks, with gamblers who were known by descriptive middle names, and I knew bookmakers by their first names. I owed all of them money. If you wanted to get me by phone, you would have to know the code: one ring, hang up; two rings, hang up. (Once, perhaps by luck, an IRS agent broke the code.)

Still, for a while, during my time at the King's Arms, I half-heartedly tried to get my life in order. After dropping out of RCC, I enrolled in St. Thomas Aquinas College in Sparkill, again taking their version of a police science curriculum, reactivating my LEEP grant. I even studied for the police entrance exam. It was as though something on an unconscious level propelled me toward being a cop. Maybe this force was trying to move me closer to my father.

The day of the test, I waited on line with my friends John Murphy and Eric Schweitzer outside a high school in Washington Heights. Both Murphy and Schweitzer had studied police science with me at RCC, though neither came from a cop family. Murphy's father was a city bus mechanic, and Schweitzer's worked at the Lederle laboratory. I think they got their inclinations toward police careers from television shows. They seemed much more enthusiastic than I was. But, then again, they didn't have my intimate knowledge that being a policeman wasn't all *Kojak* or *Columbo*.

I was on line that day for the thinnest of reasons. Not to carry on the tradition of my family, that's for sure. Rather, I was there like someone invited to a party, and going because he has no other plans. Not only was I ambivalent, but also things had changed in the police department. Long gone were the days when it was a vehicle for Irish societal acceptance as it was when my grandfather was a cop. The Irish had been accepted for fifty years in New York, and had decided there were better places to be accepted, moving en masse to the suburbs. And the department no longer offered the security so sought after by the Depression-era cops of my father's day. The year I took the test, angry cops had circled City Hall demanding raises and the back pay they had given up to avoid more layoffs. Two thousand cops had lost their jobs the year before. Cop unions printed leaflets titled "Fear

City" and were handing them out to city visitors at bus depots and airports as a way of exerting financial pressure on the mayor. No, there was no security left.

I also saw no reason to follow Frankie's path. I knew how much he had loved being a cop, and I knew that the police department as an institution did not return or reward such love. The disappointment of my brother's demotion, my father's physical condition when he retired, the stories my mother told of her father's treatment at the hands of Tammany, all combined to form a picture in my mind of the NYPD as a trash compactor that squashed lives and spat its members out broken and defeated.

I don't remember much about the test itself—what questions were asked or even how I'd felt I had done. I do remember what I did afterward, though. With my friends Murphy and Schweitzer, I went back to Pearl River and stopped in the Grasshopper. In the dimly lit bar we sat among the usual crowd of New York City cops, drank Miller Lites, and pretended we, too, were "on the Job."

Months went by. There were stories in the newspapers nearly every day about the city's budget crisis, and the freeze on hiring cops. There were also stories about the soaring crime rate. I took a job in a club called the Talk of the Town in Hillsdale, New Jersey. It was that kind of hipster joint the late 1970s had spun out after the release of the movie *Saturday Night Fever*. The place was filled with white leisure suits and matching shoes. Even I, with a face plastered with an undeniable Irish heritage, owned a pair of ivory-colored loafers, though my leisure suit (bought out of the trunk of an Impala from a huckster who also sold throw rugs emblazoned with moose and felt paintings of dogs playing poker) was lime green.

Aside from the Tony Manero look-alikes, dancing to "Stayin' Alive" on the sound system, the club was frequented by a steady clientele of Mafioso wanna-bes. They went by names like Tony Lips, Johnny D., and Matty O. In reality, most of them owned delicatessens and sliced provolone for a living, but at night, dressed in their open collars and gold chains, they talked in gangster jargon of "families" and "business."

Johnny D. did have a bookmaking operation, and lent money at five points—$25 weekly interest on $100 borrowed. And Matty O. ran a floating card game, replete with expatriate Vegas dealers. Entranced by such things as the flash of a pinkie ring on a hand dropping a $50 bill on the bar, by a gleaming hearse-black Oldsmobile 98, I forgot all about the cop test—and my family's heritage—and enrolled in gangster school.

The first class was Driving 101. My job was to shuttle players who parked their late-model Eldorados in the lot of a diner on Kinderkamack Road to a card game held in rotating locations in Hillsdale and Woodcliff Lake. I sat in my "starter" gangster car, a 1972 Thunderbird (I had cracked the axle of my LeMans on a curb one rainy night), wearing an orange hunter's hat, the signal to the gamblers—and probably most of the cops in Bergen County—that I was the taxi to the game.

Once I proved myself a capable wheelman, Matty O. made me an offer that constituted a considerable financial windfall. For $100 a night, the house I shared with two other bartenders (it was on a quiet residential block, and one of the neighboring homes belonged to the police chief of Woodcliff Lake) would be turned into a casino. At nine o'clock each Thursday evening, Matty O. backed a white Ford van, which smelled of grated cheese, into my driveway and unloaded two green felt blackjack tables. By ten-thirty my house was filled with the odors of fat men wearing fruity cologne, the smoke of Macanudo cigars, and the sounds of Tally-Ho cards being expertly shuffled. My weekly take now was $175; I wasn't exactly a full-fledged racketeer, but my career was gaining momentum. On nights off I'd drive into Little Italy, sometimes with Patricia Leahy, an almost girlfriend who, although she didn't really look the part with her auburn hair and freckles, I envisioned as my gun moll. We'd have dinner at

Umberto's or Luna's, drink labelless bottles of red wine, and have Sambuca with espresso for dessert. Fuck being a cop, I thought. This was a much better way to live.

8

After his transfer, I often saw Frankie running along the tree-shaded streets of Pearl River and the surrounding towns, a solitary figure, head down, legs pumping. Sometimes, when I passed him, driving in my car, I'd beep the horn, and he'd raise his hand in the air, a gesture of acknowledgment and a signal to leave him alone. He was a pioneer at running. It had not, in 1974, in suburbia, caught fire the way it would in the coming years, when the streets were lined with would-be marathoners wearing $100 sneakers.

Rarely did I talk to him during those days. He hardly ever stopped over the house for one of his once-cherished cop-to-cop talks with my father. There was nothing for either of them to say. There certainly were no war stories for Frankie to tell. The 50th Precinct was then, and remains, the slowest in the Bronx. It encompasses a section called Riverdale, part of which is as affluent as any in neighboring Westchester County. The money there is as old as the elm and maple trees that shade the manicured lawns of the million-dollar homes. For Frankie, this assignment was like being exiled. Back in a radio car, with partners fresh from the Academy, the biggest excitement on a tour might be a "cat call," a pet stuck in a tree.

But this solitude enabled Frankie to experience a new clarity of purpose. Just as he had after being disciplined in the navy, he turned to books by enrolling in Rockland Community College. With the exception of the Class of 1,200 in those last years of the Depression, when Mayor La Guardia championed the cause of "professional policing," the New York City police department had historically been aligned against college education for its members. Civil Service schools like Delahanty's were the educational route endorsed by the department. In 1971, only 3 percent of the entire department had college degrees. That year, a black detective had been forced to resign because he had accepted a three-year scholarship to Harvard Law School. The acceptable leave of absence was only one year—without pay. Commissioner Patrick V. Murphy overturned the forced resignation and declared that any cop would be granted any term of leave for college or postgraduate studies. His decision changed more than policy, it changed the department's attitude toward education.

Frankie didn't need, nor could he afford, a leave of absence. In uniform, he was working steady tours, which gave him the opportunity to fit in a schedule of college classes. His schooling was paid for by a combination of the G.I. Bill and LEEP, which was also available to working policemen.

His first day at the Five-Oh was also the new commanding officer's first day. After about a week, Frankie was called into the captain's office. Aaron Rosenthal's reputation had preceded him. He was a rising star in the department, and known to not take any shit. He wasn't about to jeopardize his accession to a new command with any insubordination amongst his troops. Frankie didn't know what to expect from Rosenthal, but considering how his career had gone of late, he didn't think it would be good news.

In his office, Rosenthal held my brother's file in his hand, and Frankie felt a tinge of apprehension. Rosenthal's manner was cold and aloof. But the captain looked him directly in the eye as he began to speak, and this was both disarming and refreshingly different. Bosses never looked you in the eye, especially if they were about to dress you down.

"I just wanted you to know something," Rosenthal began as he dropped the yellow folder on his desk. "As far as I'm concerned, your career starts right here and right now."

For a moment, Frankie stood in front of the captain absent of words. It was the last thing he had expected to hear, and most likely the best thing Rosenthal could have said to him. For the first time in his career, perhaps in his entire life, Frankie had received a break from a figure of authority.

Rosenthal's issuance of a clean slate reenergized Frankie. Acceptance replaced resignation. Okay, he thought, this isn't the greatest situation, but I'll deal with it the best I can. And Rosenthal hadn't spouted empty words. The captain began to match Frankie, in sort of a tutor's role, with rookies who showed promise. Among these was a young cop named Slattery. One day they sat together in a radio car on Reservoir Avenue, taking their lunch break. As they wolfed down the hero sandwiches, Frankie looked in the rearview mirror and noticed a guy walking toward them. During his time in SCU, Frankie was the undisputed champion of Pick the Perp, and the guy approaching them set off every one of his alarms: the slightly forced casual gait, the way he held his hands in the pockets of his coat. Frankie deliberately wrapped the sandwich and placed it next to him on the seat. Slattery quizzically watched as Frankie dropped his gaze from the rearview to the side-view mirror. In a voice just louder than a whisper, my brother announced: "We're taking this guy."

Frankie leaped from the car and was on his suspect before Slattery had realized what was happening. Amid a barrage of denials—"What are you doing, man? I didn't do nothing"—Frankie put him against the radio car and began questioning him. As if on cue, just then the radio blared to life with a description of the man Frankie was cuffing, wanted for a burglary. As the two cops drove back to the station house, their collar cuffed in the backseat, Slattery sat slack-jawed, staring at Frankie. Finally the rookie spoke: "How did you know?"

"You get lucky," Frankie answered.

Sometime later, Rosenthal matched Frankie with a cop named Neal Sullivan, who was newly assigned to the precinct. When the captain introduced the new partners, Rosenthal said to Sullivan: "This guy I'm putting you with is the best cop I have. Don't bring him down." But Sullivan brought something of his own to the new partnership. He was born on the Lower West Side of Manhattan, an area known as Chelsea and now an upscale enclave; but in Sullivan's youth, it had been predominantly Irish-American, filled with longshoremen, local toughs, and other sordid characters. Sullivan's father ran a saloon there, but died when Neal was only eight. After his father's death, his mother moved the family back to her native Ireland, where Neal spent the rest of his childhood. In his early teens, he came back to the old neighborhood in New York to live with relatives. Now more Irish than American, he had difficulty fitting in: he wore knickers and Bournine sweaters, and talked with a slight brogue. Because of this, he became a target of the street-hardened neighborhood kids. One day, when he was walking home from school, several local bullies jumped him and beat him severely.

Over the next year or so, Neal spent most of his after-school hours in a local gym, strapping on gloves and learning to box, the vivid memory of the beating fueling his desire. When he was ready, he knocked on each of the bullies' doors, one by one, to settle the score, and one by one, he knocked each of the bullies cold. The story was passed around the neighborhood, and made him something of a legend in Chelsea. His interest in boxing continued up until his police career. As a club fighter, he billed himself as "Irish Neally Sullivan." Later, when he was Frankie's partner, he spent much of his off time with the Police Athletic League, teaching neighborhood kids the art of pugilism.

To his complete astonishment, Frankie found out that he actually liked college. At first, the whole process was uncomfortable. He was older than most of his fellow students, and had overwhelming feelings of scholastic inferiority. But as the days passed, as he sat in the front row of the classroom, as he did his assignments at

night at home, or in the radio car on quiet shifts, a subtle transformation occurred. He realized that the same brainpower that
made him a good cop could be used to make him a good student,
even a great student. He was able to integrate his life experience,
hard duty in the biggest classroom in the world, the streets of
New York City, with what was being elaborated in his textbooks.
Like an inmate blowing dust off the jacket of a crumbling old
copy of *Treasure Island* in the far reaches of the jail's library racks,
Frankie had found the way to escape the confinements in his life.

It was during this time he realized that, in many ways, the police universe was a stagnant pool, festering with bias and narrow-
mindedness passed on from generation to generation. In college,
Frankie took his first step out of that swamp and found a whole
dry world, in which he could not only survive but thrive. His list
of priorities shifted, and with the change came a quiet confidence.
Yes, being a good cop was still on the list, but it was no longer the
most important thing in his life.

He also turned his attention to renovating his house. To cut
costs, he and his friend Bobby Myers did all the work. The first
job was putting dormers in the upstairs rooms, expanding them
into spacious bedrooms for Laurie and Patrice. Whenever I
stopped by, I'd see Frankie and Bobby hanging perilously from
the roof, hammers instead of revolvers hooked on their belts.
Though the furniture inside still looked like a collection from a
yard sale—the dining set had wobbly legs and mismatched chairs,
when you sat on the couch or one of the living room chairs you
sank nearly to the floor, and other sections of the house were in
obvious disrepair—these inadequacies took second place to bedrooms for his children.

As Laurie and Patrice grew older, Frankie found time to volun-
teer in still more organized activities, like the soccer and softball
leagues. In Pearl River and the other neighboring towns, these
coaching positions were almost exclusively filled by city cops.
Once Frankie needed to find help in coaching a team because his

work schedule was such that he couldn't make a few of the practice days. He asked a man whose daughter played on the team. But the man, who owned an auto body shop in town, and came to just about every practice and game, declined, telling Frankie that coaching kids' teams was a civil service duty, not for real citizens like himself.

With work, school, renovations on the house, coaching and finding time to get his runs in, there was no time left over for socializing. He hardly ever stopped at the Grasshopper (couldn't afford it), nor did he gather with the cops he worked with at Jesse James, the bar across from the 50th Precinct. And his family's financial burden was now heavier than it ever had been. Gone was the overtime from all the arrests he made in SCU; gone, too, was the yearly $2,500 pay increase that came with the gold shield. Out of necessity, Pam began to work more and more shifts at the restaurant. At first, Frankie had grudgingly gone along with Pam working a few lunches. But now they relied on her contribution to the family budget, and the more she could work, the better off they were. When Hoppin' John's was sold, Pam stayed on with the new owners and began to work weekends and nights. With Frankie and Pam both working nights, they arranged for several teenage girls on the block, daughters of city cops, to baby-sit.

In a way, Pam was lucky. The restaurant, now called the Steak Pub, was an instant success, and at one point she was taking home as much as her husband. But the job was exhausting. Sometimes she'd work until two or three o'clock in the morning, all that time on her feet, carrying heavy trays laden with dinner plates of porterhouse steaks. Through it all, though, she never complained. As mercurial as Frankie was, Pam's personality was the opposite: level-tempered, good-natured and, even at the roughest financial points in her marriage, optimistic. Buried beneath the burdens of the now full-time job at the restaurant and the responsibilities of motherhood was the flicker of a dream. Pam had always been interested in interior design. As a child, visiting her grandparents, who lived in a fashionable section of Park Slope, Brooklyn, Pam was taken by the opulence of the apartment: the huge living room adorned with oak furnishings, the roaring fireplace, the grand piano. One New Year's Eve, she saw her grandparents on a broadcast from the elegant Stork Club. Though the glimpse was fleeting, she had witnessed firsthand what it meant to have money. And some of that taste longed to be nourished. She greedily read *Architectural Digest*, but passed on *House & Garden*, in the racks at the checkout counter. She imagined, down to the colors, fabrics, and wood, what her house would look like, if she had the finances.

When Laurie and Patrice both reached school age, Frankie encouraged Pam to take a course at Parsons School of Design in Manhattan. She did, and immediately showed promise. Her instructor told her she had a natural flair. Pam was buoyed by the possibility of doing what she loved as a career, and for a while it looked as though she would.

By word of mouth, Pam got jobs decorating other cops' homes in Pearl River and surrounding towns. She took an ad in a local advertising letter called the *Welcome Wagon*, and received a number of responses. Charlie A, her boss at the Steak Pub, commissioned her to design a new bar and lounge for the restaurant. For a short time, she worked in a store called Nassau Decorators, in a shopping mall in Hackensack, New Jersey. But there business was slow, as the store was more of a tax write-off for the wealthy Armenian owner than anything else. When she left Nassau Decorators, she went to work for the wife of a city cop who lived in Spring Valley. But here too, things didn't quite work out (the woman had a habit of not paying Pam), and she decided to go back out on her own, where she steadily began to build a profitable business, earning over $37,000 one year. But running her own business was filled with pitfalls. People were slow in paying for her work; some didn't pay her at all. Pam cut out the middleman by buying carpeting and drapes herself. Though this increased her profit margin considerably, it was also something of a gamble. If the customer backed out on the deal, she had to hope that the carpeting could be returned, or that she could sell it to someone else. But one time when this happened, she could do neither.

The job was for a friend with whom Pam had worked in the Steak Pub. The woman, a waitress in the restaurant, was getting married and moving to a new home in Virginia. She asked Pam to decorate the home and buy furniture, carpeting, and drapes, the cost of which was $13,000. Frankie and Pam agreed to take a huge gamble: They would apply for yet another loan to cover the cost. They went to my father to cosign it.

A few days later, the friend called Pam to say that her husband-to-be had decided to use another decorator. There was no written contract; the deal had been made with a minimal deposit and a handshake. To make matters worse, Pam received a call from the trucking company she had hired to ship the already paid-for—and uninsured—furniture. The furniture, they said, had been stolen out of the truck in Virginia.

At one point, Pam and Frankie came close to losing the house. I heard all of this secondhand, at the dinner table, my father calling the whole idea "stupid" and "their own fault."

At first, Frankie, too, was angry at Pam. But in a way, the venture's failure brought them closer together. Frankie realized that most of his brooding over life's knocks had been selfish. His wife, his family, had suffered just as much as he had. So what if things didn't go as planned? he thought. At least Pam had the guts to try. Throughout their marriage they had experienced a myriad of financial roadblocks, and had always survived. Though this was the biggest hurdle yet, Frankie knew they would get through it somehow. But the bitter experience extinguished the flame of Pam's dream and, again, she went back to waiting on tables.

* * *

Though Frankie learned to live with his situation at work, he still yearned for action. It also became clear to him that he was being passed over for busier assignments. Patrolmen in the 50th were rotated to fill slots during the precinct Anti-Crime cops' vacations and sick leaves. Frankie watched as time and again younger cops were chosen over him for these assignments. One day, in a hall-way in the station house, Frankie approached the roll call officer in charge of the Anti-Crime schedule and asked why he was never picked. The cop answered him curtly, saying he wasn't on the list, and offering no further explanation. Frankie hadn't even been aware there *was* a list. Just then, Captain Rosenthal walked down the hallway and stopped to talk to Frankie. Though, because of the distance in rank, their relationship couldn't be considered a friendship, they had developed a mutual respect. When the cap-tain asked him how he was doing, Frankie seized the opportunity.

"For some reason, I'm not on the list for Anti-Crime fill-in," Frankie said.

Rosenthal leveled a stare at the roll-call cop and said: "You are now."

The Anti-Crime detail in the 50th Precinct was tame compared to the SCU, or to Anti-Crime in the 34th. But at least it was better than the "cat calls" Frankie was enduring in the radio car. The 50th Precinct wasn't fully made up of million-dollar homes. There was a section called the Hill where most of the precinct's crime occurred, and where most of the criminals—who once in a while were ballsy enough to break into a house in the fashionable sections—lived. There was also a strip along Reservoir Avenue that was a favorite hunting ground for out-of-precinct car thieves and drug addicts boosting radios and tape players. At night, especially in the winter, only cops and car thieves would be out along the quiet stretch of road. For Frankie, the apprehension of these thieves amounted to a elemental game of hide-and-seek.

My brother's prowess as an undercover cop did not go unnoticed, and one of the Anti-Crime cops who took note was the star of the unit, Artie Schwartz.

Frankie and Schwartz hit it off right away. An energetic insomniac, Schwartz seemed to go full-bore twenty-four hours a day. Like Jimmy McDermott, he had an engaging personality and would talk to anybody and everybody. Even a good portion of the criminals knew Schwartz by name and liked him—even when they were handcuffed in the back of his unmarked car. One night, after he and Frankie had arrested four car thieves, Schwartz told his handcuffed prisoners to "walk this way" into the station house, then affected a Groucho Marx–like crouch, with the willing prisoners falling into step. But Schwartz was also a "numbers man," consistently leading the Anti-Crime unit in arrests. His biggest supporter was Pat Malloy, the sergeant in charge of the unit. When Schwartz's primary partner was transferred, he went to see Malloy about who would fill the spot.

Working full-time again in Anti-Crime was bittersweet for Frankie. On the one hand, he was thrilled to be permanently assigned to the unit. But he knew that this time around, because of his demotion, he wasn't eligible for "Career Path," a system put in place to promote officers who had high arrest numbers and met other criteria. He felt as though he were still branded. Still, for the first time since his days in SCU, going to work became fun again.

Schwartz prided himself on his foot speed. In terrific physical condition, he often boasted that he never lost a race, be it just a challenge or running after a perp. If someone fled a crime scene, Frankie would fold his arms, say to his partner, "Go get 'em," and watch as Schwartz ran the guy down. In the 50th Precinct, there was a teenage gang led by the Jordan brothers, Joey and Cliff. Schwartz and Frankie knew them well, as the teens were constantly in some kind of trouble. One day on Mosholu Avenue, outside Joey Jordan's apartment, the sixteen-year-old challenged

Schwartz to a race. In front of the rest of his gang, Jordan lost by half the length of the block.

Soon after Schwartz and Frankie became partners, there was a rash of robberies in the row stores under the elevated subway train. The *Riverdale Press*, the local paper, had dubbed the perpetrators the Termite Gang, because of their method of breaking into one store, then burrowing through the walls into as many as five stores in the row. Stores on this strip had also frequently been robbed by a method called smash and dash. Thieves would wait until a train was rattling loudly overhead, then break the front windows of the stores and clean out the showcases.

The new partners decided to stake out the area from the rooftop of one of the row stores. That night, they arrested Joey Jordan breaking into the back of a hardware store (Jordan didn't try to run). Jordan told them he was only after "some spending money," and, bargaining for a lesser charge, he said that if they were interested in some information, his gang was planning a major heist the following evening.

The plan, Jordan said, was to break into a fruit stand in the middle of the block, then hammer through the walls into the adjacent stores. Captain Rosenthal, who was shouldering most of the ire of the local business community, agreed that a stake-out of the fruit stand was the right way to proceed. The owner went along, giving Schwartz and Frankie the keys to the store. Sure enough, a few hours into the stake-out, the skylight opened. One by one, the members of the gang climbed down into the store. One by one, Schwartz and Frankie cuffed them to pipes and to each other, in a back room. The lookout on the roof became impatient and called down into the store: "What's going on down there?"

Schwartz responded, in a husky whisper, "Come on down," which the lookout proceeded to do, and was promptly cuffed with his friends.

* * *

Even in the busiest precincts, a good portion of cop partners' time is spent away from stake-outs and chases. In the 50th Precinct, Frankie and Schwartz had more than their share of down time. During these uneventful hours, Schwartz's sense of humor was at its biting best. Sometimes, when there was a shortage of uniform cops, he and Frankie would be taken off Anti-Crime, put in uniform, and assigned to a radio car. On one of these occasions, at six on a rainy morning, the partners received a call about a man trying to break into a church on the Henry Hudson Parkway in a tony section of Riverdale. As they rolled up to the church they saw the man, his hair matted from the rain, wearing a soaking-wet coat, standing in front of the church and pounding on the front doors. As the partners stepped from the radio car, they heard the man screaming: "God, why have you forsaken me?" Schwartz asked the man what he thought he was doing. On seeing the uniform cop, the man tried, without much success, to make himself appear sober. Looking contrite, the man explained that he ran a men's religious retreat at the Paulist Fathers Mission House about a half-mile from the church. He said that after the evening meditation he had sneaked out to a local tavern, and had ended up closing the place. With his internal compass a bit askew from the night's festivities, he walked in the wrong direction. Then it started to rain, he explained, and as it did, he began to be flooded with guilt for his indiscretion. When he saw the church, he said, he became angry with God for his own human shortcomings. With an understanding expression, and his arm draped in comfort around the man's shoulder, Schwartz said that they would give him a lift back to the retreat. The man stiffened in horror. "Oh, you can't do that," he said. "What if someone from the mission sees me get out of the police car?" Schwartz assured the rain-soaked man, now mumbling to himself, that they would drop him off down the block where no one would see him. Instead, he pulled up right in front of the mission house. Horrified, the man stumbled from the car and, in a crouch, began to run up the driveway. Schwartz turned on the lights and siren. Shades in the windows of the mission house popped up; the man tried to hide behind a sapling tree. Several retreat members, on their way to seven o'clock mass, stood and watched the scene in astonishment. As if that wasn't enough, Schwartz drove halfway down the block, turned, and pulled up in front of the mission and hit the lights and sirens again. Throughout, he didn't even crack a smile. My brother, however, was doubled over in laughter at the thought of his partner doing the work of God—instantly administering the man's penance.

In 1975, Frankie graduated with an associate's degree from Rockland Community College and enrolled in St. Thomas Aquinas College in Sparkill, where I'd gone to school, and next to the convent where Seely and the other cops had taken their naked midnight swim. Frankie's major was political science, but his favorite courses were in the social science curriculum. He enjoyed comparing the theories of a textbook on abnormal psychology with the real-life laboratory in which he worked each night. In school he'd engage in hypothetical discussions of the social complications and treatment of drug abuse; at night he'd have a whacked-out junkie in cuffs in the backseat of his unmarked car.

Frankie rocketed through school, graduating from St. Thomas in 1976. With absolutely no college credits to start with, he obtained his bachelor's degree in the traditional four years—this with a full-time job and family responsibilities. Now that he had the degree, his goal was to obtain his teaching certificate. When I first heard him talk about it, I laughed. Was this the same guy who was the scourge of the nuns at St. Margaret's?

When he received his teacher's certificate, he put his name into a pool of substitutes for the Pearl River school system. At first, he was picked infrequently, because full-time substitutes were given priority. But even though he only taught now and then, he came to love it more and more. Most of the teaching jobs were one-day stints and in the lower grades. One day, Frankie substituted for a gym teacher in the Franklin Elementary School in Pearl River. He organized a dodge-ball game, dividing the class into two teams. One of the kids was a terror, throwing the ball as hard as he could at kids who weren't looking in his direction. Frankie knew well who the little boy was. Shaking his head, Frankie thought of his old partner. The boy was Paulie Gibbons, Jr.

Even though he was happy substitute teaching, he began to miss going to class and began explore various master's programs. At the time, the Police Academy was renting out space to Long Island University. For the university, the deal offered a central location on the East Side of Manhattan. For the police department, the motivation was primarily financial. But it also proved convenient for cops like Frankie who were interested in postgraduate studies. He began studying for his master's in the same classrooms he had sat in, twelve years earlier, as a rookie cop.

Frankie and Schwartz primarily worked the midnight-to-eight shift. They both liked the tour because it not only put them on the street at the optimum hours for crime—especially grand larceny auto, the staple of the precinct's criminal element—but also left their days free. This schedule allowed Frankie to attend day classes in his master's studies.

But in the late 1970s, a new lieutenant took over the precinct's Anti-Crime unit and changed their schedule. Frankie's new hours, two in the afternoon until ten at night, not only interfered with his classes and substitute teaching, but affected his police performance. As in his early career with Gibbons, he and Schwartz consistently led the precinct in arrests. They had developed systems, street sources, and instincts that seemed to position them in the right place at the right time. They had become so accustomed to each other, it was as though they thought as one, as the new lieutenant was to find out.

Before Frankie became his partner, Schwartz had become

friendly with a man who owned a deli on 228th Street and Broadway. Paddy Balardi was famous for his over-stuffed sandwiches and gregarious personality. A young boy named Tommy Welsh worked for him. Tommy's home life wasn't the best, and Balardi would often let the kid stay with him. Schwartz took a liking to Tommy, and later so did Frankie. Often, when Tommy was closing up the deli around midnight, Schwartz and Frankie would cruise by to make sure he was okay, sometimes giving him a ride home or to the diner on 231st Street where Tommy would order the same meal, French toast and bacon, every time. Tommy was an avid bowler, and would pester Schwartz and Frankie into having a game with him. One slow evening, while on duty, they took Tommy up on his offer. Later that day, as they were cruising in their undercover car, a radio car pulled alongside. The uniform cops in the radio car told them that their new boss, Lieutenant Quigley, had put out a 10-2, "Return to station house," for them an hour ago, and that he was good and mad that they hadn't responded.

Without even formulating a cover plan, Schwartz and Frankie drove into the station house parking lot, where Lieutenant Quigley was waiting. The lieutenant ordered Schwartz inside and questioned Frankie in the parking lot:

"Where were you?" The lieutenant was bristling.

"We were out of the car, following some guys up Broadway," Frankie answered calmly.

"How come you didn't have your radio on?"

"We did, but we had it on channel two [a different frequency] so we could talk to each other."

"How many guys were there?" asked the lieutenant suspiciously.

"There was three of them," Frankie answered.

The lieutenant told Frankie to stay right where he was, and marched into the station house to talk to Schwartz.

"Where were you?" the lieutenant asked Schwartz.

"We were out of the car, following some guys up Broadway."

"How many were there?"

"Three," came Schwartz's answer.

"Where was your radio?"

"Channel two."

Frustrated, the lieutenant ordered them back to work. An hour later, they returned to the station house with a mugging collar. As he passed, Quigley, who was still upset, asked Frankie if he wanted to go for a beer after work.

"You guys are good," Quigley said as he sipped his brew. "You got your story down pretty good."

"We didn't have a story," Frankie said. "And if you want to know how we're doing our jobs, just look at our numbers. You don't have to supervise us, Lieutenant," he said without rancor. "We're not out there drinking, fooling around, or taking money. We're out there working."

Schwartz and Frankie assembled the same story simply because they were of the same ilk. They shared the same instincts, ones that made them good cops and partners, and ones that allowed them to survive in a job where the employer was inherently suspicious of its employees. The truth is, veteran cops always have a story, and good partners always have the same one.

The following week, Quigley put them back on midnights and left them pretty much alone. It wasn't as though Frankie didn't like Quigley. As time went by, and he got to know his commander, he respected him as both a cop and a boss. They even became friendly off-duty. Quigley lived in Pearl River and had a daughter Laurie's age. The girls played soccer together.

When they went back on midnight-to-eight's, Schwartz and Frankie decided not to put chases of stolen cars over the radio. There had been too much confusion with backup teams joining the chase. Once or twice, the apprehension of car thieves had escalated into a road rally, with Schwartz and Frankie, the thieves, and several patrol cars screaming through the streets of Riverdale. On more than one occasion, when the thieves were caught, uniform cops, filled with adrenaline from the chase, had beaten them. One time, two patrol cars slammed into each other. Although there were no injuries, there easily could have been.

One night, cruising in their undercover vehicle, my brother and his partner pulled next to a late-model Mercedes, in which were two young Hispanic men. The car's ignition mechanism had been yanked out. Car thieves then employed an auto body tool called a slapper or bam-bam. The tool was used in pulling dents out of fenders, but was equally efficient in breaking the housing off the steering column. With the housing removed, starting a car was just a matter of using a screwdriver as a key. The men in the Mercedes quickly made Schwartz and Frankie as cops, and a pursuit ensued. Several blocks away, the thieves abandoned the car and ran into a building. Moments later, Schwartz and Frankie arrived and followed. There were staircases on opposite ends of the lobby. Schwartz took one, Frankie the other. When Frankie reached the roof, he paused momentarily. The worst thing a cop could do, he knew, was to stumble out into the darkness before his eyes adjusted. From the far end of the roof, he heard rattling in a small entranceway to a back staircase, not the staircase his partner had climbed. With his gun in his hand, Frankie gingerly ran across the roof and pulled open the entranceway door. It was an uncharacteristic mistake, and one that almost cost him his life.

The small compartment exploded with a deafening sound and a flash of brilliant yellow-orange light. As Frankie let go of the handle, in the millisecond it took for the door to close with a smack on its spring hinge, he saw the blue uniform standing in the stairway. With his arms spread out from the sides of his body, his palms pointed upward like he was holding a pair of pizza pies, he looked down at his Kevlar vest, positive that he would see a smoldering hole. How could it have missed? His six-foot, two-hundred-pound frame filled the entire doorway. As the shock began to subside, and the realization that, by some miracle, he had not been hit, Frankie again opened the door. The uniform cop's face was the color of chalk, he was frozen in an unblinking, horrified stare. Riding in a patrol car, the cop had witnessed the pursuit of the stolen car, and had also followed the thieves into the building.

"Are you okay?" the cop finally managed.

"Yeah," Frankie answered, still eyeing the vest for a hole. "I don't know how, but yeah."

In the confusion, the thieves escaped and, to the uniform cop's relief, Frankie never reported the incident, not even the weapon discharging, knowing that if he had, the uniform cop would be subject to an investigation and possible discipline. My brother was just happy to be alive. The next day, in his locker in the station house he found a bottle of Johnnie Walker Black Label, compliments of the uniform cop.

By 1979, with twelve years on the job, Frankie became resigned to the notion that his police career would go no higher than where it was. Not that that was so bad. He liked working with Schwartz; he liked that he was building a future outside the police department. Still, a *what if* cloud followed him: Where would his career be now if Spring Valley had never happened? He also knew that some cops had it worse.

Each morning, when their tour was just about finished, Frankie and Schwartz would stop and buy some coffee and sit in a little spot on Kingsbridge Road near the Armory, to kill the last half-hour or so of their shift. On a few mornings, Frankie noticed the same man walk by, dressed in a work uniform and carrying one of those Ralph Kramden lunch boxes. There was something familiar about the guy, but Frankie just couldn't place him.

One morning, my brother stopped into a corner grocery store to buy some cigarettes. As he was walking out he found himself face to face with the man with the lunch pail. There, it came to him. The face was older now, lined and creased, the man's hair gray and receding. But the eyes were the same, and in them was a tempered glimmer of recognition.

When my brother was a rookie cop in Washington Heights, three new detectives had been assigned to the Three-Four squad. Frankie knew them only as a uniform cop would get to know a detective—casually. Detectives were known for talking down to uniform cops, treating them as subordinates. But one of the new detectives struck Frankie as being different. The first thing Frankie noticed was that he wore expensive suits. But more than that, when Frankie led a collar up to the squad room, this fellow, unlike most detectives, wouldn't seem annoyed at the bother of booking the criminal. And he never tried to steal a collar from Frankie, as some of the detectives did. When Frankie left the Three-Four for City Wide Anti-Crime sections, he lost touch with the detective. But less than a year later he read about him in the *Daily News*. Before coming to the squad, the detective had been a member of SIU, the narcotics division special investigation unit. A member of that unit, a cop named Bob Leuci, who would become better known as the Prince of the City, testified before the Knapp Commission. As a result of Leuci's testimony, the ex-detective, now carrying a lunch pail, was sent to jail. But compared to those of other cops involved in the scandal, his punishment was light. Two of the convicted cops killed themselves. One, a detective by the name of Cody, who had also been transferred in Frankie's early days to the Three-Four, shot himself in Van Cortland Park in the 50th Precinct, where his brother worked as a detective. As Frankie stood in the doorway, the ex-detective managed a crooked smile. "Still on the Job, huh," he said. Frankie nodded. Just out of jail, the ex-detective, once nearly rich from working in narcotics, was now a night watchman. Then, making Frankie think of his Academy days, and his father's advice, the man said: "Well, keep your nose clean."

By 1980, the Anti-Crime partners had their act, literally, down to a mathematical science. Artie Schwartz kept the statistics. He carried a logbook in which he kept track of arrests and pertinent information on criminal trends in the precinct. By his count, he and Frankie averaged sixty or seventy collars a year. In comparison with other, busier precincts, and certainly with Frankie's time in the SCU, these numbers are not overly dramatic. But considering that the 50th Precinct was the quietest in the entire Bronx, the numbers become astounding. Schwartz also carried what he called his bag of tricks. Although Frankie knew that in the bag Schwartz kept his logbook, an extra pair of handcuffs, and other items, he was never entirely sure of its contents. Even in partnerships as close as theirs, some territory was considered personal, and those boundaries were strictly respected. Schwartz's bag of tricks lay within those bounds.

One night, over the radio they heard a call about a robbery in progress. A man driving up the Deegan Expressway saw some kids breaking into a Mobil station and called 911. Though they mentally noted the call, it wasn't of any real interest to them because it would be answered by radio cars.

When the uniform cops responded to the call, the thieves fled the gas station into a swath of woods, about 500 yards wide, that separated the Deegan from the Mosholu Extension. Schwartz and Frankie listened to the radio as the initial responding cars called for backup to intercept the kids on the Mosholu. As those cars arrived, the kids doubled back toward the Deegan. The radio banter between the two groups of cops began to sound comical, as if the kids were playing the game of "running bases." Each time they headed up through the woods, the cops below would warn the cops above that the suspects were coming in their direction, and then vice versa. Though at first Schwartz and Frankie listened to the antics with a sort of amused detachment, as the situation lingered it began to become embarrassing.

"The whole sector is listening to this," Frankie grumbled.

Schwartz wheeled the car around and headed toward the scene. They approached the uniform sergeant and offered their assistance.

"What are you guys gonna do that we haven't?" the sergeant

asked sardonically. But, reluctantly, he agreed to give them a chance.

Schwartz grabbed his bag of tricks. Standing at the edge of the woods, he shouted: "Fuck this—get the shotgun, Frankie."

Frankie slammed the car door, then followed his partner into the woods. From his bag of tricks, Schwartz removed an M-80 firecracker. He lit the fuse and tossed it into the thicket. As the M-80 exploded, the kids appeared like grouse from the brush and began running down the hill. Frankie and Schwartz took off after them. This was Schwartz's element, and Frankie, in top shape from his daily runs, kept in step. Side by side, the partners high-stepped over fallen trees and stumps, holding their hands in front of their faces to push away the branches. For some reason, about a hundred yards into the race, Schwartz began to let out an Indian war whoop, and then Frankie did, too. A few hundred yards into the chase, they caught their suspects. Tackled, and now cowering on the ground, two of the three thieves looked up in astonishment as these men, whoever they were, danced around them like Apaches, pretending they had tomahawks.

A few weeks after the Indian chase, Lieutenant Quigley met Frankie in a hallway in the station house.

"You got a few minutes?" the lieutenant asked.

He told Frankie that headquarters had decided to bolster the Detective Division. They asked each precinct commander to recommend one or two cops, preferably from the Anti-Crime units. Getting his gold shield back was something Frankie never allowed himself to think about. Why be disappointed? Even as the words came from Quigley's mouth, he wasn't quite sure what the lieutenant was saying.

"Frankie. If you want the division, it's yours," Quigley said succinctly. "I'll give your name to the captain."

For a moment, Frankie stood there unable to formulate any words. His mind, however, was a rush of memories: the thought of those bony white fingers throwing his gold badge into the cardboard box, the look of disappointment on his father's face, the talk with his brother Eugene, and how close he had come to quitting. Then his thoughts went to his partner.

"What about Artie?" he asked.

"If he wants it, he goes too," Quigley answered.

9

A few years before Frankie got back his gold shield, a kid I had grown up with was released from jail. He had shocked Pearl River, filled with its commuting New York City cops, by robbing the Nanuet National Bank. A few years older than me, Eddie had always been in trouble at school—a teenage marijuana bust and numerous suspensions for fighting or stealing from lockers. But he was, to my knowledge, the first and only bank robber from Pearl River.

One night, after his release, he walked into the Talk of the Town. The adolescent face I remembered was now hardened by his three years behind bars; his body, once skinny, had taken on jailhouse proportions from hours of lifting weights. He swaggered, and he spoke in black jargon. As he glanced around the barroom, he liked what he saw: the girls, the steady stream of white jackets headed to the bathroom for a snort of cocaine, the undercurrent of illegal activity that he instinctively sought. A smirk cut across his face as if to say: This is home.

For all their bravado, Matty O. and the boys steered clear of Eddy. Making book or running a card game was one thing; walking into a bank with a loaded shotgun, something else. I, on the other hand, wasn't repelled by his infamy. We had known each other all our lives, and no matter how big and bad he had grown in jail, in some sense he was still the kid with whom I had ridden bicycles.

Eddie began to spend a lot of time at the house in Woodcliff

Lake. One night, I walked in as he was cutting lines of an amber-tinted white powder on the dining room table. He handed me a rolled-up $100 bill; his expression was cut in a sneer, daring me. If there was ever a moment in which I drove a stake through the heart of the idea of my becoming a cop, it was then. I don't remember if my father or brother came into my thoughts as I took the bill and bent over the table. But on some level I knew that this was the ultimate act of defiance against them. From my earliest memories, that childhood eavesdropping on my father's conversations, I knew that heroin was the enemy of cops, I knew that it had taken the Bronx from them, that it fueled the demonic army that had defeated them. My father never railed against the evils of heroin. Rather, when he talked about it he seemed to drift off, like a survivor remembering some unfathomable tragedy: "An elderly woman stabbed forty times for her Social Security check . . ." He would shake his head and mumble something about "those god-damned junkies."

As we sat at the table, both, to different degrees, high on his smack, my friend told stories of his time in jail, the "brothers" he was in with, and the crimes they had committed.

I fought a wave of nausea from the heroin that turned my stomach upside down, and told him in turn of a restaurant owner and entrepreneur who owed me a thousand dollars. I had worked for him briefly as a bartender and as a salesman in his big-screen TV business. Though, as the first of their kind, the TVs were terrible—their pictures snowy and constantly blurred—I was able to sell one to a sports bar near Giants Stadium, and another to a pizza restaurant in northern Bergen County. The TV business, however, quickly went bankrupt, and I was never paid my commissions. My friend listened with only passing interest. That is, until I told him that a skylight in the restaurant was easily jimmied open, and that the weekend take was kept in a beer cooler behind the bar. At five o'clock that morning, my sense of justification fortified by cognac and heroin, we drove in my Thunderbird to Englewood Cliffs, and within an hour, were back sitting at the dining room table dividing up $1,600 worth of $5, $10, and $20 bills.

As the effect of the heroin and booze began to wane, I was flooded with guilt. Sunlight poured through the kitchen window onto the table, giving the scene an unbearable cheery feel. I pushed myself back from the table, leaving the money there, went to my bedroom, and pulled the covers over my head.

When I awoke, hours later, I was happy to see that both Eddie and the money were gone, and had the sincere hope that I would not see either again. That day, I drove up to my parents' home. As I pulled in to the driveway, I noticed the ladder leaning against the side of the house. My father, dressed in a plaid flannel shirt, was on the roof, cleaning out the gutters and leaders. His hair, now just about all white, resembled a cloud against the pale afternoon sky. He gave me a curt nod as I stepped from the car. I asked if he needed help, and he shook his head no, without saying a word. I walked inside and picked up a pile of mail addressed to me. There in the stack was a letter from the New York City Civil Service Department. The list for appointments to the police department had been frozen until further notice. The letter didn't say whether or not I had passed the test or made the list, just that appointments were, for now, not going to be made from it. I sat at the kitchen table, my head throbbing, my insides churning from the events of the night before, as my mother made me a ham sandwich. Her voice was soothing and happy. I wanted her to grab hold of me, the way she had so often when I was a child. I wanted the forbidding feeling within me to just go away, to not have happened. I felt as though I had betrayed something intrinsic inside me. Something instilled from childbirth, taught by example from a father and, later, a brother, and reinforced by the community in which I grew up. The masses, the regular people in the middle, didn't matter. The world was made up of only two camps—cops and bad guys. I had crossed over to the enemy, and I wanted a do-over. I wanted another chance. As I sat there, my thoughts swirling, I held to the slightest of hopes that it was all just a bad dream, that from the kitchen, where I now sat, my mother would call up the stairs that I was late for school, and I would yawn and stretch and see the light tumbling through my bedroom window, the one with the geraniums in the flower box outside. It didn't happen. At least, not right away.

I never went back to the house in Woodcliff Lake, and I vowed to change. A month or so later, Eddie was arrested for armed robbery and sent to jail again, and I counted myself lucky that I didn't go along with him.

Some years later, in 1981, I moved out of the house in Pearl River for good. Twenty-six years old, the police test a distant memory, and just becoming an adult, I took a small apartment over a coffee shop on the East Side of Manhattan. Once a week I'd hop on a bus to the Talk of the Town in Hillsdale. There I would leave an envelope with a hundred dollars in it for a loan shark, every week until my debt was paid off. Then I'd continue on to my parents' house for a visit and a home-cooked meal.

During this period, my relationship with my father began to change. It didn't happen all at once. For months, even years, he sized me up with a suspicious glare when I walked into the house, wondering if I had reverted to my old ways. And it took at least as long for me to forgive him.

In Manhattan, I again worked in the restaurant business. But this time my aspirations did not lie with gangsterdom or the racetrack. Instead, I took acting lessons and even joined a small theater company. Frankie, and even my father, came to a couple of my performances. I also began to write, first just scenes and monologues for my acting class, then one-act plays and later, short stories. One day, when I visited my father in Pearl River, he presented me with a gift—an old-style Underwood typewriter. For fourteen years that typewriter had sat on his desk in the 41st Precinct squad room. It weighed a ton, and had several crooked keys. But as I sat in front of it, hunt and pecking my nascent prose, I felt as close to being a cop as I ever would.

On October 1, 1981, Frankie arrived at the 52nd Precinct Detective Squad, in the north-central section of the Bronx. He was assigned to a team of veteran detectives: John Borris, Tony Martin and Mike Kelly, all of whom had worked together for some time. For the first week or so, he didn't catch a case; he spent most of those days trying not to get in anyone's way. The squad was housed in a converted garage next to the station house. More than the physical separation of the squad room, there seemed to be a discernible rift between the uniform cops and the detectives. Or was this cool breeze only blowing his way? By nature, cops are suspicious toward new assignees, especially those assigned to detective squads. Most times, the initial reaction is: Someone must have put in a contract. "Who the fuck does he know?" is a favored line. This exclusion is not overt by any means. Its signals are subtle—conversations held as if you weren't present; eye contact kept to a minimum; official interaction handled in a slow, detached manner. Once or twice, Frankie felt the urge to scream: "Listen, I just spent a good part of the last fourteen years in uniform!" He didn't, though. And it was just as well. The police department's rumor mill would deliver his tale soon enough. And when it did, the cops would know that he had won this assignment with no one's help.

Precincts in New York City are classified by letters: A is the busiest, B, the second busiest, and so on. The alphabetical codification, however, is deceiving just to the south of the Five-Two. The 46th Precinct was an "A" house, but staffed by almost twice as many detectives as the 52nd, which was then a "B," with only fourteen detectives in its squad. What's more, the 52nd was huge. Just before Frankie arrived there, the city charter was amended to provide for something called co-terminality. Simply explained, precincts would share boundaries with community boards. Because of this, the 52nd Precinct annexed a half-dozen blocks from the 46th. These blocks, in the 1980s, were the highest-crime area in the Five-Two.

Once it started for Frankie, it never slowed down. Though part of his new precinct, on the west, bordered Frankie's old one, there was no comparison between the two. The 50th Precinct and its midnight car thieves seemed like suburbia next to the crime in the Five-Two. Frankie's partner, Tony Martin, a DeNabli cigar–smoking detective, often told him that the Five-Two had "good crime." What he meant was that their precinct did not have the depraved crack-addled crime that happened in the South Bronx or parts of Brooklyn, where crackheads killed their mothers for stealing their pipes. "Good crime," to Martin, meant a lot of it, and a lot of different kinds of it: real, professional burglars, stick-up men who lasted more than a week in their careers, and murders that were harder to solve than just following the bloody footprints to the apartment next door.

But Martin's statement didn't mean there wasn't a crack co-caine problem in the Five-Two. In my father's time, it took years for neighborhoods to deteriorate, but in the early 1980s crack destroyed them seemingly overnight. One of those shattered neighborhoods was Fordham: Sedgwick Avenue, Devoe Park, St. Nicholas of Tolentine, lay square in the middle of the 52nd Precinct. In his time there, Frankie would work countless mur-ders, rapes, and robberies, and every other conceivable crime, on the same blocks where, as a kid, he played and walked to school.

One day, early in his time in the 52nd squad, Frankie's team caught a robbery case. A nun from St. Nicholas of Tolentine was mugged as she entered her building on University Avenue, just a few blocks from the church. All four detective team members— Frankie, John Borris, Tony Martin, and Mike Kelly—were as-signed. The reason for the unusual manpower (usually only a pair of partners caught cases) was because the chief of the Bronx at the time, a man by the name of Ciccarelli, was a daily communicant and a personal friend of the cardinal. Any crime against the church got his complete attention, and therefore the attention of all his detectives. As the team arrived at the scene, uniform cops filled them in on the particulars. The detectives were told that the nun, who was shaken and bruised, but not badly hurt, had been knocked to the floor in the vestibule of the building, and that the thief made off with her bag. But, the uniform cops said, the mugger left something behind: his German shepherd. Apparently the suspect had been walking his dog and saw the opportunity but, in the struggle, lost hold of the leash, and the dog was trapped in the nun's building.

John Borris and Tony Martin conferred and came up with an idea. Their plan was to let the dog loose and follow it—a *Lassie Come Home* strategy. Because they were in the best shape of the team, Frankie and Martin were designated as the runners. With the uniform cops looking on with amused expressions, John Borris walked the dog out to the sidewalk, and Frankie and Martin took runner's stances. When Borris unhooked the leash, the dog shot down University Avenue and across busy Fordham Road, with Frankie and Martin in close pursuit. As the cars whizzing by just missed them, the two detectives raced up Kingsbridge Terrace after the German shepherd. Sure enough, about three quarters of the way up Kingsbridge Terrace, the dog ran into the open door of a building. From the vestibule, and over their loud gasps for breath, Frankie and Martin could hear the dog scratching on a door a couple of floors above. Up they went, and knocked on the door, which was opened by a small Hispanic woman. Do you live alone? the detectives asked. With my husband, she said. Is your husband home? She shook her head no. Do you mind if we come in? She shrugged. Just inside the apartment was a hall closet with the door open. On the floor of the closet was the nun's bag.

The woman in the apartment refused to cooperate. She told

Frankie and Martin that she did not know where her husband was. Days went by and she was brought to the station house and questioned several times, but she still would not give any information. The detective team did find out that the husband had relatives in the East Bronx, and Frankie and John Borris took trips there each day—and each day, Chief Ciccarelli checked on the progress of the case. But like the wife, the relatives wouldn't tell them the husband's whereabouts.

Days stretched into a couple of weeks, and the husband was still in the wind. One day, while Frankie and Borris were on the way to the East Bronx, a call came over the radio: a bank robbery in progress on Fordham Road, right nearby. The two detectives joined in canvassing for witnesses. My brother spotted two deliverymen standing near their straight-rig truck, which sat in front of Devoe Park.

"Yeah, I saw the whole thing," one of the deliverymen began. "There were four young kids in ski masks—they ran out of the bank and hopped into a car down here." Frankie asked the routine questions: What kind of car? Did you get a license plate? And so on. But the man said he didn't get that close a look.

While he was interviewing the witness, my brother's eyes were drawn to the man's partner. Emaciated, with sunken cheeks, red eyes, and a cigarette hanging from his lip, he looked to Frankie as though he'd been on the wrong end of a chase a couple of times himself.

You see anything? Frankie asked. The man let the cigarette drop to the ground. "See that guy over there?" he said. "The fat one in the army jacket, getting into his car? He was part of it. We tried to stop the kids and he ran over and got in our way."

For whatever reason—years of police experience, instinct, or just a hunch—Frankie gave credence to the skinny man's words. With Borris, he walked up to the man in the army jacket, and amid a flurry of protests, escorted him to their car.

When they arrived at the station house there was utter pandemonium. Because it was a bank robbery, the FBI was there; so were most of the bosses from the Bronx, including Chief Ciccarelli.

As Frankie escorted his suspect into the interrogation room, he was approached by a smallish man with heavy-lidded eyes and a few days' growth of beard. Politely, the man asked Frankie if he could talk with him. Just then word was received that four kids with ski masks, suspects in the bank robbery, had been caught in Queens. In the back of a patrol car on the way to the Bronx, the four kids gave up a description of the heist's mastermind: heavyset, wearing an army jacket.

Frankie turned to the little man and explained that he had no time to talk to him at that moment, but if he would be patient, and take a seat, he would get to him as soon as he had the chance. Although most of the bosses there were elated that Frankie and Borris had already apprehended the suspect, Ciccarelli chose that moment to ask Frankie about progress on the nun's case. Jesus, Frankie thought, what does this guy want from me? After an hour and a half of questioning the bank robbery suspect, Frankie, needing a break, walked out of the interrogation room, where he was again approached by the small man. "Please, sir," the man implored, "I have to talk to you." By this time, Frankie had almost had it. "Can't you see I'm busy right now?" he said, bristling. "But this is very important," the man pleaded, as he followed Frankie to a Coke machine. Finally, Frankie turned to the man and said: "What? What the hell is so important?"

"I'm the guy who lost the dog," the man said.

If there were any doubts in Frankie's mind about whether he was going to be accepted in his detective team they were dispelled that day. He and Borris got credit for collaring the bank robbery suspect, and the team was credited for breaking the nun case. Both suspects were ultimately convicted.

* * *

As was the case with every aspect of police work Frankie was involved with, he quickly found out that he was inherently good at being a detective. By just his second year in the 52nd, Frankie was frequently taken off the schedule and assigned to important and high-profile cases. One of these was the investigation into an attempted murder of a policeman.

Mike Palladino worked as an Anti-Crime cop in the 52nd Precinct. At the time, he was dating a local girl who lived on Jerome Avenue. Very early one warm late-spring morning in 1982, as the couple sat in Palladino's Trans Am in front of the girlfriend's apartment, Palladino saw two men breaking into a car. The young cop jumped from the Trans Am, and after a short chase apprehended the men. Across the street from where Palladino stood with his two suspects was an Italian social club, in front of which sat several patrons. The club members knew Palladino from the neighborhood—they called him "Mikey the Cop." Without backup, Palladino enlisted the club members' aid to watch his suspects as he went to retrieve their burglar tools. When Palladino returned, the suspects were gone. Later, in front of a grand jury, one of the patrons of the social club explained: "We threw the guys a beating, then kicked them in the ass out of the neighborhood."

The very next afternoon, in his girlfriend's apartment, Palladino was told by a neighborhood kid that two carloads of teenagers were waiting for him out front. Palladino took his service revolver and slid it into the waist of his pants. Outside, one of the suspects from the night before—a guy who was missing most of his teeth—pointed to Palladino. The two cars rumbled to life, heading in opposite directions down Jerome Avenue. When they were separated by a few blocks, they turned and headed back toward where Palladino stood. From one of the cars, a teenager was held by his belt as he leaned out the window. In his hand was a nine-millimeter automatic. It was a warm afternoon, and along Jerome Avenue, a residential block, neighborhood people sat in lawn chairs. Later investigators recovered fourteen shell casings from the automatic and from a revolver fired from the other car. Miraculously, neither Palladino nor any of the neighbors was hit.

During the shooting, someone from the neighborhood copied down the license plate of one of the cars and reported it to the police. Although the plate turned out to be registered to a fake address, the plate number and a description of the car were issued to all boroughs. Two nights later a uniform cop, John Turino from the 34th Precinct, spotted the car in front of Junior's restaurant in Washington Heights. The driver of the car, who had also been the driver the night of the shooting, was arrested.

Afterward, Frankie and John Fox, the lead investigator on the case, began to assemble important information on the driver's cohorts. During this time, the early 1980s, crime in New York City's subway system was rampant. Muggings by teenage gangs were commonplace. Funded by an infusion of cash—the result of community outrage that put pressure on politicians—the transit police had formed special squads to investigate organized gang crime. One of the most infamous gangs of that day called themselves the Ball Busters. Their leader was one Oscar Fernandez. According to the driver, it was Fernandez who'd fired the nine-millimeter at Palladino.

Riding in a van with a small peephole in its side, Frankie and a team of five other detectives, dressed in bulletproof vests and carrying shotguns, cruised the streets of north Harlem as—looking through the peephole—the driver pointed out his fellow gang members, one by one. After just a few hours, seven of the eight members had been apprehended. Only Oscar Fernandez remained at large.

During interrogation, one of the gang gave up Fernandez's address, an apartment on West 148th Street. Four of the team of detectives entered the building and approached the suspect's apartment door. Frankie and a detective named Fuselli covered the alleyway in the back of the building. Just a few moments later, the back window of Fernandez's apartment slid open. Though the apartment was on the first floor, the window was some twenty feet above the dark alleyway. Fuselli had positioned himself at one end of the open corridor, with Frankie at the other. As Fernandez readied to jump from the window, both detectives raised their shotguns to their shoulders. When the suspect hit the ground, Frankie yelled, identifying himself as a police officer. Just then there was a popping sound and a flash of light, from a small handgun. Though Fernandez was only some fifteen feet from Frankie—and from the shotgun he held against his shoulder—my brother didn't fire. In the darkness of the alleyway, he couldn't be absolutely sure that the spray of the blast wouldn't hit Fuselli. Instead, he took off after the suspect, tackled him from behind, and wrestled a small derringer from him. The bullet from the gun was later pried out of the wall only a few feet from where Frankie had stood.

All eight members of the Ball Busters were arraigned on charges of attempted murder. Several of them, including Oscar Fernandez, made bail and fled to their native Dominican Republic. Several years later, Fernandez returned to the United States and killed two people during an armed robbery. This time, when he was arrested, he was held without bail, and was ultimately convicted of the murders and sent to prison for life.

In his other world—Pearl River—Frankie coached his daughters, Laurie and Patrice, in Little League softball. The teams were called the Phillies and the Chargers. The girls wore brightly colored sweatshirts and baseball caps pulled down to their ears. A good portion of the fathers who watched the games from the stands of Anderson Field were cops, and almost all of the coaches were New York City policemen.

Much like Eugene and Frankie, Laurie and Patrice were strikingly different. In Little League, Laurie, the classic overachiever, worked hard in practice and gave a hundred percent during the games. For Patrice, being good at sports was just a matter of showing up. With little effort, she was the pitcher and star of the Chargers, and was picked for the all-star team. As the years passed, Laurie grew tall and slender, with a natural beauty accented by dark chestnut hair and perfect features. Patrice was also pretty but, as though she didn't believe it, she covered her face with layers of makeup, and streaked and bleached her hair. At one game when Patrice was about twelve, she came on the field wearing makeup and earrings. Her first boyfriend was in the stands, and she wanted to look her best. Embarrassed by his daughter's garish appearance, Frankie banished her from the pitcher's mound to left field. Patrice gave her father a steely stare as she walked to the outfield.

From very early on, there was noticeable friction between Frankie and Patrice, perhaps because they were, in personality, so alike. While Laurie played the role of doting daughter, Patrice met her father head-on, as if to show him that she could be every bit as rebellious as he had been. Laurie was an A student; Patrice hated school with a passion equaled only by her father in his early life.

By the time Patrice went to high school, her rebellious streak really did rival her father's. But the temptations of high school in Patrice's day were far more dangerous than they'd been in the tame 1950s-greaser era of Frankie's youth. By the eighties, crack cocaine showed little respect for the distance city cops had moved from New York City. Where once the joke among the habitués of the Bronx Criminal Court was "Criminal justice? Yeah, *just us,*" crack had changed the very complexion of crime. Streets like DeKalb Avenue in the far northern section of the 52nd Precinct—which, not too long before, had been a stable working-class neighborhood—became a kind of drive-through crack market for white suburban customers: lawyers and store managers and secretaries who drove Toyotas and Nissans. The market also served white high school students behind the wheel of Mom or Daddy's car. Some of them were cops' kids.

* * *

In the summer of 1982, a detective named Kenny Dudonis, a fellow Little League coach, asked Frankie if he would like to teach his class at Rockland Community College. A year and some months earlier, on St. Patrick's Day, 1981, Dudonis, a member of the NYPD's Bomb Squad, had been severely burned when an incendiary device he was trying to disarm exploded. The bomb was located in front of the Youth International Headquarters on Bleecker Street. Doctors had to reconstruct his face and hand. Though he was not able to teach during his recuperation, he wanted to keep his position at Rockland while he counted the days until he was eligible to retire from the NYPD.

Not too many years earlier, Frankie had walked into that college without a single credit. Now he jumped at the chance to teach there. The course was in criminalistics, more commonly known as forensics, the scientific side of investigation. That summer, a few weeks before the semester was to begin, Frankie took the course textbook with him on vacation to the New Jersey shore. He read it twice, and, while lying on the beach, dreamt about leading stimulating class discussions. For three days before the first day of class, he wrote and rewrote his opening lecture several times, in the same black-and-white marbled composition books where he kept his case notes. He even practiced in front of the mirror. For the first day of class, he wore his best blue blazer and khaki pants, trying hard to look less like a cop and more like a college professor. When the class began he was so nervous he kept his hands in his pants pockets because they were sweating profusely. He forgot everything he'd memorized. His lecture lasted all of ten minutes, the longest ten minutes of his life. Flustered, he finally said to the class: "Why don't you just go buy your books?"

He took good-natured ribbing from the detectives in his squad. They called him professor, just to break his shoes. He didn't mind. He liked being called professor. And teaching the class made him a better detective: He learned more about crime labs than he could have in a career on the street. For his students, his enthusiasm brought excitement to the class. As the semester went on, he found he didn't have to spend time memorizing lessons; much of what he taught, he already knew. What he didn't know, he learned along with his students. He brought in guest lecturers: detectives, Anti-Crime cops, and forensics experts. He even brought an old squad commander in to speak to his class. My father was in top form with the built-in audience for his war stories.

During those days at Rockland Community College, Frankie found out there was a job he could do that was more fulfilling than running after bad guys, and that he could actually fit in with civilians in a normal lifestyle. But it was always only a matter of time before Frankie caught a case that would, again, make being a cop the most important thing in his life.

On August 12, 1985, a burning furnace of a summer evening, Briggs Avenue was filled with kids playing games in slow motion. The sidewalks around them, strewn with every imaginable color of broken glass, glinted in the setting sun. Men stood on the corner under red and white corrugated-metal awnings, drinking beer from cans clothed in brown paper bags. The night hummed with a high-pitched crackle, like a radio station not quite tuned in. The street reeked with the sour odor of poverty, the kind that squeezes your nasal passages deep below the bridge of your nose, like the smell of a rat dead in a wall for weeks—not unbearable, just always there.

On the television show *Missing Children*, Frankie stood with Terry Hodrick on the porch in front of her home on Briggs Avenue. Her golden-brown skin was moist with sweat. She wore a loose-fitting housedress, which draped her pregnant stomach. She listened to Frankie's words intently, but did not look at him. Her eyes were distant and worried as they stared out over the street that had swallowed her eight-year-old daughter whole.

Later on, in a close-up shot, Frankie's face filled the screen. "Probably half my working hours are spent on this case," he said in the interview. "A lot of my thoughts go into this case—a lot of all of our thoughts. But we have to deal with facts. And the facts are: Equilla ran down the block that night. Turned the corner. And hasn't been seen or heard from since."

What Frankie didn't say into the camera was that he thought of little else but Equilla Hodrick. From the day of her disappearance that August, to the day he retired as a policeman, and beyond, in every quiet moment, during every drive home in his car, each time he sat at his desk at work, even in his dreams, the picture of her bright, engaging smile, her disarming hazel eyes, her delicately smooth, brown skin haunted him. For Frankie, this was even more than a missing-child case, it was an obsession. And, in some ways an act of atonement.

I never really knew—didn't want to know—what my brother had said to those six black men in Spring Valley that foggy night. But any stain of bigotry on him disappears in light of the attention and care he lavished on Equilla Hodrick's case—and the love he had for the little girl he searched for for years, but never knew, never found.

Both as a uniform and as an undercover cop, Frankie entered people's lives like a car accident: lights, siren, and shouts; an arrest, or sometimes not; and on to the next collision. Now, as a detective, he dealt with emotions that weren't fueled by adrenaline. Instead of shouts there were whimpers; instead of chases, there were sighs. Instead of thinking of victims as crime statistics, he found that they were human beings with lives and families. He knew that Terry Hodrick wasn't an addict. She didn't sell her body or peddle drugs. She was a mother who tucked her daughter into bed each night and stroked her head. She prayed on her knees and hummed gospel hymns all the time. Frankie stopped by her house at least once a day, even though, as time wore on, he could offer little more than support and optimistic words. One night, several weeks after her daughter's disappearance, Terry hugged him. At first, as the pregnant black woman draped her arms around him, he held her woodenly. But as she laid her head on his shoulder, and as he could feel her moist sobs against his neck, his arms tightened around her and tears filled his own eyes. He held her that way for some time, as curious neighborhood people walked slowly by and looked at them.

With his partner, John Borris, Frankie conducted hundreds of interviews with neighbors, shop owners, family members, anyone who might offer even the smallest insight into Equilla's disappearance. For all intents and purposes, Borris and Frankie worked the case alone. Several years earlier, a young boy in Greenwich Village named Etan Patz disappeared, almost the way Equilla had. For Etan Patz, the NYPD mobilized an entire task force; a hundred detectives worked the case for months, years. But Equilla didn't live in Greenwich Village, nor did she have blond hair or white skin.

To be fair, in the days immediately after her disappearance, the police department did use helicopters and bloodhounds. One of the dogs picked up her scent and led police to a hole in a fence that ran along a Metro North train right-of-way. The tracks cut a canyon through this section of the Bronx, ferrying commuters back and forth from Westchester. Along the edges of the tracks, homeless people lived in a squatter's camp filled with cardboard-box homes, shopping carts, and junk. Frankie and Borris decided to conduct a thorough search of the canyon. It was about eleven a.m. on a Thursday when Frankie called Metro North. On the phone, he was told that an official would be sent to speak to him in person. During the months prior, Metro North had been under scrutiny by commuter groups and the city for inadequacies in service: shortages of trains and frequent equipment problems.

In a construction trailer beside the tracks, Frankie and his squad commander, Sergeant Malvey, met with the official from Metro North. The man nervously played with his beard and glasses as he told Frankie that a shutdown of the trains would be impossible.

"Do you know how many people you want to inconvenience?" he asked.

Though Frankie was inwardly seething at the man's valuing commuters' convenience over a young girl's life, his outward response was measured:

"This is an urgent police matter," Frankie said. "We're searching for a missing eight-year-old girl. We need your cooperation."

"I'm sorry," the man replied. "There's nothing I can do."

"Well, who can?" asked Malvey, glaring at the official, who was now sweating profusely.

By phone, Malvey was connected to a Metro North supervisor in Manhattan, and was given pretty much the same answer: no. Malvey then asked for the supervisor's boss. Finally, he heard a sympathetic voice. Although the Metro North vice president wouldn't go as far as stopping the trains, he did agree to slow them down to thirty miles per hour—a safe enough speed, he said, for the cops to search the sides of the track. Frankie and Borris, with a half-dozen uniform cops and the same number of Emergency Service officers, conducted the search. As they rooted through the debris, they could feel the suction from the trains zipping by.

The executive from Metro North had agreed to a half-hour search. But once the cops were in the tunnel, there was nothing the railroad could do to get them out. The search stretched to almost three hours. Meanwhile, the slowing of the trains began to have a domino effect on service. By the time rush hour arrived, there was total havoc in Grand Central Station, with hundreds of thousands of commuters stranded and delays of several hours.

The search of the tunnel produced a dozen homeless people, each of whom was interrogated exhaustively, and one possible lead: a man with obvious emotional problems, who had several children's dolls in his possession. But after several hours of questioning the man, it became clear that he was innocent, and he was released.

Disappointed, Frankie began making phone calls from his boss's office, checking on sightings. He had been in contact with several missing-children agencies, which were now distributing fliers and information about Equilla around New York and in several other cities. A hot line had been set up, and every lead, no matter how unlikely, had to be followed up.

As Frankie sat there behind the desk, phone cradled under his chin, a local TV reporter knocked on the door. As she did, TV lights behind her filled the squad room. The reporter thrust the microphone in Frankie's face and asked if he had made the decision to disrupt the commuter traffic.

"Nobody made that decision," he said. "We made the decision to search for a missing child."

When the reporter pressed for an answer, Frankie stopped her in mid-sentence.

"What is your story?" he asked contemptuously. "That an eight-year-old girl is missing? Or that a few assholes from Westchester came home to a cold dinner? I don't have anything more to say to you."

Over the coming weeks, with the aid of a couple of Emergency Service cops, Frankie searched nearly fifty abandoned buildings, storefronts, and apartments. Terry Hodrick insisted she come along on these searches. And for those weeks, Frankie sat next to her in the squad car, promising her he would find Equilla.

The people of the neighborhood around Briggs Avenue were very involved. The flier with the little girl's picture was in just about every shop window, and residents, most of whom knew Frankie was the detective in charge of the case, would stop him in the street to ask about any progress. One Saturday afternoon, a block party was held on 194th Street. Fernando Ferrer, then a congressman from the Bronx, stepped onto the bandstand to thank the neighborhood for its help in the Equilla Hodrick case and ask for continued assistance. From the bandstand, he introduced Frankie, who was standing in the crowd, and announced the phone number that anyone with information should call. As Frankie walked back to his car from the block party, he passed a shriveled old woman, rooting through a garbage can. As he did, he heard her say: "You're never gonna find that little girl alive—she is buried up in Yonkers." Frankie knew the woman as a "can gatherer" and a little bit of a nut. Her words didn't register until he was driving back to the squad room, and then he spun the car around and raced back. Frantically, he ran through the crowd, looking for her, asking people if they had seen her. Nobody had.

Yonkers. Terry Hodrick had a boyfriend who sometimes lived in a house right next to hers on Briggs Avenue. But the rest of the boyfriend's time was spent in an apartment in Yonkers. On the night of Equilla's disappearance, the boyfriend had been seen running, shirtless, on Hoe Avenue, just a few blocks from the Hodricks' home. Later that same night, witnesses placed him riding in a red car with another man. By interviewing at least a dozen people, Frankie was able to identify the other man. His address was the apartment Terry Hodrick's boyfriend lived in in Yonkers.

During the first months of the investigation, Frankie had brought the boyfriend in for interrogation half a dozen times. More. One night, alone with him in the 52nd squad room, Frankie asked him how he was going to live with himself. Every day, Frankie told him, Equilla's little face would appear in his thoughts, and would never let him forget. The boyfriend began to cry—deep, heaving sobs. Slowly, he lifted his head from his hands and turned to Frankie. His eyes were a watery red, with blood and tears. He began to speak, and Frankie was sure he was about to confess. But all the boyfriend said was "I didn't do nothing."

The interrogation of the boyfriend's Yonkers roommate proved as fruitless. For months, Frankie searched for the woman who had been rooting through the garbage. But she disappeared like an apparition. Indeed, several times Frankie even doubted her existence. Perhaps she had been admitted to a psychiatric ward and was now in the labyrinth of New York City's institutional system. Or maybe she had died. Her words, though, lived in his thoughts for the rest of the Equilla Hodrick investigation. How, he often wondered, did the old woman know about Yonkers?

Two years after her daughter disappeared, Frankie still talked to Terry Hodrick four or five times a week. Two years after Equilla had disappeared, Frankie still followed up every lead that came from the private sector's missing-persons network. Equilla's picture was on the back of milk cartons and tractor-trailers. Her story was on national television. Two years later, there were still plenty of leads coming in. None led anywhere.

By this time, Frankie was certain that Equilla was dead. During the investigation, he had come to know her like she was his own daughter. She was smart, with street smarts that inner-city kids learn the way country-club kids learn golf, by just being there. Frankie knew that she loved her mother, and in some ways took care of her. Terry Hodrick was not the brightest of people—she couldn't have been, to get mixed up with a junkie boyfriend. If Equilla was alive, she would have found a way to come home by then.

Yet, on some level, Frankie couldn't allow himself to believe the inescapable. The Equilla Hodrick case was the biggest disappointment of his career. More than almost anything, he wanted to solve it. More than that, he wanted to find her alive. Just a week before he retired, he took out the twenty-five-pound case folder and placed it on his desk. One last time, he looked through it, as if, magically, this time he would find the answer.

That afternoon, he went to see Terry Hodrick to tell her he was leaving the force and another detective would be assigned to the case. She slowly shook her head back and forth, her eyes were dull, as if there were no more tears left to shed. "Well, that's the end of it," she said simply, the words as empty as they were final. For a few moments they stood together on the porch in awkward silence. Then Frankie walked down the steps and out of Terry Hodrick's life. Eleven years later, Equilla is still listed as a missing child.

10

Built atop the Palisades, cliffs that drop hundreds of feet to the Hudson River, and through a forested tract of land bequeathed by the Rockefeller family, the Palisades Parkway is about as lovely a drive as any in the New York area. In spring, with the windows down, the cool rush of pine- and maple-scented air fills the nostrils; in fall, you're surrounded by explosions of reds, yellows, and maroons as the foliage changes. In the winter, when the leaves have fallen, you can see the Hudson River, and across to Riverdale and north to Westchester. So beautiful is the vista, there are lookouts along the parkway with binocular stands, like the kind you find on the observation deck of the Empire State Building.

It takes no longer than twenty minutes to drive the Palisades Parkway from the George Washington Bridge, through a corner of New Jersey, to the exit for Pearl River. There are only two lanes in each direction, there are no trucks, no tolls (except for the bridge), no billboards. For cops, the drive is like the first cold beer after a hot summer tour, when they can finally stop holding their breath.

There is a story that city cops in Pearl River tell. One of their brethren, who worked four-to-twelves, drove the Palisades home early each morning. Each time he did, he noticed a small, perfectly shaped pine on the side of the highway. One day, a few weeks before Christmas, as he left for work, he threw a shovel into the trunk of his car.

Coming home from work that night, he pulled his car off the highway and onto the winter-browned grass near the tree he admired. As he began to dig, he imagined how perfect the tree would look in front of his house, first wrapped with Christmas lights, and then, in the spring and summer, shading the new steps and walkway he had just put in that fall. When he had almost finished digging up the tree, a Palisades Parkway police car pulled off the highway behind him.

"What the hell do you think you're doing?" the Jersey cop sternly asked.

"Listen," his New York counterpart said, his mind in full engagement. "I'm a cop in the city. This tree is from my front yard, and I just put a walkway in. I didn't have the heart just to cut it down, so I dug it up and thought I'd plant it here, on my way home from work."

"You can't do that," said the Jersey cop. "You're going to have to get it out of here."

But for New York City cops who live in Rockland, the Palisades Parkway is more than a pleasant drive and a chance to unwind. It serves as the demilitarized zone, the buffer between their two worlds. No matter how far the crime stain of New York spread, they believed that it could never, ever reach Pearl River.

In denial, city cops wouldn't believe that Pearl River was not safe anymore from crack cocaine. It *had* to be, because if it wasn't, they had lost the crime war not only in New York City, but in their homeland, too. By the time Patrice was in Pearl River High School, the homeland was no longer safe.

I often wondered how my brother must have felt when the very agent he fought in his latter police career broached the moat of the Hudson River and crawled up the Palisades Parkway and past its reeling elms to his own backyard? As heroic as he was, battling drugs as a cop in the Bronx, did he think he had failed as a father in protecting his daughter from them in Pearl River?

In his defense, riding through the inner city in an unmarked police car, and watching your daughter climb the stairs to her bedroom after being at a high school party, are two distinctly different vantage points. And, at first, none of us had any clue. Patrice's personality bubbled over with a quick wit accentuated by smiling, clear, aqua eyes. She called me Uncle Brian, which made me feel so very adult around her, and she never missed a family get-together. We—my entire family—knew all of her close-knit group of friends. In fact, at family gatherings, visits from Patrice's friends were a high point. They were funny and harmlessly mischievous. One of her friends, Michael, even aspired to be a stand-up comic. A natural mimic, he had Frankie down pat.

But in Patrice's junior year in high school, it became clear that she had problems. Though certainly a bright kid, she was failing every subject. She just didn't go to class. She had been suspended from school on at least one occasion. Although the reason for the suspension was never discussed—at least not with me—it was known to have something to do with drugs. That year, my brother and Pam arranged for Patrice to live with Pam's brother Clem's ex-wife in Scottsdale, Arizona. Their thinking was to remove her from the bad influences in Pearl River. But the problem lay in Patrice, not in outside influences.

About a month after Patrice moved to Scottsdale, her aunt called Pam to say it wasn't working out. Patrice wasn't going to class in Arizona either, and the aunt was worried about her own daughter, who was Patrice's age, and who was now spending far too much time with her cousin. Pam flew to Scottsdale to talk to school officials. She was told that Patrice was doing just fine—but obviously the school didn't have its information correct. Pam rented a small apartment, planning to live with Patrice until the school year was over. But Patrice was already immersed in the illegal-drug culture of Scottsdale. She would borrow Pam's car to go for cigarettes and not return until the next day. One of these disappearances stretched to three days. Frantic, Pam called Frankie, and my brother booked the next available flight.

For the first couple of harrowing days, Frankie and Pam weren't really sure what had happened to Patrice. But when Patrice's cousin, also seventeen, turned up missing too, they knew the girls had gone somewhere together. Three days later, when the cousin returned home, she told Pam where Patrice was staying.

As Frankie packed a carry-on bag to go to Arizona, he looked at the gleaming Colt Cobra, his off-duty weapon, in the sock drawer. In some ways, at least symbolically, he had always reached for the gun as the answer when drug addiction was the issue. But, in this case, that symbol was the last thing he needed. Whether or not police guns work to stop illegal drugs on the streets of the Bronx is debatable. Whether a gun would help in rescuing his daughter was not. He closed the drawer with the Colt still in it.

For a moment, as he sat in his rental car in the parking lot of the run-down roadside motel, his thoughts again went to the gun. He didn't know what he would find in the motel room, but he feared the worst, and he felt almost naked without the Colt. So many times he had gone through the same motions in the Bronx, and the gun was always there to reassure him—the biscuit, he called it.

He pulled himself from the car and walked toward the door of the motel room. When he knocked, the door was opened a crack, but held by the chain. "I'm Patrice's father," he said to the squinting eyes that looked out at him. The eyes darted away, but before the door could be slammed, Frankie threw his shoulder into it, snapping it open. Inside, there were two men in their early twenties in the room, and another girl about Patrice's age. Patrice lay half asleep on the bed; her eyes had sunk into her skull, with dark circles underneath. She had lost a great deal of weight, and the sight of her shocked Frankie. It wasn't as though he hadn't seen the likes of what lay before him. The Port Authority bus terminal, the streets of Times Square, and sections of the Bronx were filled with such forlorn souls. But the skeleton he now looked at wore the just barely recognizable features of his own daughter. One of the men, who had a hardened face and greasy jet-black hair, began to yell: "Get the fuck out of my room!" From experience, I can easily imagine what Frankie looked like in that moment: the glaze descending over his eyes, the skin on the back of his neck crimson—the only tell-tale signs that beneath the otherwise placid exterior his blood raced fiery hot.

The other man silently leered at Frankie. My brother could see the outline of a handgun under his shirt. For a moment, my brother and the man held each other's eyes in a sizing-up stare, and in that moment my brother thought of the Colt he had left behind. Though Frankie didn't know this then, the young man knew he was a cop; Patrice had told him. Undoubtedly, he thought Frankie had a gun, too. A heavy silence engulfed the room. Then the young man slowly walked past Frankie, brushing up against him as he did. For a few seconds my brother's cop instincts took over. He listened intently to the man's footsteps climbing the stairs outside the door. In that moment, he imagined the man positioning himself for a clear shot. But as he looked again toward his daughter, cop worries were swept aside. Frankie walked to the bed, cradled Patrice in his arms, and carried her from the room to the car, glancing over his shoulder only once. The man with the gun was nowhere in sight.

Perhaps it was then that Frankie first realized that, for the whole of his daughters' lives, his priorities had been, at the very least, divided between being a good father and being a good cop. In some ways, you can't be both. The job not only steals cops' time from their families, it takes words from their mouths. Witnessing lives sliced apart, seeing horrors upon horrors, dulls cops' ability to express love.

With Patrice, Frankie was given another chance. Soon after he brought his daughter home, I sat in a room and watched as he told her how much he loved her. I saw his eyes flood with tears that began to drip down his tough cop face, as he told her how he didn't want her to die. I saw him hold her tenderly, like the best of fathers, and watched as she cried, too. In that moment, a police shield no longer covered his heart.

The day Frankie retired, he drove up the Palisades as a civilian for the first time in twenty years. Snow still swirled from the white-gray sky and clung to the bare branches of the trees. For the first time in twenty years there wasn't a badge on his person, there wasn't a service revolver in the glove compartment of his car. The thought came to him of how much space those articles had occupied, and he felt uneasy and vulnerable in their absence. He thought about the offer that had lured him away from the job that had defined him all his adult life. He hoped that, with time, his pension and his new salary would fill the longing. When he was out from under the weight of his debts and bills, leaving the job he loved wouldn't seem so painful.

By accepting the offer, he had completed the trifecta mirror image of his father's life: the navy, the police department, and now airline security—working for TWA. That snowy day, he pulled in to his father's driveway to tell one last war story, the events of Patrolman Michael Reidy's murder investigation.

Over the coming weeks and months, Frankie was by turns fascinated with his new career—in a world of white-collar criminals, of credit-card fraud and airline ticket forgery—and melancholy over his departure from the police department. At TWA, his first assignment was to investigate a lost-luggage claim—thirteen Halliburton aluminum suitcases belonging to a Hollywood producer. He flew to Orlando to interview ticket and rental-car agents. No longer a cop, he realized on his way to the first interview that these people didn't have to talk to him if they didn't want to. They did talk, though. The aura of authority from his twenty years on the force still draped Frankie like a uniform.

The claim turned out to be false. A retired detective, working as a security manager in a New York hotel, told Frankie that the hotel bellhop had records of the producer checking the Halliburton bags there—days after he had reported them lost or stolen in Florida.

When the *Daily News* or *New York Post* headlines blared another major crime story, Frankie couldn't help but think that he had made a mistake; he desperately missed the action of the street. Even the perks of the new job (with flying privileges, he and Pam once took a weekend in Rome) didn't quell the yearning for some squad-room banter and a greasy meatball hero. But as time went by, he slowly became acclimated to the corporate world, and even though the commute from Kennedy Airport to Pearl River was on some nights a two-hour push through bumper-to-bumper traffic, he liked being home each night for dinner and, for the first time in his life, having the normal hours of a working father.

About a year after he began the job at TWA, he started to teach again, part-time, for a university in New York City. Throughout his time at TWA, and later, when he went into academia full-time, Frankie's classes in police science were filled to capacity. Young, scrubbed faces of every hue looked toward him for guidance—and a grade—in the hope of fulfilling their dreams of careers in law enforcement. He began each first class of the semester with the same words: "A cop's life is not for everybody. But," he would add, "it was for me." He knew what he was talking about.

A few years ago, I met my brother in downtown Manhattan, in Foley Square, outside the federal courthouse. The college where he worked was just a few blocks away. I was there covering the trial of a drug dealer for a story I was writing freelance for *The New York Times*. We grabbed a couple of hot dogs from a vendor and sat on a green city bench. All gray now, with a St. Anthony bald spot on the crown of his head, his body thick around the middle, my brother began the conversation in his usual way: the joke of the week. The square was filled with those on both sides of the law rushing for a quick lunch before afternoon court sessions and work. It was a beautiful April day, and a young cop in shirtsleeves walked by. I watched my brother's eyes, their blue a match for the cop's shirt, as they followed the patrolman. It was as though he was looking into his own past.

"Being a policeman," he said wistfully, "was the only thing I ever wanted to do."

11

Some sixty years after my grandfather's death, over thirty years since my father retired, and now some twelve years since my brother left the job, we are still a family delineated by the badge and gun of the NYPD.

Each Christmas Eve, Frankie hosts a party at his home, which is now completely paid for. The festivity is held in the "new" room, an extension off the side of the house that Frankie and Paul Gibbons built. Thanks to Pam's expertise, the room looks like a picture out of *Architectural Digest*: cream-colored walls, recessed lighting, walnut shelves, forest-green couches and chairs. The shelf over the fireplace is lined with mementos of Frankie's police career: a plaque with a replica of his gold shield presented to him on his retirement by his old squad; a photograph of him as a rookie cop.

All of my family attends the party, even Eugene and Diane, who make the four-hour drive from an affluent Boston suburb where they now live. Patrice is always there too, with her boys, Mikey and Danny. Patrice and Frankie have worked hard at their relationship over the years. Family loyalty is strong—as is Frankie's pride in his grandsons. There is one chair left empty. My mom passed away last year, and the celebration has lost much of its heart. For all of the strong, brave men in uniform who surrounded her throughout her life, it was her passion that pumped the blood through my family's veins. Though she never held a gun or ran down a bad guy (that I know of, at least), my mother was the true hero of my family, and we are not the same without her.

Inevitably, though, after the plates of lasagna and roasted turkey are scraped clean—and the Dewar's bottle shows more clear than amber—Frankie and my father will begin to regale us with their war stories (somewhere my mother is rolling her eyes).

Even though we have all heard the stories many times now, as each is told everyone in my family leans forward on their chairs. But no one in my family listens as intently as me.

My father had no way of knowing what he had started when he gave me the Underwood—that it would lead to all the windows and doors of our home being thrown wide open. Then again, perhaps he did. He was never big on expressing feelings through the spoken word. It was between the covers of books where his emotions found freedom. I'd like to think that the gift of the typewriter was his way of saying: "Write, Brian. Write it all."

One thing is for sure, each time I look at the old typewriter, I'm reminded of that long-ago day when I held his .38 special in my hand. Indeed there are times when I think that the typewriter is the service revolver I never owned. There are times I think it is my father's gun.

The typeface used in this book is a version of Janson, a seventeenth-century Dutch style revived by Merganthaler Linotype in 1937. Long attributed to one Anton Janson through a mistake by the owners of the originals, the typeface was actually designed by a Hungarian, Nicholas (Miklós) Kis (1650–1702), in his time considered the finest punchcutter in Europe. Kis took religious orders as a young man, gaining a reputation as a classical scholar. As was the custom, he then traveled; because knowledge of typography was sorely lacking in Hungary, Kis decided to go to Holland, where he quickly mastered the trade. He soon had offers from all over Europe—including one from Cosimo de' Medici—but kept to his original plan, returning to Hungary to help promote learning. Unfortunately, his last years were embittered by the frustration of his ambitions caused by the political upheavals of the 1690s.